JOHN FREELY
The House of Memory

John Freely was born in Brooklyn in 1926, served in the U.S. Navy from 1944 to 1946, graduated from Iona College, received a Ph.D. in nuclear physics from New York University, and did postdoctoral work at All Souls College, Oxford, England. He taught physics for more than fifty years at Bosphorus University—formerly Robert College—in Istanbul, where a building was recently named for him. He is the author of more than sixty books on Turkey, Greece, biographical figures, and the history of science. Freely died in 2017.

Also by John Freely

Aladdin's Lamp (2009)

Jem Sultan (2004)

The Lost Messiah (2001)

Inside the Seraglio (1999)

Istanbul: The Imperial City (1996)

Strolling Through Venice (1994)

Strolling Through Athens (1991)

Classical Turkey (1990)

The Western Shores of Turkey (1988)

Crete (1988)

The House of Memory

The House of Memory

REFLECTIONS ON YOUTH AND WAR

John Freely

VINTAGE BOOKS
A Division of Penguin Random House LLC
New York

FIRST VINTAGE BOOKS EDITION, FEBRUARY 2018

Grateful acknowledgment is made to the following for permission
to reprint previously published material:

Alfred Music: Excerpt of "Don't Fence Me In" (from *Hollywood Canteen*), words and
music by Cole Porter. Copyright © 1944 by WB Music Corp, copyright renewed.
All rights reserved. Reprinted by permission of Alfred Music.

Alfred Music and Songs of Peer, Ltd.: Excerpt of "Skylark," words by Johnny Mercer
Music and music by Hoagy Carmichael. Copyright © 1941 by the Johnny Mercer
Foundation and Songs of Peer, Ltd. All rights for the Johnny Mercer Foundation
administered by WB Music Corp. All rights for Hoagy Carmichael administered
by Songs of Peer, Ltd. All rights reserved. Reprinted by permission of
Alfred Music and Songs of Peer, Ltd.

Hal Leonard LLC: Excerpt of "Lili Marlene," words and music by Mack David,
Hans Leip, and Norbert Schultz. Copyright © 1943 by Universal-Polygram
International Publishing, Inc. and Chappell & Co., Inc., copyright renewed.
All rights reserved. Excerpt of "(There'll Be Bluebirds Over) The White Cliffs of
Dover," words by Nat Burton, music by Walter Kent. Copyright © 1941 by
Shapiro, Bernstein & Co., Inc., New York, and Walter Kent Music, California,
copyright renewed. All rights outside the United States controlled by Shapiro,
Bernstein & Co., Inc., New York. International copyright secured. All rights
reserved. Used by permission. Reprinted by permission of Hal Leonard LLC.

Library of Congress Control Number: 2016963012

Vintage Books Trade Paperback ISBN: 978-1-101-97468-1
eBook ISBN: 978-0-451-49471-9

Book design by Iris Weinstein

www.vintagebooks.com

Printed in the United States of America
10 9 8 7 6 5 4 3 2 1

In memory of Charles Shelmerdine,
John Jacob Esau, and Ching Ging Too

These are the men who laid down the splendor of their manhood . . . they are no more, but they have left the fairest memorial of their valor.

—*Epitaph of the Greek warriors who fell at the Battle of the Eurymedon in 466 BC*

When I remember them, those friends of mine,
Who are no longer here, the noble three, . . .
In vain I stretch my hands to clasp their hands;
I cannot find them. Nothing now is left
But a majestic memory. They meanwhile
Wander together in Elysian lands,
Perchance remembering me, who am bereft
Of their dear presence, and, remembering, smile.

— HENRY WADSWORTH LONGFELLOW,
   "Three Friends of Mine"

Contents

PART ONE · YOUTH

1. Sailing Against the Tide   3

2. Depression Brooklyn   32

3. The Shadow of War   52

4. All Will Be Well   64

5. I'm in the Navy Now   75

PART TWO · WAR

6. Preparing for War   103

7. Shipping Out   135

8. Lost Horizon   145

9. Jade Dragon Snow Mountain   169

10. The Rivers of Paradise   187

11. The Ungovernable Sea   215

PART THREE · MEMORY

12. Waves Washing the Sand   247

Part One

Youth

m y mother was born in Ireland as Margaret Murphy, but everyone called her Peg. She never used her married name, Mrs. John Freely, always identifying herself as Peg Murphy. This was not uncommon among the Irish women of her time, but it was mostly her fierce spirit of independence that made her keep her own name, for she was Peg Murphy and not Mrs. Somebody Else, she always said. We were led by her to believe that she had been born in 1904, but I learned many years later that her true date of birth was 1897. I never found out why she subtracted seven years from her age. Perhaps it was to be eternally young, for she often spoke of going off to Tir na nÓg, the "land of the heart's desire," where in Celtic myth no one grows old. So Peg told me one day. Many years later I read Eavan Boland's numinous rendering of this whispered promise:

Fair woman, will you come with me
to a wondrous land where there is music?
Hair is like the blossoming primrose there;
smooth bodies are the color of snow
There, there is neither mine nor yours;
bright are teeth, dark are brows,
A delight to the eye the number of our hosts,
the color of fox-glove every cheek.

She was one of eleven children, all but one of whom left Ireland and emigrated to the United States. They were helped by relatives in Lawrence, Massachusetts, from an earlier family migration. Her paternal grandfather had "died on the roads" when he and his family were evicted from their home in the last years of the Great Hunger, after which his widow and surviving children had emigrated to America and found refuge in Lawrence. But her eldest son, Peg's father, Tómas Murphy, had not taken to life in America and returned to Ireland, though none of his family was left there.

Tómas was born in County Kerry on the Dingle Peninsula, which together with the Kenmare Peninsula to its south forms the southwesternmost extension of Ireland. When Tómas returned from America he found work as a porter for the Irish Railways, on the narrow-gauge line that operated between Tralee, capital of County Kerry, and Dingle, the main town on the peninsula. At the beginning of his first day of work an English tourist, getting on at Tralee, pointed out his trunk on the platform and arrogantly ordered Tómas to put it up on the luggage rack. "Put it up yourself," said Tómas proudly, walking away to help an old Irishwoman board the train. The conductor, observing this, said, "Murphy, you will not grow gray in the service of the Irish Railways."

Tómas kept the job for about a year, but then he was dismissed for giving another English tourist a piece of his mind about Britain's treatment of Ireland. It was just as well that he left, for the following Whitsunday there was a terrible accident on the Tralee–Dingle line. Locomotive Number One swerved off the tracks on the Curraduff Bridge and fell thirty feet into the river, killing the engineer, the conductor, the porter, and ninety pigs, who were the only passengers that day. An old woman in Dingle remarked to Tómas that he had been spared by the hand of God, to which he responded, according to Peg, "I'm sure the Almighty had more important matters to think about that day than the fate of three Irishmen and ninety pigs."

Soon afterward Tómas met and fell in love with a pretty young schoolteacher named Maire Ashe, whose father was the postmaster in Anascaul, the only town of any size between Tralee and Dingle. Tómas and Maire married and settled down in a tiny cottage by the sea four miles east of Inch, the enormous transverse sand cape on the south coast of the Dingle Peninsula. Tómas became a fisherman, making himself a small currach, a wickerwork boat covered with tarred canvas. He also built a little dock to moor his currach, in a cove below his cottage, that is still called Murphy's Landing. On the hillside behind the cottage he cleared and walled in a small plot of land and planted it with potatoes, cabbage, barley, and hay, building a small barn that sheltered a cow, a donkey, and a score of chickens. He farmed his little plot and at intervals set his nets and lines for codfish and herring in Dingle Bay, searching the rocky strand at low tide for periwinkles and mussels. With these resources, Tómas and Maire raised eleven children, five of them boys and six girls, all of whom survived their childhood, something of a miracle in rural Ireland at the time.

The Murphy children learned reading, writing, arithmetic, and not much more at the Kerry district school, a two-room schoolhouse three miles west along the coast from where they lived, making the journey barefoot in all seasons. Their schoolmaster was named Daniel Quill, whom Peg always referred to as an "ignorant tyrant." Once he announced that there would be no school the following day, for it was the Feast of the Circumcision. Peg, who was then about eleven, raised her hand and asked, "What is circumcision?" Master Quill called her up in front of the class, and then with all of his might slapped her across the face, knocking her down. She later said that there were two possible reasons for Master Quill's violent response: one was that he knew what circumcision was, and the other was that he did not—but either way he would have been driven to rage by his embarrassment.

The other figure of authority in Inch was the local Catholic priest, Father Mulcahey, whom Peg hated as much as she loathed Master Quill. One rainy winter day she was walking home from school, barefoot as always, accompanied by a classmate, the daughter of a neighbor who was prosperous enough to buy shoes for his children. Father Mulcahey was driving their way in his horse and carriage, but when he stopped he offered a lift to the other girl but not to Peg, who was left to walk home three miles alone in the freezing rain, consumed with a bitter rage that welled up again in her later life whenever she told the story. I often wondered whether that incident was the root of Peg's atheism, for although she sent us to Catholic schools she never once went to church herself. When her granddaughter Maureen graduated from Harvard, Peg, who was then nearly eighty, interrupted Derek Bok, the university president, when he mentioned the name of God in his address, to shout out in her melodious Irish brogue that "God should be abolished!"

The Murphy children all left school in turn after four or five years and went to work, usually on their own farm or those of their neighbors. Peg found a place at Foley's Public House at Inch, where she looked after the publican's infant son, Jerry, and also helped out in the bar. She gave part of her wages to her parents, and saved the rest in the hope that she would

My mother, Margaret Murphy, known by all as "Peg"

eventually have enough money to go off to America, the dream of every young person in rural Ireland at the time, for their homeland had nothing to offer them.

Peg was the only one of the children to inherit their mother's love of reading. Her mother, Maire, had been sent to a convent school by her father, Thomas Ashe, who had been appointed postmaster of Anascaul after he returned from the Crimean War, in which he had served in the British Army. He had been badly wounded in the last battle of the war, the attack on the Redan, and had recuperated in Florence Nightingale's hospital on the Asian side of the Bosphorus across from Constantinople. He was illiterate when he joined the 88th Regiment of Foot at the age of seventeen years and nine months, but while he was in the British Army he seems to have learned how to read and write, as well as to speak English, which qualified him to serve as postmaster in Anascaul when he returned to Ireland. Maire taught school for a few years before her marriage to Tómas, who was illiterate. (I discovered this only many years later when I first saw Peg's birth certificate, where her father's signature appeared as a scrawled X.)

All but one of the children went off in turn to America. Peg was the sixth to leave, after her sisters Hannah, Bea, Annie, Mary, and Nell, with her brothers Jerry, Tommy, Mauris, and Gene following soon afterward. Her younger brother John was the only one who remained at home with Tómas and Maire, helping to look after their farm, which, tiny though it was, still required a lot of manual labor. He too would have gone to America, but he had consumption, which they now call tuberculosis, or so Peg told me.

Peg had saved enough money from her wages at Foley's to pay for her passage to the United States in steerage, and she had put aside a bit to buy her first pair of shoes, but the friends who emigrated with her went barefoot. The same thing was happening all over Ireland, as the Irish once again left their native land, just as they had during and after the Great Hunger of the mid-nineteenth century.

The story was much the same in the cottage where my father was born, near the town of Ballyhaunis in County Mayo, in the northwest of Ireland. All the Freelys in the world come from in and around Ballyhaunis, the descendants of an O'Friel who moved there from County Donegal in the north around 1800, the date of the thatched cottage in which my father was born. O'Friel was illiterate, and in registering his name the English authorities had written it down as Freely. Otherwise, like most Irish of the soil, the Freelys were a family without a history, just a succession of simple farmers, who at least owned their own plot of land. This is why they survived the Great Hunger, when tenants were evicted and either "died on the roads" or emigrated, diminishing the population of Ireland from eight million to four million in just a decade.

My father, John, was uncertain about the date of his birth. He always said that he had been born the "year of the great wind," which he thought was 1898, but eventually we learned that he, like my mother, was born in 1897. Neither he nor Peg knew the day on which they were born, so we assigned them birthdays: August 4 for Peg, July 1 for John, to make him a bit older than her. He was the second of the nine children of Michael and Ellen Freely, who had eight boys and one girl: Jim, John, Willie, Tom, Pat, Mike, Charlie, Mary, and Luke. All nine emigrated from Ireland, some to England but most of them to America. Jim, the eldest, eventually returned with his wife, Agnes, to run the family farm after the death of his parents.

There were no books in the house, for Michael and Ellen had never gone to school and were illiterate. Their children went to school up to the age of twelve or so, but since there was no public library in Ballyhaunis they never developed the habit of reading. Thus Peg could never talk to John about literature, nor to anyone else among our relatives and friends, which was one of the reasons she looked down upon Irish immigrants and did not want to live among them—another reason being their addiction to drink.

John left home in the spring of 1916, along with his younger brother Willie, hoping to find work in England. They had not tuppence between them when they decided to leave, as John told me many years later. The only cash in the house was their mother's "egg money," a few pennies that she had accumulated by selling eggs now and then when she went to the weekly market in Ballyhaunis. One morning, well before dawn, John awoke and dressed quietly, waking Willie, and went to the cupboard and took his mother's egg money, vowing to replace it as soon as he found work in England. Then they left the cottage and headed for Ballyhaunis, five miles distant, to catch the weekly train that stopped there at six in the morning. They cut across the fields to intercept the train a mile or so before it reached the town, and when they saw it approaching they stepped out on the track to flag it down. The train stopped for them and the conductor let them come aboard, for he was from Ballyhaunis and knew the family. He didn't bother to ask them for their tickets, for he knew they wouldn't have been able to pay for them.

The train had two cars, one for mail and the other for passengers. The seats were all taken, so John and Willie sat down on the floor at the back, covering their faces when the train stopped at Ballyhaunis so they wouldn't be recognized by anyone who might come aboard there. But no one did, and after the mail was loaded the train chugged off, just as the sun rose over the hills of Roscommon, the next county to the east. Then Willie went to sleep, while John took one last look at Ballyhaunis, which he would never see again. It was Easter Sunday, and he could hear the church bell tolling for the first mass of the day. He blessed himself, and then he too fell asleep.

A while later, the other passengers in the car began waking up, and some of them in the back seats started talking to John and Willie. It turned out that all of them were Irish sailors who had been aboard a British freighter that had been sunk by a German submarine off the northwest coast of Ireland. They had come ashore in lifeboats and were put on the first train leaving for Dublin. They had been given their full pay, and when they were all awake they took up a collection and gave John and Willie enough money to buy shoes and tide them over till they could find work. Pint bottles of Irish whiskey were passed around, and it was then that John had his first taste of hard drink, which started him on the "downward path to ruination," as Peg would later say.

When they arrived in Dublin John asked for directions to a "model rooming house," which he had been told about in Ballyhaunis, and he and Willie spent the night there for a single penny, paying a ha'penny each. They and the other occupants did not sleep on beds, nor even on the floor, but hung by their armpits on ropes suspended from the walls in parallel lines. The rooming house—and others like it—was known as a "Ha'penny Hanger," catering to the hordes of young Irishmen who came to Dublin on their way to England in search of work.

When the ropes were let loose the next morning John and Willie went out to buy a loaf of bread for their breakfast. As they headed for the center of Dublin they heard the sound of gunfire and cannonades, and soon they came within sight of the general post office, where the Irish Republican Army was being besieged by British forces. It was the beginning of the Irish revolution, they learned, and a "terrible beauty" was being born in Dublin, but John and Willie knew naught of that, as my father told me long afterward, for on their isolated farm they had had little news of the outside world, with neither radio nor a newspaper.

They quickly made themselves scarce, for the British forces were rounding up every young Irishman they came upon, shooting some of them down where they stood. John and Willie walked all the way to the port at Dun Laoghaire, still barefoot and on empty stomachs. They were lucky to find a British freighter due to leave for Liverpool the following day, and they were hired as cargo handlers to pay for their passage across the Irish Sea. In Liverpool, they found work as longshoremen; the port was full of troopships and freighters carrying British soldiers and supplies across the English Channel to France. Willie wanted to enlist in the British Army, but John talked him out of it, for they had to save enough from their wages to pay for their passage to America, and also to send money home—the theft of his mother's egg money was weighing heavily on his conscience.

Willie eventually married an Irish girl in Liverpool, where he lived for the rest of his life. But John was determined to get to America, and by 1921 he had finally saved enough to buy a one-way ticket to Boston on a Cunard liner, crossing the Atlantic in steerage, the lowest-class accommodations, in the bowels of the ship, in which immigrants always traveled. During the crossing he gambled away the little money he had saved. But he soon found work as a ditchdigger, staying in a rooming house that catered to young Irishmen recently arrived in Boston, a big improvement on the Ha'-Penny Hangers of Dublin and Liverpool.

*My parents, John and Peg Freely,
in Boston*

The Irish immigrants in Boston held dances on Saturday evenings, and at one of these *caleighs,* as they were called, John met Peg Murphy, who was working as a maid for a wealthy family on Beacon Hill. They were married in September 1924 and moved into a furnished room in Roxbury, where I was conceived about a year later.

Peg was dismissed from her job on Beacon Hill the moment her employers learned she was pregnant. That same day she told John that they had to pack their bags and leave Boston without delay. She felt that there would be more freedom and opportunity in New York, particularly in Brooklyn, where John had an aunt who could help him find a better job than ditchdigging.

Early in the spring of 1926 they took the train to New York and moved in with John's aunt Helen Moran, whose husband, Paddy, was a supervisor for the BMT, the Brooklyn–Manhattan Transit Corporation. Paddy used his influence to have John hired as a conductor on the trolley line that ran between Canarsie Bay and the Williamsburg Bridge, and Peg began looking for an apartment somewhere along the route. She finally found a ground-floor flat halfway along the trolley line, on Cooper Street at the corner of Wilson Avenue in the Bushwick section of Brooklyn, a predominately German neighborhood. They moved in just before I was born, on June 26, 1926, already an experienced traveler.

Peg told me that whenever John's trolley passed he would ring the bell and she would rush to the window and wave to him, and sometimes on a fine day we would ride with him to the Williamsburg Bridge and back.

Years later Peg said that the main reason she decided to leave Boston was that there were too many Irish there, penned up in shantytowns and looked down upon by upper-class Yankees like the Brahmins she worked for on Beacon Hill. "I did not leave Ireland to live among the Irish," she said, usually when we moved from one apartment to another when the rent was overdue, to neighborhoods with varying mixtures of Germans, Italians, Poles, and eastern European Jews, but never to one where the Irish predominated. Our successive apartments were all in what were once working-class neighborhoods. When I first heard this term as a boy, I asked my mother if we were working class, and she said, "We would indeed be of the working class if your father could find steady work."

But the Irish soon began moving into Bushwick, beginning with John's younger brothers Tom and Pat and Mike, and Peg's younger brother Mauris, all of whom married girls recently arrived from Ireland. Then all of the girls began bringing out their younger brothers and sisters from the "old country," and before long we had created what Peg called a "Gaelic ghetto" in German Brooklyn.

I never asked Peg why she wanted to avoid the Irish, because I knew that she missed Ireland terribly and was very proud of her Irish heritage. It was just that she was in a new world and wanted to start a fresh life, she said, free of the hopelessness she had left behind in what she called the "desolation of Ireland."

Peg had also chosen the apartment on Cooper Street because it was, in a curious way, "out in the country." It was just a couple of blocks away from the entrance to the Evergreens Cemetery, one of the largest burial grounds in New York City, laid out along the border between the boroughs of Brooklyn and Queens. The Evergreens dated back to the mid-nineteenth century, and preserved the origi-

Me in the arms of my dad in the Evergreens Cemetery, 1927

nal topography of what had been open countryside outside the old town of Brooklyn. From its tombstone-studded hills, the skyline of Manhattan can be seen across the miles of featureless urban landscape in between. One of the photographs in our family album shows Peg holding me in her arms as she sits on the marble steps of the Schaefer mausoleum, the huge neoclassical tomb built for the founder of one of the two largest German breweries in Brooklyn. The Trommer family, owners of the other large brewery, had an even more grandiose tomb in the Evergreens, but Peg preferred the Schaefer mausoleum for our outings, because it reminded her of a classical temple she had seen in a lithograph illustrating a book of travels in Greece, and she imagined that we were on Delos or one of the other Aegean isles, and not in a Brooklyn cemetery. I suppose it was this that first started me thinking about the Greek islands and other faraway romantic places—the gift of daydreaming that I inherited from Peg.

We were still living on Cooper Street when my sister Dorothy was born on December 19, 1927. John's brother Tom and his wife, Chris, were looking after me while Peg was in the hospital, where she had been taken by her sister Nell. Tom waited outside on the front steps of our apartment to tell John the news when his trolley passed. John then left the trolley, telling the passengers that he would be right back, while he and Tom went into a "speakeasy" saloon on the corner run by Paul Hesse, who poured them each a schooner of beer on the house. One drink led to another, and the party went on until the saloon was raided by the police, who had been called in because of the long line of trolleys that had stopped behind the one John had abandoned. A reporter and photographer from the *Daily News* arrived together with the police, and a photo of the scene appeared on the front page of the newspaper the next day, under the headline STORK SNARLS TRAFFIC.

John returned to his trolley, but at the end of his run he was fired by the supervisor in Canarsie. During the next two years he worked intermittently as a longshoreman on the Hudson River docks whenever a cargo ship arrived. But his pay was very irregular and we were eventually evicted from the Cooper Street apartment.

Peg then managed to find a cheaper apartment a few blocks away, on Chauncey Street. There were a number of other Irish families on the block, which led Peg to say it was no wonder the rents were lower there.

Among them were the Gleasons, whose son Jackie would later become a famous star on television and in Hollywood. His extremely popular sitcom, *The Honeymooners,* was set in a flat on Chauncey Street exactly like ours; in one skit he described the decor as "Early Depression."

By then the Great Depression had begun, and John could find no work at all, nor could most of our relatives and Irish neighbors. It became the custom at the end of the month to give "rent parties," several of which we held in our apartment on Chauncey Street, the guests making a contribution to the rent and bringing along something to drink and a bit of food. There was always someone playing a fiddle or an accordion in the kitchen, and I remember fearing that the floor would give way as everyone danced the jig or reels or the stack-of-barley. Between the dances there were songs, some in Irish if there was someone from the Gaeltacht, the Irish-speaking areas in the west of Ireland, otherwise in English. There were rousing songs of rebellion, dirges of the famine years, laments of immigration and exile, and ballads of lost love.

The rent parties usually cost more money than they brought in. So on the first of the month we never had enough to pay the full rent, and eventually we were evicted. We then moved in with John's aunt Helen and her husband, Paddy Moran, who had a big house in Flatbush, all four of us sleeping in the hall bedroom that they usually rented out to bachelors. Peg felt the situation was hopeless, she said, and after a few weeks there she decided she would take me and Dorothy with her and go back to live with her parents in Ireland, and she would stay there until John found work.

Peg's sister Nell gave her the money for our one-way third-class tickets on a Cunard liner, which came to eighty dollars, forty for Peg and half fare for me and Dorothy. Nell gave Peg some extra money to buy new clothes for all of us, for she didn't want their parents to know that the Irish in America were as poor as they were in Ireland.

I remember very little of that first trip to Ireland and back, which Peg later told me began early in 1931. We were in Ireland only a few months when John wrote to say that he had found work, and that he had saved and borrowed enough money to pay for our return tickets. He had found a cheap furnished apartment on Chauncey Street, he said, a block away from where we had lived before, and we moved in there as soon as we returned.

John's job was with a gardening firm called Perpetual Care, which looked after burial plots in the Evergreens Cemetery, cutting grass and planting and watering flowers. The work wasn't steady, peaking in the spring and summer, particularly on Memorial Day, tapering off in the autumn except for All Souls' Day, and then leaving him virtually no work in the winter except shoveling snow for the City when blizzards struck New York.

Peg never had enough money to pay the rent, and she continually had to ask the landlord for an extension. Finally, when our rent was long overdue, we were evicted once again. Helen offered to take us in, but Peg thanked her and said that she was going to return to Ireland again until John had found a proper job and could afford a decent place to live. Nell bought tickets for us on a Cunard liner, and gave Peg as much money as she could for her expenses, for she knew that their parents wouldn't have a penny to spare.

We left New York early in the spring of 1932, a few months before my sixth birthday. I can remember our departure, which endures as one of the most painful of my early childhood memories. I can still see John's receding figure on the dock, waving up to us as the ship moved slowly away, Peg beside me holding Dorothy in her arms, weeping as she waved back to him. I can also remember passing the Statue of Liberty, which most immigrants see when they first arrive in New York, but which we saw when leaving—and for the second time, because of what Peg called our "contrary ways," always "sailing against the tide."

All I can remember of our voyage is the Atlantic itself, for we were all alone in the middle of the boundless ocean, our wake churning up behind us as far as I could see. Our cabin was partially below the waterline of the ship, and on calm days all we could see through our porthole was the bubbly blue-green sea coursing by. But in rough weather, the ship pitched and rolled and our porthole emerged above the surface periodically, waves smashing against it in a shower of spray. We were seldom in our cabin except to sleep, for Peg loved the sea and she kept us up on deck in all weather. Fortunately none of us were subject to seasickness.

We landed in the Cobh of Cork, which Peg still called Queenstown, its name under British rule. We took a train to Tralee, where we changed and boarded the narrow-gauge railway to Anascaul, halfway out along the Dingle Peninsula. The sea was in view on either side, Tralee Bay to the north and Dingle Bay to the south and beyond that the Kenmare Peninsula. We were now deep in Kerry, the ancient Kingdom of Munster, land of heroes, scholars, and minstrels, Peg said, quoting from a poem describing "King Aldfrid's Itinerary Through Ireland."

I found in Munster, unfettered of any,
Kings, and queens, and poets a many,
Poets well skilled in music and measure,
Prosperous doings, mirth and pleasure.

Tómas was waiting for us at the station in Anascaul, and he loaded the three of us and our trunk aboard what he called his "trap," a cart pulled by a donkey whom he addressed in a language Peg said was Irish. He spoke to Dorothy and me in English, and as we drove off, heading eastward along the southern shore of the peninsula, he gave us a lesson in local geography, myth, and history, tipping his trilby to those he passed along the way and greeting them in Irish.

Off to our south, on the other side of Dingle Bay, we could see the Kenmare Peninsula, and along its spine the Macgillycuddy's Reeks, the highest range of mountains in Ireland, its peak at Carrantuohill reaching over 3,400 feet. The Slieve Mish Mountains, which formed the backbone

My grandfather Tómas Murphy driving Dorothy and me in his trap on the Dingle Peninsula, 1933

of the Dingle Peninsula, were almost as high, the tallest peak, Mount Brandon, rising to more than 3,000 feet. The two peninsulas formed the southwesternmost extension of Ireland, and Tómas said that it was from the end of the Dingle Peninsula that St. Brendan the Navigator had set sail fifteen centuries ago on the voyage to the Isles of the Blessed.

Tómas told us all of this and more as we jogged along, relating the history and myths of the Dingle Peninsula, pointing out the cove where the "King of the World" had tried to invade Ireland, the megalithic standing stones left as monuments by the pre-Celtic people, the Fir Bolg, or "Bag Men," and the places where the "fairies," or "little people," had been seen on nights like May Eve and Halloween. As he talked on I could see why, as Peg had told me, he was known locally as Tómas a' Bhreag, "Tom of the Winds," because of his never-ending flow of talk, full of fascinating information that he must have gathered from the four winds, they said, for he could neither read nor write.

We slowed down when we reached Inch, where a spit of sand three miles long almost closes the inner end of Dingle Bay, protecting the harbor of Castlemaine from the great waves that I could see rolling in from the Atlantic. There we stopped for a brief visit at Foley's Pub, where Peg said she had worked when she was a girl. The Foleys and their customers welcomed Peg back and gave me and Dorothy a thousand million welcomes, as they say in Irish. They were all speaking Irish, though most everyone east of Dingle town on the peninsula spoke English too these days, Peg said. West of Dingle was part of the Gaeltacht, where the first language was Irish. Tómas spoke it fluently because he had been born out on the western end of the peninsula, and it was not until he went to Boston that he learned proper English.

After leaving Foley's we continued along the shore road, passing the church and the seaside graveyard where Tómas said some of my ancestors were buried. I counted four milestones before we came to the tiny hamlet of Lach, just four houses, two on either side of the road. The donkey, without being instructed, stopped at the first house on the left, a little stone cottage with a slate roof, set back a bit from the road, its door and two windows facing out to the sea. My grandmother Maire was waiting at the door to greet us, and she gathered the three of us into her arms, welcoming us in Irish and then switching to English. My uncle John was there too, looking frail and wan as he greeted us, trying to shield us from his hacking tubercular cough.

*My grandparents Maire and Tómas Murphy with Dorothy and me,
in Lach, Ireland, 1933*

When we entered the cottage Peg stood and looked around her for a moment with tears in her eyes. Years later she told me, speaking of that moment, that she remembered the cottage when it was full of life, eleven children and her parents crowded exuberantly into its three rooms, and now only her aged mother and father and her invalid brother were left, living out their last years in a house of silence and shadows. Then, while Maire made us tea on the turf fire of the great hearth, Peg went upstairs to the attic, and Tómas said to me with a smile, "Your mother will be up there with her novels, lad, there's been no one here to read them since she left."

Peg always said that summer twilight in Kerry was a thing of wonder, particularly out on the Dingle Peninsula, ten and a half degrees west of Greenwich and still on Greenwich time, so at the summer solstice the sun sets around ten o'clock, with its last light still glowing on the hilltops as midnight approaches. It was early spring when we arrived, but the peak of Mount Brandon was still alight when we finished supper that evening in the Murphy cottage, which soon began to fill with neighbors who had heard that Peg was back and came to greet her and us.

The first to arrive were Barry Callaghan and his daughter Peig, my mother's dearest friend, who lived in the next cottage along the road. My mother had wanted Peig to leave with her when she emigrated to America, but it wasn't possible, for her parents were old and she was the last of the children and was needed at home. Her mother had since died and Peig was living with her father, who though he was in his eighties still had some red left in his full beard.

The Sayers family from across the road had brought a jug of poteen, home-brewed Irish whiskey, and they all sat around the glowing turf fire and drank while they talked in Irish and listened to Barry play the fiddle, which made Peg happy, she said, for this was the Ireland she had missed and longed for in America.

The Murphy cottage had no electricity, running water, central heating, bathroom, or toilet, inside or out. Oil lamps and candles provided light, and heat came from the turf fire in the hearth, where Maire cooked our meals and baked bread that we covered with butter that she made in her churn. Everything we ate was from their tiny farm, except the fish that Tómas caught. Drinking water came from the barrel that captured rain running off the roof, or from the brook half a mile down the road where the local women did their laundry. Each of us took a bath once a week in a large wooden tub filled with rainwater that had been heated in a kettle over the turf fire. Bath time was early Saturday evening, in preparation for church the next day.

Every Sunday morning Tómas drove Maire and me and Dorothy to the church at Inch in his trap, while Peg stayed in the attic to catch up on her reading, she said. My uncle John always claimed that he walked to church, though Maire told me he wasn't going to mass but to Foley's, where he'd have his weekly pint of porter—the only joy in his life, poor man. Tómas always stayed outside in the trap while we attended mass, which was in Latin, though the sermon was in English. Maire told me in a whisper that some of the older people in the congregation didn't understand English, which she said was a blessing in disguise, for the priest, Father Mulcahey, was an ignorant old bore who always ranted on about sin and damnation. I asked her why Tómas didn't come with us into the church, and she explained that he was a free thinker, like my mother, who had inherited her atheism from him, "and may God have mercy on them both," she said, crossing herself.

Peg often took Dorothy and me down to the rocky strand across the fields below the Sayers house. Peig Callaghan would come along too, and she and Peg would sit on a great boulder at the top of the strand with Dorothy while I explored the beach looking for shellfish and minnows in the shallows, venturing as far as I could out on the rounded rocks, listening to them clatter as they rolled in and out with the ebb and flow of the tide.

I often went down to the cove with Tómas, watching him as he set his nets and lines, listening to him as he explained how the tides were influenced by the moon and the sun and the wind. Occasionally he would catch a big codfish, which he would salt and hang outside the cottage door, so at suppertime he could cut off chunks of it to add to our meal, which usually was a dish called pandy—mashed potatoes formed into a cone with butter filling its peak—which reminded me of a picture of Mount Fujiyama that was hung up on the wall above the hearth, next to an image of the Blessed Virgin.

I was very curious about the books in the attic, so Maire began teaching me to read and write, starting with the primers she had used when she was a schoolteacher. When I had finished with those I began reading the books I found in the attic, the first one I can recall being *A Pictorial Journey Around the World,* a travelogue illustrated with engravings. Maire told me that her father, Thomas Ashe, had bought this in Constantinople after he had recuperated from his wounds at Florence Nightingale's hospital. One of the chapters was entitled "A Voyage on the Limpopo," and another was "A Journey by Train Across the Ameri-

Bringing home freshly cut peat in a wicker basket atop a donkey's back, Ireland, 1933

can West." The chapter that fascinated me the most was about Constantinople, particularly the engraving showing mosques and minarets rising from the seven hills of the ancient city at the confluence of the Golden Horn and the Bosphorus, the historic strait that divides Europe and Asia, as Maire told me. She said that her father had talked about Constantinople till his dying day, and it was this that started me thinking about the city, now known as Istanbul, where I was fated to spend a large part of my life.

Once I accompanied Tómas when he took his donkey up to the bog in the hills above the cottage. There he cut turf with a flat spade called a slane, loading the bricklike pieces into a pair of wicker baskets on either side of the donkey's back. All the way along our way to and from the bog Tómas kept up a constant flow of talk, pausing to point out places of interest in the Slieve Mish Mountains that towered above us, rising up to the cloud-plumed peak at Caherconree, nearly three thousand feet above the sea. He pointed with his walking stick to a rocky knoll that he called the Magical Fort of Caherconree, which dated from thousands of years before Christ.

Tómas told me that the fort was built by the legendary hero Cu Roi Mac Daire, who was later killed there by an even greater hero, Cúchulainn, the two of them having fought over the maiden Bláthnaid. Cúchulainn and Bláthnaid were then slain by Cu Roi's druid Ferchertne, who threw them to their death from the peak of Caherconree.

He pointed out another site below Caherconree that he called the Giant's Table, three colossal standing stones, called *galan* in Irish, and on top of them an enormous stone slab. He said the monument had been built thousands of years before by another legendary Irish hero, the giant Finn Mac Cool, for only he could have lifted these colossal stones into place.

I was tremendously impressed by these monuments and their great antiquity, which seemed to be as old as the Egyptian pyramids and the Sphinx that I had read about in *A Pictorial Journey Around the World.* I mentioned this to Tómas, and he said that unlettered men like himself could comprehend vast intervals of time only in terms that they were familiar with in their daily life. He walked me up the hillside above his farm to show me a corn ridge, known in Ireland as a *crich,* a place where the earth had been piled up in ridged beds by generations who tilled

Dorothy and me on Tómas's donkey

the soil here back in the night of time, their furrows now covered with heather. A *crich* like this would have been worked over and over again in successive generations, he said, quoting an old Irish saying:

Three life-spans of a horse: a man;
Three life-spans of a man: an eagle;
Three life-spans of a yew tree: a corn ridge;
Three life-spans of a corn ridge: the end of the world.

Tómas said that his own people came from a culture much older than that of those who tilled the soil, for they and others like them earned their livelihood on the margin of the land and sea, fishing in the deep and gathering cockles, mussels, and periwinkles in the shallows, as well as the eggs of seabirds who nested on seagirt crags, tending goats who could live on the sparse vegetation out on the end of the Dingle Peninsula and on the Blasket Isles off its westernmost promontory, where he had spent his early years before going off to America.

Tómas took me out to the end of the peninsula in his trap in the late spring of 1932, a few weeks before my sixth birthday. It was an all-day outing, and we stopped several times on the way, first at the South Pole Inn in Anascaul. The publican, Tom Crean, was a veteran of the British navy and had been on Robert Scott's tragic expedition to Antarctica in 1911–12 as well as Roald Amundsen's voyage and trek to the North Pole the following year—or so Tómas told me. He introduced me to Crean, saying that I was newly arrived from America, and I shook hands with the great explorer, feeling that my knowledge of the world had expanded by just meeting him.

A short way beyond Anascaul we stopped at the seaside hamlet of Minard, where Tómas showed me a ruined tower that had been built almost a thousand years before by the Normans, when they crossed over to southwestern Ireland after conquering England. He told me that I had Norman blood in my veins, for my grandmother Maire was an Ashe, which in Irish is spelled Agassi, and it pleased me to think that I had some romantic foreign ancestry.

We saw another Norman tower, Ferriter's Castle, farther along the coast at Ballyferriter, which took its name from the ruined fortress. Tómas said that the most famous member of this Norman family was the poet Pierce Ferriter, who was sent to the gallows by the English in 1653 for rebelling against the Crown. Years later I read one of his poems, written while he was in prison awaiting execution.

O God above, look down on my lonely bed,
Where no light falls from dawn to dusk, and no
Sound but the rain dropping beside my head
On the stony pillow, and the roar of the waves below.

We then drove for miles without seeing a single house except beehive-shaped stone dwellings that Tómas said dated from the Stone Age. During the Great Hunger some of the dispossessed tenant farmers took shelter in them, as had his own family for a time after his father "died on the roads."

The road now took us along the heights above the outer end of Dingle Bay's northern shore, where Tómas pointed out the Blasket Isles, the little archipelago off the tip of the Dingle Peninsula, and beyond that a seagirt crag called Skellig Michael, the westernmost point of Europe, site of one of the oldest monasteries in Ireland. Above us to the north was Mount Brandon, where, according to Tómas, there were the ruins of a monastery founded by St. Brendan the Navigator.

We then rode on to the end of the peninsula at Dunquin, the westernmost village in Ireland and all of Europe. There we stopped at the famous Kruger's Pub, which Tómas told me was so called because the publican, Maurice "Kruger" Cavanaugh, supported the Afrikaners during the Boer War and took his nickname from their leader.

Peg had already told me that when the American aviator Charles Lindbergh made the first solo flight across the Atlantic in 1927, his first sight of Europe was the tip of the Dingle Peninsula. When I was introduced to Kruger, he told me that he had waved up at the plane, and that Lindbergh dipped its wings in response. Kruger pointed to an autographed photograph on the wall, showing Lindbergh standing in front of his plane, the *Spirit of St. Louis,* which in my imagination I could see flying over the pub and dipping its wings.

After Tómas and I left the pub we stood out on the promontory behind it and looked down on the little cove that served as the harbor of Dunquin, as huge combers rolled in from the Atlantic and smashed against the cliff beneath us in showers of rainbowed spray. "We're at the edge of the world, lad," Tómas said. "Here in Dunquin they say that the next parish is in America." America never seemed farther away than then, truly over the edge of the world, and I wondered how Lindbergh could have flown all that way like a seabird in his little plane, when we had taken more than a week on our huge Cunard liner.

Below us a long flight of stone steps led down to the cove below Dunquin, where the islanders beached their currachs when they rowed in from the Blaskets. There were just a hundred and fifty or so still living on the archipelago, Tómas said, most of them on the Great Blasket, by far the largest of the half-dozen inhabited isles. Only much later did I learn that twenty years or so just before I got there Irish scholars had been out on the Great Blasket, where they were listening to and transcribing the folktales of the islanders. One of these was *Twenty Years A-Growing,* by Maurice O'Sullivan, which came out in the fall of 1932 in both Irish and English. By then the stories of two other islanders had been published, again in both Irish and English: *An Old Woman's Reflections,* by Peig Sayers, and *The Islandman,* by Tómas O'Crohan. All three books became international best sellers and were translated into many languages. I read them in the early 1950s, just when the final few islanders had to leave the Blaskets. Most of them resettled in Worcester, Massachusetts, where on a St. Patrick's Day in the mid-1980s I came upon some of them in the Dingle Pub, all of them, even the younger generation, still talking and singing in Irish. A line from *The Islandman* comes to mind when I think of the day when I first saw the Blaskets, just two decades before they were abandoned forever: "The likes of us will never be seen again."

Soon afterward my cousin Lizzie Tish Murphy came to stay with us during what Peg called Lizzie's "last days," for she had been diagnosed by a doctor in Tralee as having "brain fever," which I now think was a brain tumor. Lizzie was about seventeen and had been ill for more than a year. She had been living in a remote cabin up in the foothills of the Slieve Mish Mountains with her parents, both of whom were consumptive and unable to care for her properly, and so my mother and Peig Callaghan had offered to look after her in the Murphy cottage, where she would have some company and could enjoy the sea air.

Lizzie and I became very good friends, and it pained me to see how much she was suffering, though she never complained and always smiled at me even when she was wracked by the worst of her headaches. Then she began lapsing into comas, and when the doctor from Tralee examined her again he said that she was "not long for this world."

One afternoon a visiting priest came to our cottage to give Lizzie what I was told was the Last Sacrament, Extreme Unction. After he left, the Callaghans and the Sayers and other families came to say the rosary, which was repeated over and over again by everyone except Peg and Tómas, who took turns checking on Lizzie, who was lying in our bedroom. Then not long after sunset Peg came out and told us that Lizzie had passed away.

Two of the women present then went into the bedroom, and Peg told me they would be preparing Lizzie for burial, washing her body and dressing her in clean clothes. One of the younger men went off to inform Lizzie's parents, and another went to tell the parish priest so he could arrange for her funeral and burial. Meanwhile, Lizzie was laid out in front of the hearth, with a veil covering her face and candles burning at the head and foot of her cot.

Then an old woman I'd not seen before sat in front of the hearth and began keening, singing what Peg told me were ancient Irish funeral laments called *caioneadh*. She said that sometimes, particularly at the death of a child or a young woman who had died in childbirth, the mourners would hear a woman wailing outside the house, the cry of the banshee, the supernatural death messenger of ancient Ireland. The few who claimed to have seen one always described her as a beautiful young woman, who was sometimes observed to be combing her long black hair.

I asked Peg if we might hear a banshee that night. She said that we might, for Lizzie Tish had died before her time, and it was for young women like her that the banshee most often appeared.

When the old woman finished her keening everyone resumed saying the rosary, as one by one they went up to kiss Lizzie and say a silent prayer for the salvation of her soul, or so I was told by Peg. I went up to kiss her myself, saying goodbye to her rather than a prayer.

The rosary went on as other families farther along the road on either side of our cottage began arriving to pay their respects to Lizzie. I went outside to get some fresh air, for the fumes from the turf fire were making me sleepy and I wanted to stay awake for Lizzie's sake, wondering what had become of her. It was then that I heard from the field across the road what I thought might be the wail of a banshee, which Peg had said sounded like the cry of a heartbroken young woman or a vixen fox. I considered for a moment crossing the road to see if I could catch a glimpse of the banshee, but the soughing of the wind in the trees frightened me and I went back inside the cottage.

I wanted to tell Peg what I had heard, but she was in deep conversation with Peig Callaghan. Then I thought to tell Tómas, but he was nowhere to be seen, until after a few minutes he appeared at the cottage door and went up to kiss Lizzie goodbye. I was puzzled at the time, and only years later did I realize that the banshee was actually Tómas, who had played the part of death's messenger for my sake, knowing that someday I would understand why.

Lizzie was buried on June 23, the eve of St. John's Day, one of the major holy days in Ireland. Tómas told me that this was the remnant of a pagan festival held at the time of the summer solstice, which the druids celebrated at a holy well. The following day he drove me to the Minard Castle to see a holy well dedicated to St. John—not the Baptist, as I later learned, but the "Light Giver," because of his association with the summer solstice, when the noon shadow is the shortest of the year. Pilgrims were circling the shrine while they chanted the rosary, throwing pebbles toward the well every time they completed a circuit. Tómas shook his head, saying, "Druids have been replaced by priests, lad, but superstitions remain the same. Last evening here they were leaping over bonfires, just as they did when they were pagans."

I celebrated my sixth birthday two days later. It was a beautiful day, and Peg gave a party for me on the huge boulder overlooking Murphy's Landing, where Tómas beached his currach. I still have one of the photographs Peg took that day, showing me and Dorothy and some of the Sayers children standing on top of the rock with Peig Callaghan, all of us gazing across Dingle Bay toward the Macgillycuddy Reeks and the Kenmare Peninsula, which formed the background to my world.

Late in the autumn Peg received a letter from John, saying that he had found a job, and as soon as he saved enough money he would send our return tickets. Then a few weeks later he wrote again to say that he had bought us tickets on one of the Cunard liners, scheduled to leave from Queenstown on February 1, 1933. He also asked Peg if she would take me and Dorothy to see his parents in Ballyhaunis, and he enclosed a money order to pay for our expenses.

A few days before Christmas the postman delivered a package from John, with presents for Peg and me and Dorothy. My present was an American Indian chief's war bonnet, with a nimbus of colored feathers, which I immediately put on and showed off to everyone who visited the cottage on Christmas Day. Because of the headdress, the local boys invited me to join them the following day, the feast of St. Stephen, to celebrate the "Hunting of the Wren," which they pronounced as "wran." All of us, "the wren boys," dressed up in bizarre costumes, my Indian headdress making me an instant celebrity.

We started the day by searching for a wren's nest in the thatched roofs of the local cottages. The other boys had already made an elaborate wicker cage, and when we found a wren we put it inside and paraded with it all the way to Inch, stopping at every cottage along the way, singing the "Song of the Wren," begging for a "trate," which was usually a sweet.

The Wran, the Wran, the king of all birds,
St. Stephenses Day, he was caught in the furze.
Although he is little, his honor is great,
Rise up, kind sir, and give us a trate.

We followed this Wran ten miles or more
Through hedges and ditches and heaps of snow.
We up with our wattles and gave him a fall
And brought him here to show you all.

For we are the boys that came your way
To bury the Wran on Saint Stephenses Day.
So up with the kettle and down with the pan!
Give us some help for to bury the Wran!

The Wran, the Wran, the king of all birds,
St. Stephenses Day, he was caught in the furze.
Although he is little, his honor is great,
Rise up, kind sir, and give us a trate.

Early in the New Year we took the train to Ballyhaunis, where my grandfather Michael Freely was waiting at the station. There was no mistaking him, for he looked just like my father, with a little red left in his hair, though he was in his early seventies, Peg said. He was driving a horse-drawn cart, and he put Peg and Dorothy in the back with our baggage, setting me beside him for the five-mile ride out to the farm.

The Freely cottage was larger than that of the Murphys, as was their farm, which was on the brow of a hill above the road, looking across a valley to another hillside covered with blackberry bushes. The cottage was made of whitewashed fieldstones, with walls a yard thick, and it was covered with a thatched roof. I later learned that the cottage was built around 1800, when the Freelys first settled in Ballyhaunis.

My grandmother Ellen was waiting there with my uncles Charley and Luke, and they all embraced us and welcomed us into the cottage. Peg had told me that Ellen was about sixty, though she was very pretty and looked much younger than that. Charley was twenty-three, and Luke, the youngest of the family, was going on seventeen. My father and his brother Willie had never met Luke, for he was born a few weeks after they left home in 1916.

We had tea around the great hearth, which was also the room in which all the children had slept, in a series of niches hollowed out of the walls on either side, each with a little curtain that could be drawn closed at

*The Freely house in Ballyhaunis, with my grandparents Michael and Ellen
Freely on the far right and Dorothy and me in front of my uncle Charley*

night. Ellen said that the niches were called "hags," and she pointed out
the ones that John and Willie slept in the night before they left home.

Though it was midwinter the weather was beautiful, and we spent a few
days wandering around the farm and the surrounding fields. During the
long evenings we sat around the hearth talking, and Peg had such a good
time, she said, that she was sorry we had to leave so soon, for we would
be boarding our ship in Queenstown at the beginning of February.

A few days later Michael died. He had been working in the barn and
fell down against the door, and I could hear Charley and Luke shouting
as they forced their way in to help him. They finally managed to open
the barn door and then carried him to his bed, and I could hear Charley
saying that he was not breathing and had no pulse. Ellen sent Charley
off with the horse and wagon to bring back the doctor from Ballyhaunis,
who said that Michael had died of a sudden heart attack or stroke.

Ellen took it very well, and sent Charley off to Ballyhaunis to arrange
for the funeral and burial. Then the rest of us left the room, for she said
that she was going to wash Michael's body in preparation for his burial,
and as we waited in the kitchen I could hear her weeping.

When I saw Michael again the next day he was dressed in his Sunday
suit and laid out in a plain wooden casket, which had been placed on
two chairs in front of the hearth, with tall candles at his head and feet.

Throughout the day people came in from Ballyhaunis and the surrounding towns to pay their last respects; many of them were Freelys, as I learned when they were introduced to us.

Then the priest arrived and led the mourners in a rosary, blessing Michael and placing a crucifix against his forehead. Next they all went up in turn to kiss Michael and say a prayer for him, after which they offered their sympathy to Ellen, Charley, and Luke.

The moment the priest left, Charley opened a jug of poteen and Luke brought out a tray of glasses, handing them around to the men, while Ellen and Peg made tea for the women. Someone had brought along a fiddle and someone else an accordion, and when they began to play all of the younger people got up to dance the jig and the stack-of-barley, which I recognized from our rent parties in Brooklyn.

This was the first time I had ever been to a wake, the traditional Irish farewell party for someone who had passed away in the fullness of their years, though I would later go to many more when we returned to Brooklyn. I learned that this was another pagan Irish custom, now banned by the Catholic Church, which eased the pain of death for those who had lost their beloved, as I could see from looking at Ellen, who was tapping her feet to the music, though I knew that she was grieving.

We left Ballyhaunis a few days after the funeral and took the train back to Anascaul, where Tómas was waiting for us in his trap. He was not his usual talkative self, and as we drove along in silence I realized that he was saddened because we would soon be leaving, and that made me sad as well.

Peg was silent too on our ride back to the cottage and in the days afterward. As the time of our departure approached she spent much of her time in conversation with Peig Callaghan, talking of the mixed feelings she had about returning to America. She hadn't been happy there, I heard her tell Peig, but there was no way we could remain in Ireland, for we would be a burden on her parents and her ailing brother John, who could barely support themselves.

I was troubled myself about returning to America, for the mountains and the sea around me had replaced virtually all of the vague memories I might have had of Brooklyn. The Dingle Peninsula was the only world I knew, and I began wondering if there was some way that I might stay there when Peg left with Dorothy.

I had been spending most of my days down in the cove at Murphy's

Landing. On rainy days I took shelter there under the huge rock where I had celebrated my sixth birthday. Beneath the overhang of the rock there was a small hollow where I could sit and look out across Dingle Bay, listening to the stones on the strand rattling as they rolled when the tide changed, watching the seagulls that dove down to catch minnows in the shallows, then joining them to search for periwinkles among the seaweed-covered rocks. By putting some tree branches across the mouth of the hollow I made the entrance all but invisible, and when I sat inside even the seabirds that perched within reach of me seemed unaware of my presence.

This was where I would hide, I decided, as the day of our departure approached. When the time came to leave I would hide in the hollow for a day or so, and after Peg left with Dorothy I would return to the cottage. The day before our departure I took some bread and dried codfish and put them in a burlap sack along with a jug of rainwater, and when I thought no one was looking I brought my supplies down to the hollow, where I had already left some candles and matches, along with an old burlap sack from the barn.

Our train would be leaving at noon from Tralee, and Tómas had arranged with a friend in Anascaul who had a motorcar to pick us up in the cottage at eight in the morning. We went to bed after supper on the eve of our departure, and as soon as I thought everyone was asleep I got dressed and snuck out of the cottage. It was pitch-dark and I was a bit frightened, but I had no trouble making my way down to the cove, where I crawled into the hollow and lit a candle, wrapping myself in the burlap sack.

I was prepared to sit up all night, but I must have fallen asleep right away. I was awakened by the mewing of seabirds on the strand outside the hollow, and I could see that dawn was approaching from the faint glow on the peaks of the Macgillycudy Reeks across the bay. The car from Anascaul would be arriving at any moment, I thought, and I began to wonder whether I had done the right thing by hiding here, for Peg would be very upset when she found that I was missing.

Just then I heard the sound of someone approaching across the rocky strand, and I peered through the branches. It was Tómas, with a lantern in his hand, and he was heading straight for my hideout. He pulled aside the branches at the mouth of the hollow and called in to me, "Come along, lad, 'tis time for ye to be leaving."

He took me by the hand and led me back to the cottage, where Peg gave me a tongue-lashing and told me to get properly dressed, for I looked like a young tinker, she said. A short while later the motorcar arrived, and the driver loaded our baggage in the boot. When all was ready we said our tearful goodbyes and boarded the car, as Tómas sent us off with the traditional Irish farewell:

May the road rise up to meet you and the wind always be at your back; may the sun be warm upon your brow and the rain fall softly on your fields; and may God hold you in the hollow of his hand.

As we drove away I looked back to see Tómas and Maire and John waving goodbye to us from the door of the cottage, which I would not enter again until many years had passed, when they were long gone and their world lost forever except in my memory.

The voyage from the Cobh of Cork to New York was my fourth trip across the Atlantic, which gave me a feeling of great pride, for though I was only six and a half I could already claim to be a world traveler. We were out on deck all day throughout the voyage, which was unusually calm for that time of year, as one of the crew told us. When we approached New York I stood out on the prow so I would be the first passenger to spot the Statue of Liberty, which I was now passing for the fourth time, though I hardly remember the first two trips.

John was waiting for us on the dock when we moored at Pier 92, and I recognized him at once, though Dorothy barely remembered him. Peg was very happy to see him, and I could tell that she was more hopeful about the future than she had been in Ireland. He had written to tell her that he was now working regularly as a gardener at the Evergreens Cemetery, and that he had found an apartment in Brooklyn, not far from where we had lived before we left for Ireland.

Our apartment was on the top floor of a three-story building on MacDonough Street, in the Bedford-Stuyvesant district of Brooklyn, which disappointed Peg, since she had been hoping for a ground-floor flat with a yard in front and a garden in back. I could see that she wasn't too pleased with the secondhand furniture that John had bought on credit, putting down ten dollars that he had borrowed, the rest to be paid in weekly installments for two years—though he had already missed the first two payments. There was no refrigerator or icebox, but there was a cabinet attached to the outside of the kitchen window that served as a fridge during the winter. The bathroom was in the hallway, shared by the family in the other apartment on the third floor, but we did have a private toilet off the kitchen. There was central heating, but there was no hot water other than what could be heated in a kettle. Peg didn't complain about any of the accommodations, which to her were luxurious compared to the Murphy cottage in Kerry, though she did miss the turf fire, and so did I.

Peg had asked John to buy her a canary, because she thought its warbling might cheer up the apartment. And so on his next payday he went to a pet shop and came home with two cages, one of them with a canary and the other containing a macaw, which he said the shop owner had given him free of charge, just to get rid of it. That evening we discovered why the man had been so generous: the canary never sang, while the macaw, which became my pet, squawked unless Peg covered its cage with a towel.

A week or so after we moved in there was a fire in the apartment downstairs and we were forced to flee from the building down the fire escape and stand in the freezing cold until the firemen put out the blaze. I was carrying the squawking macaw in its cage, which amused the firemen. After we were allowed back in the building Peg wept when she saw the condition of our apartment, for all of our belongings were soaked. We had to stay with Tom Freely and his family until our bedding and furniture dried out a bit, though everything was still damp and mildewed when we moved back in; I could tell that Peg was beginning to regret that she had come back to America.

My mother came down with a bad cold soon afterward, and I had to do the shopping until she recovered. The shops were all just around the corner on Saratoga Avenue, so I didn't have to cross any streets when I went first to the Jewish grocer, then to the Italian fruit and vegetable store, and finally to the German butcher shop, where on Saturdays there was a three-piece brass band playing outside to attract customers. Peg wrote out lists for each one of the shops and warned me to count the change carefully and to make sure that the Italian in the fruit and vegetable store didn't give me short weight on his scales. I managed all right in the first two stores, but the butcher shop was very difficult, particularly on Saturdays, when it was crowded with big German women who pushed me out of the way so I was always the last to be served, though the clerk did give me a slice of baloney to eat as I left.

Most of the food that I bought was very different from our fare in the Murphy cottage, where we had porridge or boiled eggs for breakfast, a mound of pandy and a piece of codfish for supper, and in between buttered bread and a cup of tea. Now at the grocer's I bought Wonder Bread, which was sliced, white, and so soft you could compress the whole loaf into a small fraction of its original size, but it had no taste at all. The first brand of cereal I bought was Wheaties, because the package had a picture of Jack Armstrong, the All-American Boy, but the next time I chose Kellogg's Corn Flakes, because the box had a drawing of Buck Rogers with cutouts of his rocket ships that I put together. In Ireland Dorothy and I always drank milk still warm and frothy from the cow, but now in the evening before going to bed we always had a glass of Ovaltine, which had a picture of Orphan Annie on the jar and a coupon inside that I mailed away to get her magic ring.

I did so well on these shopping expeditions that Peg sent me out to buy newspapers at the stand under the El station at Broadway and Halsey Street, for she wanted to learn what was going on in the world after being completely out of touch in Ireland. I bought the *Daily News* in the morning and in late afternoon the five-star edition of the *Journal-American*, which John wanted because it had the odds for the horse races and also the figures for the U.S. Treasury bond sales for that day, whose last three integers gave the winners of the illegal numbers lottery.

I read every page in both papers, starting with the comic strips and going on to international affairs, American politics, New York crime and scandals, editorials, columnists, both gossip and political, and, finally, the obituaries. My favorite columnist was Danton Walker, whose column in the *News* was entitled "Baghdad on the Subway" and filled with witty gossip about café society in Manhattan. My grandmother Maire had read me tales from *The Thousand and One Nights,* many of them set in medieval Baghdad, and now it pleased me to think that I was living in a great metropolis whose life could be compared to that of the fabled city of the caliphs.

Around the corner on Saratoga Avenue there was a branch of the Brooklyn Public Library, which I entered with much hesitation one day after passing it several times. The woman at the desk inside asked if she could help me, and I said that I wanted to look at the books. She asked me if I knew how to read, and when I told her that I could she began filling out an application for a library card, but when she learned that I hadn't started school yet she said that after I enrolled I should come back with one of my parents and then she would give me a card. Before I left she gave me a tour of the library and said that she looked forward to seeing me again soon.

The block on Halsey Street between Saratoga Avenue and Broadway had several saloons where my father and his brother Tom would drink on Saturday afternoons, while I waited outside and watched the passing crowd, which included the first black people I ever saw, all of whom were waiting for the trolley that would take them to their own neighborhood farther away in the Bedford-Stuyvesant section. One day I saw a black man lying on the sidewalk, and someone said that he had dropped dead while running to catch the trolley. The people passing by stopped to look, as I did, but no one tried to help him, and he was finally carted away in an ambulance.

Across the street from the biggest saloon, Boyle Brothers, there was a huge building called the Broadway Arena, where I went with John and Tom to see Irish Pat McCoy fight a black boxer named Kid Chocolate. We all cheered for Pat McCoy, but he was knocked out in the third round by Kid Chocolate, who received no applause because there were no blacks in the audience.

Farther down Halsey Street there was a big building called the Halsey Theater, where Peg took me and Dorothy to see *King Kong,* the first movie we had ever seen. On Saturday afternoons we sometimes went there for a vaudeville matinee, the performers including singers, musicians, jugglers, acrobats, magicians, and comedians, the most famous of whom was Joe Penner, whose opening line was "Does anyone wanna buy a duck?" But Joe Penner wasn't nearly as funny as my uncle Tom, who could make Peg laugh even when she was depressed.

Tom had been the caretaker at the American Legion Social Hall in Ridgewood, the next district to the north beyond Bushwick, on the Queens border. Whenever the Legion had a dinner or dance Tom and his wife, Chris, would clean up afterward, and then all the Freelys and Murphys would have their own party with the leftover food and drink.

Tom was eventually fired for helping himself to the liquor in the Legion Social Hall, but he soon found work as a janitor at the Fourteen Holy Martyrs Catholic Church in Bushwick, which also had a parochial school and a convent for the nuns of the Dominican order who taught there. The pastor, Father Multz, liked his whiskey, and Tom made sure he had a plentiful supply, part of which he diverted to his own use, along with some of the wine he smuggled in for one of the nuns, Rosey the laundress. He never took any of the sacramental wine from the sacristy, though—not because it would have been sacrilegious, but because it was too sweet.

A couple of weeks after we arrived Peg took me and Dorothy to enroll us at the parochial school of Our Lady of Lourdes, which was about a mile from our apartment. The Mother Superior of the Dominican nuns who ran the school put me in first grade and Dorothy in kindergarten. The spring term had already begun, so as soon as we were registered we were taken to our classrooms. I was very frightened at first, for I had no idea what to expect, but I soon relaxed when I saw that I was well ahead of my classmates; they were just beginning to form the letters of the alphabet and add one-digit numbers, whereas I could read and write as well as add and subtract big numbers, thanks to my grandmother Maire.

The first Saturday after we started school I went with Peg to the public library on Saratoga Avenue. The librarian gave me my library card as she had promised and I checked out my first book, Robert Louis Stevenson's *Treasure Island*. I finished that within the week, and the following Saturday I checked out Jules Verne's *Twenty Thousand Leagues Under the Sea*. The librarian said that at the rate I was going I would soon have read all the books in the library, which worried me, and I wondered if I should proceed at a slower pace.

A few days later I was playing on the street outside our flat after school when I was hit by a car. I wasn't hurt at all, but Peg was so frightened that she decided to move somewhere that had less traffic and was closer to our school. Besides, our apartment was infested with cockroaches, and though Peg tried everything she couldn't get rid of them, which led her to say, "If the roaches won't leave, then by God we will."

She soon found a place two blocks from Our Lady of Lourdes on Aberdeen Street, just inside the Brooklyn-Queens border. The apartment was on the ground floor of a two-story building just outside the boundary fence of the Evergreens Cemetery, with houses on one side of the street and open fields on the other. It also had a glassed-in porch at the back looking out on a little garden, which made Peg very happy. And there were no signs of roaches, although Peg worried that some of them might have gotten into our belongings, which had been moved from MacDonough Street in a hearse that Tom had borrowed from the Collins Brothers Funeral Home, near Fourteen Holy Martyrs Church. When the hearse parked outside our apartment our new neighbors thought that someone in the family had died, which mortified Peg, though Uncle Tom thought it was very funny.

John won a few dollars on the numbers lottery and bought us a secondhand radio, which we listened to in the late afternoon and after supper. My favorite program was *Og, Son of Fire,* a drama set in the Stone Age that came on at five in the afternoon, and after that I listened to *The Lone Ranger* and a mystery program called *The Shadow,* whose announcer began and ended each episode by saying "What mysteries lurk in the hearts of men, only the Shadow knows."

The lesson that I enjoyed most at school was the weekly art class, taught by an older woman who was not one of the nuns. I did a chalk and crayon drawing of Lindbergh's plane, the *Spirit of St. Louis,* as Kruger Cavanaugh would have seen it looking up from his pub in Dunquin. It was awarded first prize in my class, and when I told the story behind the drawing, also mentioning my meeting with Tom Crean at his South Pole Inn, I gained the reputation among my classmates of being a world traveler.

Our weekly assemblies at school were usually very boring, and I passed the hour daydreaming. But one week we had a special show about the American Indians that I will never forget, though I can't remember the name of the chief who sat cross-legged in front of his wigwam at the center of the stage, wearing a feathered war bonnet that was far more elaborate than the one I had worn as a wren boy in Ireland.

The chief never spoke except to say "How" at the beginning of the assembly, and he sat there silently while one of the nuns told us about the various Indian tribes and their customs. That Saturday I went to the library to find a book about the Indians, and I checked out *The Last of the Mohicans,* by James Fenimore Cooper.

John took me and Dorothy to mass every Sunday at Our Lady of Lourdes, where I made my first holy communion early that spring,

Dorothy and me, back in Brooklyn. I'm in my Indian chief's outfit.

My first communion. I'm dressed in
my new blue suit, Brooklyn, 1934.

wearing a navy-blue suit with knickers that my aunt Nell bought me and that I never wore again because a boy in my class said that I looked like a sissy.

At the end of the first month I brought home a perfect report card from school, with a note from my teacher saying that I was the top student in the class. When Peg read the note she said, "In the land of the blind the one-eyed man is king," which, as I learned, was her way of keeping me from developing an inflated ego. That concerned my personal appearance as well, as when she sighed one day and said, "To think that I, Peg Murphy, have a homely son." She was referring to what she called my "Irish pug nose," which she compared unfavorably with the features of her handsome younger brother Tommy, who had "a spear of a nose," she said, which led me to tie a string around my head to bend down the upward tilt of my nose.

Tommy was a merchant seaman, and when his ship docked in New York that spring he came to see us on Aberdeen Street. He was indeed handsome and very funny and charming, and I could see why he was Peg's favorite. He sat me on his lap and told me of his adventures, which included surviving storms in the North Atlantic and a hurricane in the China Sea, as well as knocking out a Russian policeman during a drunken brawl in the Arctic port of Archangel. He gave me sips of his whiskey while he was spinning these tales, and I woke up the next morning with a terrible headache. Peg gave me an aspirin and told me that I had a hangover, saying, "And may that be a lesson to you," while she took two aspirins herself.

A few months later Peg received a letter from her mother saying that Tommy had been lost at sea off the coast of Madagascar, and she cried for days afterward. I was very sad too, for Tommy had become a hero to me, and it was he who put the idea in my head of spending my life at sea.

So I started reading books about the sea, beginning with Richard Henry Dana's *Two Years Before the Mast.*

Not long after that a letter arrived from Peig Callaghan, who told Peg that a flu epidemic had virtually wiped out their little hamlet of Lach, killing off her own father, Barry, as well as Peg's father and mother and her brother John, along with several of the Sayers family. Peg again wept for days, and I was deeply saddened as well, both for Peg and for the loss of the first home I ever knew, and to which I could now never return.

One day in class our teacher announced that we had a new president named Franklin Delano Roosevelt, and she wrote his name on the board so we would know how to spell it. I already knew about Roosevelt because I read the *Daily News* and the *Journal-American* every day. There I learned about the New Deal that he promised the American people, particularly his plan to provide work for the unemployed, which now included most of the men of our extended family.

Roosevelt also promised to end the prohibition of alcohol, which made him even more popular with all of our family except Peg, who said that if the saloons were allowed to operate legally that would be the end of the Irish in America, who were already drinking themselves to death. When Peg heard someone say that alcohol was all right if taken in moderation, she said, "With the Irish, it's either dead drunk in the ditch or no brandy on the Christmas pudding!"

Prohibition ended at the beginning of December 1933, and saloons opened up all over our neighborhood, many of them former speakeasies well known to John and his brother Tom. One Saturday afternoon they took me to Paul Hesse's saloon on the corner of Wilson Avenue and Cooper Street, where the picture on the front page of the *Daily News* for December 20, 1927, was still framed on the wall above the bar, showing John and Tom drinking schooners of beer against the background of a line of stalled trolley cars, the headline above reading S T O R K S N A R L S T R A F F I C. I knew enough not to tell Peg about this, for the merest mention of that legendary episode would send her into a fury, followed by tears and a silent supper.

The newspapers were full of articles about the Great Depression, an expression I first heard in reference to Peg's mental condition, for she often complained about being depressed, and now it seemed as if all of America had the same problem. John at least had a job, but he was paid only when someone hired him to look after their funeral plot in the Evergreens Cemetery, and on days when there was no work he came home without a penny, though he was sometimes able to trap a rabbit for our supper.

When there was no money in the house we would get help from one or another of our relatives who lived nearby, although most of them were as badly off as ourselves. Peg's younger brother Mauris was the only one of our relatives who had a steady job, reading meters for the Brooklyn Edison Company. Mauris didn't spend his money in saloons like other Irishmen, Peg said, but he always brought his full pay packet home to his wife, Madge, so we could always count on them for help.

We could also rely on my aunt Nell, who worked as an orderly at the Creedmor insane asylum on Long Island. Nell not only lent us money, but she also brought us bags of stale bread from the asylum, which Peg used to make bread pudding. She also gave us scores of toilet paper rolls that had been used except for the last turn or two, which she would leave in a burlap sack at the change booth in the Halsey Street subway station. It was my job to carry it home, to the jeers of all the kids I passed on the way.

Many people in our neighborhood had been evicted for not paying their rent, and on my way to and from school I often saw families with all of their furniture and belongings piled on the sidewalk. One woman was feeding her baby in a high chair while her husband and three other children were sitting on the curb. Ten million Americans were unemployed, according to a headline in the *Daily Mirror,* and below the headline there was a photograph of a breadline in Brooklyn. The Our Lady of Lourdes Church provided free sandwiches at lunchtime for the poorer students, and Dorothy and I brought home some of the leftovers when there was no other food in the house, though Peg felt deeply shamed that we had to live like "miserable paupers."

Late in the autumn of 1934 the Perpetual Care company went bankrupt and John was totally without work. He tried shaping up on the docks as a longshoreman, as he had before we left Ireland, but there were many hundreds of unemployed men doing the same, and he was never hired; he came home at the end of the day minus the ten cents he had spent on subway fare. It seemed as if we would have to move in with the Morans again, which upset my mother, though she knew there was no other way for us to survive.

Peg said that she couldn't bear the shame of being evicted once again, so she began packing up our belonging so that we would be ready to leave as soon as our next month's rent was due, for our landlord refused to give us an extension. We wouldn't bother taking our furniture, she said, because we were several months behind in our payments and might just as well let the company repossess it.

On the first of the month my uncle Tom arrived driving the Collins Brothers hearse to take us and our belongings to the Morans' house in Flatbush. I was carrying the macaw's cage, but Peg said that Helen would never tolerate such a filthy creature, so I had to leave it with Tom. He promised to look after it, though it screeched when he carried it away, as it always did when it was disturbed.

We moved into the Morans' house in January 1935. They lived in the part of Flatbush that is now called Flatlands, a marshland that had originally been part of Jamaica Bay. I could smell the sea from where we lived, near the corner of Flatbush and Flatlands avenues, and it reminded me of Ireland.

The Morans had a big house, though there were just the two of them and their daughter, Mary, who at the time we moved in was living in her own apartment in Manhattan. They no longer rented out rooms to bachelors, for they were too old to deal with the bother that tenants involved. Now there was more space for us, and Helen let us have two large bedrooms instead of the single small room that we had lived in before we left for Ireland. We had the full use of the rest of the house, and Peg was quite happy, cheerfully doing all of the cooking and housework, though she would have preferred a place of her own.

John spent the first couple of weeks looking for work and finally managed to find a part-time job as a laborer with the Works Progress Administration, one of the new agencies created by President Roosevelt. The pay wasn't much, but it was enough that we weren't a financial drain on the Morans, and Peg didn't need to hang her head down like a beggar, as she said to me one day.

Peg enrolled me and Dorothy at a public school in Flatbush, where for the first time I had classmates who were not Catholics, but mostly Protestants and Jews. The only other Irish boy in my class was Jack Reynolds, who was much bigger than I was and tried to bully me until I bloodied his nose in a fistfight. We then became good friends, but his family soon moved away and I began to make friends with some of the Jewish boys in my class. Their families were mostly from eastern Europe, and when I visited their homes I heard the older people speaking a strange language that I learned was Yiddish.

Many of the teachers were Jewish, too, and they seemed to know more about the world than the nuns who taught at Our Lady of Lourdes. We had different teachers for each of our subjects, which included science, of which I had learned nothing in parochial school. I heard the name of Albert Einstein for the first time, and I wrote a term paper on the relativity of time, which I had to present in front of the class. It was the only time I ever spoke in public in my school career, for in parochial school we only listened and never spoke, which is no cure for the crippling Irish handicap of shyness.

Our science teacher also told us of the amazing advances being made in astronomy, the most dramatic being the discovery of the planet Pluto in 1930. There was a branch of the Brooklyn Public Library only a block from our house, and after I received my new library card there I checked out a book on astronomy. The book had been published ten years before and said nothing about Pluto, but when I told this to my science teacher he lent me a copy of a more recent text that had a chapter on the new planet and other recent discoveries, including the theory of the expanding universe.

I knew then that I wanted to be a scientist, but I still dreamed of spending my life at sea like my uncle Tommy. When I asked Peg about this she cried thinking about Tommy, saying that she'd never let me go to sea, and how could I even think of being a scientist, when the likes of us couldn't even dream of going to college. She said that when I came of age I should take a civil service exam and become a policeman or a fireman, for I'd have a regular salary and afterward a pension. I agreed with her and then went to my room to read the two books I had just checked out of the library, a new astronomy textbook and Joshua Slocum's *Sailing Alone Around the World*.

The ocean was only seven blocks away down Flatbush Avenue, which led to an inlet of Jamaica Bay in Marine Park. I walked out on the frozen bay until I fell through the ice up to my waist, and then as I waded back

I lost my way and it was nearly dark before I reached dry land again at the end of Flatbush Avenue. Peg was so glad to see me that I got off without the usual scolding, and I promised her I wouldn't go wandering off again, though I was already planning my next exploration of the surrounding seashore.

Our public school had one period a week devoted to physical education, which was usually just boring calisthenics, but I learned to play basketball and softball. I was already very interested in baseball from reading the sports section in the *Daily News,* and I wrote away to become a member of the Brooklyn Dodgers Knothole Gang. Club members were given free tickets to a half-dozen games at Ebbets Field, usually when the Dodgers were playing some other team low in the standings and there were plenty of empty seats.

In mid-May 1935 I went to Ebbets Field with a group of other boys from the neighborhood to see the Dodgers play the Boston Braves. I had been following the sports pages closely and I knew that the great Babe Ruth would be playing for the Braves, who had bought him from the New York Yankees at the end of the previous season. The sportswriters were saying that the Babe was finished, and that it was just a matter of time before he hung up his spikes. But when he came out for batting practice everyone rose to their feet and gave him a standing ovation, which he acknowledged by doffing his cap. While he waited for his turn to hit he stood leaning on his bat, gazing out to the bleachers in right field where I was sitting, and I had the feeling that he was looking directly at our Knothole Gang. The Babe did nothing much in the game that I watched, but two days later, playing against the Pittsburgh Pirates, he hit three home runs. The following day he announced his retirement, and when I read the story in the *Daily Mirror* I knew that he had been saying goodbye to us that day at Ebbets Field.

My sister Nancy was born on November 1, 1935, while we were living in Flatbush. It now became very crowded at the Morans', and Peg decided that we had to have a place of our own, though she had no idea how we could afford one.

Then the saints in heaven worked a miracle, as Peg said to me one day when I returned from school, for John had finally found a full-time job. Paddy Moran knew Mike Quill, head of the Transport Workers Union, who used his influence with the BMT to have John rehired as a trolley car conductor. Paddy said that to do this they first had to clear up John's file by removing the record of what had happened on December 19, 1927, though those who drank in Paul Hesse's saloon could still see the incriminating news article from the *Daily News* on the wall.

When John returned to the Morans' house that evening, we had a party to celebrate our good fortune. "God doesn't close one door but that he opens another," Helen said, and all of the grown-ups drank to that, though I knew that Peg thought otherwise.

John was once again assigned to the trolley line that ran between Canarsie and the Williamsburg Bridge, beginning late in the autumn of 1936. Soon afterward we left the Morans', once again loading all of our possessions into the Collins Brothers hearse. My uncle Tom drove us back to our old neighborhood in Bushwick, where he had found us a flat directly above his own on Central Avenue between Eldert and Covert streets, across from the Fourteen Holy Martyrs Church and School.

As soon as we had moved our belongings into the flat, my aunt Chris invited us to have supper in their apartment downstairs. After supper I asked Tom about my macaw and he said it had died. When I seemed upset about this he took me down to the candy store on the ground floor of the building and bought me a Baby Ruth candy bar. Then he brought me with him as he drove the hearse back to the funeral home, which was just a block away to the left, just next to the Evergreens Bar and Grill on the corner of Central Avenue and Eldert Street.

After Tom returned the hearse he took me with him into the bar and bought me an orangeade, which I drank while he had a whiskey with a beer chaser. Tom told me that this was his office, for he could sit at the bar during the day and keep an eye on Fourteen Holy Martyrs, which was just across Central Avenue on the next block. Above the bar there was a mosaic photograph that extended the full length of the room, showing the saloon's annual Fourth of July picnic from the days when it was still a speakeasy, a rear view of about a hundred men peeing simultaneously into Lake Ronkonkoma, setting up a beautiful pattern of intersecting waves.

When I got home I could see that Peg was unhappy with our new flat, which was on the third floor of what she called "a filthy roach-infested firetrap." But she made the best of it, because it was, at least, a place of our own, and the next day she put me to work with her as she cleaned up the flat and tried to drive out the roaches—or just make them move next door, as she said when she saw them scurrying under the door that led to the hallway.

The flat was unfurnished, and Peg had to start from scratch once more, buying kitchen and living room and bedroom furniture on time at Mason's Department Store on Broadway, making a down payment with money Nell gave her. She also began to accumulate dishware by going to the Colonial Theatre with me every Tuesday evening, when they gave away a set of fifty-two pieces one at a time; for the next year we didn't miss a film for fear of not completing the set. The best movie I saw that year was *Lost Horizon,* starring Ronald Colman, which led me to add Tibet to the list of faraway romantic places that I planned to see when I resumed my travels.

As soon as we were settled Peg took me and Dorothy across the street to enroll us in the Fourteen Holy Martyrs School, which was directly above the church. The teachers were all nuns of the Dominican order, and their principal was the Mother Superior, who assigned me to the fourth grade and Dorothy to the third. She said that we were obliged to attend mass every morning at 8:15 before school, and she showed me and Dorothy the pews to which our classes were assigned, boys to the right of the aisle, girls to the left, the lower grades in front.

The spring term began on January 15, 1937. Peg got us up early, and we crossed the street to the church at eight o'clock sharp. No one was there except our uncle Tom, who was sweeping up after the six-thirty mass, and we talked to him for a few minutes before going to our seats.

I took Dorothy to her pew and then went to find mine. I saw that a boy about my age had come in and was sitting in the first row of the fourth-grade pews, and he motioned for me to come and sit beside him. He said his name was Jimmy Anderson, and the Mother Superior had told him that I would be joining the class and he should look after me. Then the other boys in our class began filing in, and Jimmy whispered their names to me. The girls in our class were sitting across the aisle with our teacher, a ferocious-looking old nun whom he identified as Sister Saint Peter. Even though he had barely whispered her name, she turned and silenced us with a look that I very soon learned to fear.

After mass I followed Jimmy up to our classroom, where Sister Saint Peter read out our names, thirty-one girls on the left side of the room and twenty boys on the right. I was put by the window in the last row next to Jimmy, who told me that Sister Saint Peter seated her students according to their final grades, and that Jimmy had ranked last among the boys. "That means she thinks you're just as dumb as I am," he whispered, and when we laughed Sister Saint Peter smacked us both on the side of the head, making my ears ring.

But I found that Jimmy wasn't dumb, for he seemed to know a lot about the street life of Brooklyn, though he wasn't particularly interested in book learning. I thought I would show Sister Saint Peter that I was as smart as Richard Holtzman, John Mione, and Albert Kreyl, the three top boys, whose marks were higher than those of Mary McCabe, Muriel Rogers, and Ruth O'Kane, the three smartest girls. But that would mean I would be moved up to the front of the room, where it would be more difficult to look out the window and daydream. Besides, I wasn't interested in anything Sister Saint Peter taught except geography, and when she pulled down the maps from the roller above the blackboard I would take to daydreaming about the faraway places to which I would travel one day.

Sister Saint Peter gave daily quizzes, and by memorizing the principal products of Peru and other such information I eventually worked my way up to the head of the class alongside Richard Holtzman. Richard was very smart and knew far more than I did about things like American history and politics, which he had learned from his father, who was a lawyer. He was also very witty and told me some terribly funny jokes, but when I laughed out loud at one of them Sister Saint Peter had me up in front of the class and whacked me with her yardstick ten times across the palms of my hands. She then changed my seat and sent me back to the last row next to Jimmy.

Jimmy's father was dead, and his mother was an invalid. His older sister, who was about twenty, supported the family on her wages as a secretary, but one day she disappeared and was never seen again. Jimmy's mother had a small pension, but it wasn't nearly enough to support them, and he made ends meet by delivering newspapers and other odd jobs.

One of his jobs was making the rounds on Saturday and Sunday with a homemade wagon in which he collected old newspapers, discarded furniture, household appliances, broken radios, scrap metal, and other assorted junk, which at the end of the day he sold to a junk dealer. I became his helper, although he wasn't able to pay me anything other than buying me a Baby Ruth chocolate bar if it had been a good day. But the reward for me was getting to learn things about Brooklyn that I would otherwise not have known: the garbage dumps where he found most of his newspapers and other junk, the boarded-up houses where he helped himself to whatever could be carried away, the railway freight yard where he picked up scrap metal along the tracks, and the abandoned ice house where he stripped the lead roofing and ripped the copper refrigeration pipes from the walls.

The ice house had lost all of its floors in a fire, so Jimmy and I had to climb the walls by shimmying up the pipes that he hadn't yet ripped out. Most of the roof was still in place, and when we climbed up there we straddled one of the pipes and hung upside down in the darkness like bats, shouting and laughing to make echoes that sent the doves cooing and flapping from their nests in the rafters.

The ice house was next to the railway yard, which had tunnels at both ends that were used by the freight trains as well as the subway line that led from Canarsie to Fourteenth Street and Eighth Avenue in Manhattan. Jimmy and I would climb the chain-link fence above the railway yard and make our way along the ledge of one of the tunnels, where there was just room enough for us to sit and look down on the freight trains passing below, counting boxcars. Once we made our way in along the subway tunnel in the direction of the Wilson Avenue station, taking care not to touch the electrified third rail and backing into recesses in the wall when a train approached. One of the subway motormen must have seen us, because when we approached the station we noticed a policeman shining a flashlight in our direction, so we raced back along the tracks to the tunnel entrance and made our escape, hiding for a while in the ice house before we went home.

Later I made my own wagon and scavenged for junk independently of Jimmy, once I had learned the ropes from him. We scoured the neighborhood on separate blocks, meeting up at the end of the day in the junkyard, after which we would go to the abandoned ice house. We had built a little ramshackle clubhouse there, where we counted our earnings and talked about our day's adventures until it was time to go home.

Peg knew how much I loved baseball, so she bought me a bat and ball for my tenth birthday. The bat was a Louisville Slugger, and the ball was inscribed with the name Babe Ruth, which made it my most treasured possession. Jimmy and most of the other boys in my class came to my birthday party, and after we ate the cake and had a tug of war with the bat in our living room we went out to play baseball in a vacant lot beside the railway yard, using a piece of cardboard for home plate and rocks for the bases. The back half of the lot was about ten feet higher than the front, with a thirty-degree slope between the two levels, which complicated the ground rules of the game. Also, the railway yard was below the back of the lot, so when someone hit a homer one of the outfielders would have to climb over the fence and retrieve it. But then Jimmy hit the ball into the open boxcar of a passing freight train, and that was the end of our game and season, because we could never accumulate enough money to buy another baseball.

After that we played stickball on one of the side streets off Central Avenue, using a sawed-off broomstick for a bat and a Spalding rubber ball that we chipped in to buy. The game usually ended when we broke someone's window, after which we scattered before the police car came.

During the fall we played roller skate hockey in the street. I had neither skates nor hockey stick, so I substituted for anyone who was winded or worn out, which was usually Joey Bausch, who had a heart condition. Billy Decker would often lend me his skates and stick when his mother called him in to do his homework, and Martin Kaiser would sometimes do the same. Both of them were from German immigrant families, and I was struck by how much quieter and more restrained their way of life was compared to that of the recently arrived Irish like ourselves.

Bobby Doyle was Irish too, but his parents had been born in the United States, and the extra generation from the immigrant ships made a difference, for his family seemed more refined than our clan, though I never told this to Peg, for she'd have killed me. But after a few visits to the Doyles' I found that they had lost their native gift of gab, and their talk was not nearly as interesting or as wildly funny as in our flat, particularly when my aunts and uncles were gathered for an evening of the *craick*, which is what the Irish call an explosion of mirth, often followed by a deep Gaelic melancholia.

The other Irish in my class were all born here except for Theresa Mahr, who had come from Ireland just the year before. She still had a strong Irish brogue, much more pronounced than mine, but she was so shy that she rarely spoke, so Sister Saint Peter put her in the back of the class and forgot about her, which suited Theresa fine, she told me.

Then one day Sister Saint Peter announced that the class would put on a play before the Christmas holiday. The play was a one-act comedy about an Irish immigrant who comes to rent a room at a lodging house run by an ill-tempered old Irish widow. All eyes turned to me and Theresa, who blushed crimson when Sister Saint Peter ordered the two of us up in front of the class and gave us our scripts, telling us that we had just two weeks to learn our lines.

Theresa had a very good memory, as did I, and by the end of the first week we knew our lines by heart. We practiced in the classroom at lunchtime under the watchful eye of Sister Saint Peter, who never smiled even at the funniest lines, some of which I ad-libbed, for I was beginning to enjoy myself and so was Theresa, although we were both terrified at the prospect of performing in public. And we'd have to do the play twice, first in front of the class, and then after school before the parents. I didn't tell Peg about the play, which was broad stage-Irish burlesque, which she would hate, particularly the scene where the Irishman becomes ensnarled in the rolls of flypaper hanging from the ceiling of the lodging house parlor. That bit of stage business was my idea, for I remembered that in the summer my grandmother Maire hung a roll of flypaper inside our cottage, "to catch the unwary creatures before they take up residence with us," she said. Peg would know immediately who was behind the flypaper farce, and for sure I would catch hell for giving the impression that the native Irish lived in such squalid conditions. At our last rehearsal I whispered to Theresa that to make the scene even more realistic we should have a pig in the room, and she laughed so much that Sister Saint Peter knocked our heads together.

The play turned out to be a great hit, particularly the flypaper scene, which brought down the house at both performances. It took a long time to get the flypaper off my clothes, though, and I didn't want any of it sticking to me when I went home, lest Peg should learn what I'd been up to.

The only other girl in my class I came to know well was Jean Caputo, whose father owned a barbershop on Cooper Street. He and his wife were both from northern Italy, and they had met and married in New York. Jean told me that her parents had decided to settle in the Bushwick area for the same reason Peg had—to not have to be among their own kind, particularly in the tough Italian ghetto around the church of St. Rose of Lima on Palmetto Street, where everyone was either Sicilian or Neapolitan.

I heard Italian opera for the first time in the Caputos' living room, listening to Enrico Caruso singing an aria from *Rigoletto.* I borrowed the record and played it for Peg that evening, and she said that Caruso sang like an angel. She thought that he sang even more beautifully than the best tenor that Ireland had ever produced, and so to compare them I put on a recording of John McCormack singing "The Dawning of the Day."

No cap or cloak this maiden wore, her neck and cheek were bare,
Down to the grass in ringlets fell her glossy golden hair,
A milking pail was in her hand, and she was lovely, young, and gay,
She bore the palm from Venus bright, by the dawning of the day.

On a mossy bank I sat me down, with the maiden by my side,
With gentle words I courted her, and asked her to be my bride.
She said, "Young man, don't bring me blame," and swiftly turned away,
And the morning light was shining bright, at the dawning of the day.

Ordinarily that would have put Peg into a despondent mood, reminding her of what she called "the lost Ireland of days gone by," but she only laughed and said it wasn't fair to compare an Italian aria with a sentimental Irish folk song. So we gave Ireland another chance by playing something I'd not heard before, a recording of McCormack singing an aria from *La Traviata,* and we agreed that he was no match for Caruso.

Peg went on to talk cheerfully about Brooklyn, saying it was grand that I had a classmate who could introduce me to Italian opera, and to have a public library nearby from which I could borrow novels and books on history and science, and a school across the way where I could study, whereas in Ireland she had had to walk for miles barefoot to learn nothing from an ignoramus of a teacher.

This surprised me, because up till then Peg had always been so negative about living in New York, and I realized that recently she had seemed happier than I had seen her in a long while. That evening I learned why, when she told me and Dorothy and Nancy that we'd soon have another baby sister or brother.

My brother, Jimmy, was born on June 10, 1937. I saw him for the first time a week later when Peg returned from the hospital. "What a pity," she said, as she showed him to me and Dorothy and Nancy. "He has red hair just like his father."

John wasn't there to hear that compliment, for after returning from the hospital he had gone with Tom to Paul Hesse's bar to celebrate the birth of his second son. It was his day off, so this time there was no fear that the stork would snarl traffic. When I passed the bar with Jimmy Anderson, John came out to say hello. He gave me a dime, which I realized was a bribe so I wouldn't tell Peg where I'd seen him, though I never would have done so anyway. I appreciated the money all the same, and I used it to buy two frozen ice cream sandwiches, one for myself and the other for Jimmy. We put them in our pockets and ran all the way to the railway yard, where we made our way out on the ledge above one of the tunnels. We ate the ice cream sandwiches there, watching the trains pass by beneath us. Life in Brooklyn was indeed grand, now that I had a baby brother and Peg was happy again.

S oon after Peg returned from the hospital she began looking for a new apartment, because she hated the flat on Central Avenue, even more so now that she had to bump Jimmy's pram up and down two flights of stairs every time she wanted to give him an airing. And she was afraid to let Nancy and Dorothy play outside because she thought they might be hit by a car, as I had been years before on MacDonough Street. There was also the noise from the Fourteen Holy Martyrs School, particularly after classes were let out and all the kids hung around on the sidewalk in front of the candy store on the ground floor of our building.

I didn't join the others at the candy store myself because I had no time between doing chores for Peg, scavenging with Jimmy, and checking books in and out of the library on Hopkinson Avenue. But I did go to the candy store if I had earned a few pennies scavenging or taking empty milk or beer bottles back to the grocers for the deposit, which was then three cents, although I could get away with that only when Peg lost count of the empties.

Most of the money I spent in the candy store was on chewing gum, which I hated because it tasted like perfumed rubber, but I had to buy it for my collection of the picture cards that came in each package. My first collection was of pictures of Indian chiefs, of which my favorites were Geronimo and Tecumseh. I also collected baseball cards, particularly of the Brooklyn Dodgers, and I had to do a lot of trading before I had pictures of everyone on the team. Then a new set of cards appeared with colored drawings of the atrocities that the Japanese soldiers were committing in China, particularly their massacre of the people in Shanghai in 1937, which I had read about day by day in the *Daily News* and the *Journal-American*. Nobody else was interested in the Japanese-atrocity cards, so I was able to complete my collection by trading duplicate pictures of Indian chiefs and Brooklyn Dodgers. But Peg took a dim view of what she called my morbid collection of mass murders, and I had to keep the Japanese cards out of her sight, in the secret hiding place I had created in a hole in the wall behind the closet in the bedroom I shared with Dorothy and Nancy. I also hid there the diary in which I had been recording my thoughts, which I wrote in the invisible ink I had learned to make from the Dick Tracy Boy Detective kit Aunt Nell had given me for Christmas.

Peg finally found a new apartment late in July 1937. It was about half a mile west of Fourteen Holy Martyrs at 225 Cornelia Street, near the corner of Wilson Avenue, which was on the route of the trolley car that John drove. We moved there on the first Sunday that John had off in August, and Tom once again borrowed the Collins Brothers hearse, though Peg refused to ride in it, preferring to walk, pushing Jimmy in his pram and accompanied by Dorothy and Nancy. Tom had to make several round-trips with the hearse, because we now had our own furniture, and so the move took all day—in part because in between loads he and John stopped off at a bar at the corner of Wilson Avenue and Jefferson Street. Jimmy and I moved all of the household appliances and odds and ends in our wagons, and on the return trips we took a different route each time to scavenge old newspapers that we stored at our hiding place in the abandoned ice house.

Our new apartment was what they called a "parlor floor and basement," in a three-story brownstone house owned by Harry and Josephine Simmons. Peg didn't know what nationality Mr. Simmons was, although she thought he might have changed his name to hide his origins. Mrs. Simmons was Polish and proud of it.

The Simmonses lived on the top floor, while we had the ground floor and two rooms on the middle floor. The front room on the ground floor was the parlor, the middle room was a bedroom where my parents slept, with Jimmy's crib beside them, and the back room was our kitchen. Dorothy and Nancy had the front bedroom upstairs, and I had the middle room, the first time I had had a room of my own. When visitors came, I had to share my bed with them, usually my uncles Pat or Mike sleeping with me, while my aunt Mary or my cousin Mary Moran slept with Dorothy and Nancy.

Mrs. Simmons rented out the back bedroom, and we had to share the bathroom with whoever lived there, for that was off the second-floor hallway. When we first moved in, an old Italian widower was renting the back bedroom, and I hardly heard him except when he was playing operatic arias on his phonograph, sometimes singing softly in Italian along with the music.

There was a yard in front and another yard and garden at the rear, all of which we had to ourselves. There was also a full basement, where John looked after the furnace, and where he could hide his extra bottles of beer, for Peg allowed him only two a day. I bought the beer for him at the corner grocery, where I cashed in the empty bottles. The store was owned by a Jewish couple, the Hellmans, who kindly gave us credit when we were short of money, starting from the first week that we moved to Cornelia Street. Mrs. Simmons was also very kind, and she told us not to worry if we didn't have enough to pay the rent, right as we moved in.

During what was left of that summer we settled into our new apartment, which was by far the nicest place we had ever lived in, and Peg was never happier than she was there. When John was on the day shift we would sit out on the front steps in the early evening with Mr. and Mrs. Simmons. I would fill a bucket with cold water so John could cool his feet after a long day of standing at the controls of his trolley. Then I would "rush the growler," Brooklyn slang for fetching a pitcher of draft beer for John from the local saloon, making sure the bartender didn't give me too much foam, which I would lick off on the way home.

Then I would have a game of stickball with the other boys on the street, or sometimes Ringelevio, while Dorothy and her friends would play Potsy or Hide and Go Seek. But all the games would stop when we heard the bells of the Good Humor ice cream truck, and we would line up to buy popsicles or ice cream sandwiches or cups of ice cream, hoping that we'd uncover a lucky number that would win us a free treat. But I never won anything, and I began to suspect that the vendor kept the lucky numbers aside and sold them separately, for the street knowledge I had picked up with Jimmy made me believe that everything in New York was a racket, even a free popsicle.

A few months after we moved in, the old Italian man in the back bedroom died and his relatives came to take him away. Then a young woman named Audrey moved in, though against the better judgment of Mrs. Simmons, who said that she usually rented only to respectable bachelors. On weekends Audrey was joined by her boyfriend, a middle-aged Jewish gentleman named Norman, who kept his pigeons on the roof and gave me twenty-five cents a week to feed them.

On Saturday nights, while I was trying to read or do my homework, Audrey and Norman always listened to a radio program starring Mr. Anthony, a psychologist who counseled men and women complaining about their emotional problems. I don't think Audrey and Norman were really listening to Mr. Anthony, though, because their bedsprings were pounding and squeaking during most of the program. Mrs. Simmons must have heard them too, for she asked Audrey to leave, telling her that Norman's pigeons were making too much of a mess.

Mrs. Simmons then rented the back bedroom to an elderly Irish American man named Mr. Dwyer, whose first name I never learned. He made no noise at all except when he talked to himself, always speaking to a woman called Marjory, who I later learned was his wife, as he revealed when he told his troubles to Peg. Peg would often invite him down for a cup of tea in the evening, to keep her company when John was on the night shift, and listening to him rambling on about his unhappiness reminded me of the stories I had heard on Mr. Anthony's program. It seems that Marjory was much younger than Mr. Dwyer, and that he had married her just two years before, after his first wife died. Soon after their marriage he learned that Marjory was carrying on with a young Italian man who was renting their hall bedroom, and when he confronted her she said that if he didn't like it he could leave. Eventually he did leave, for he was afraid that Marjory was trying to poison him so she could cash in on his life insurance and marry the Italian man. Peg asked Mr. Dwyer why he didn't divorce his wife, and he said that he couldn't because he was a Catholic. Besides, he still loved Marjory, as I learned from listening to his imaginary conversations—that is, until I bought a set of earplugs with the money I had accumulated from feeding Norman's pigeons and the deposit on John's empty beer bottles.

I also bought kits to make model sailing ships and airplanes. The first model ship that I made was a three-masted schooner, complete with rigging and sails. At the time I was reading *Mutiny on the Bounty*, by Charles Nordhoff and James Norman Hall, and I imagined that my model ship was the HMS *Bounty*, with Captain Bligh in command.

The first airplane I made was a model of Lindbergh's *Spirit of St. Louis*; it reminded me of the day my grandfather Tómas introduced me to Kruger Cavanaugh at his pub on the western tip of the Dingle Peninsula. I realized what a long way I had come since that day, and I wondered if we'd ever return to Ireland. I asked Peg about that one evening, and she said there was no way we could go back to Ireland now, particularly since her parents were dead. My paternal grandmother, Ellen, had died too, as John learned that summer in a letter from his brother Luke, who was thinking of selling the Freely cottage and moving to England, as there was no money or work in Ireland. We were exiles, Peg said, just like all of the other Irish of the diaspora, and the only way we could return was in our memory and in our songs. Then, as she often did when she was homesick, she played a recording of John McCormack singing "Come Back to Erin." I can never remember more than the first stanza, though even now I recall his splendid voice crackling on the gramophone.

Come back to Erin, Mavourneen, Mavourneen,
Come back, Aroon, to the land of thy birth,
Come with the shamrocks and springtime, Mavourneen,
And its Killarney will ring with our mirth.

My uncle Tom spent his days at the Evergreens bar, where one of his drinking buddies was a character known as Jiggs. Jiggs was a roofer by trade, and everyone wondered how he survived, for he was perpetually drunk even when he was working on the highest buildings. Before Christmas Jiggs put a roof on the big new crèche that Father Multz had built in the courtyard of Fourteen Holy Martyrs, for which he had bought life-sized statues of the holy family and the other figures in the nativity scene. Everyone in the parish was present on Christmas morning when Father Multz unveiled the new crèche, only to see that Jiggs was lying in the manger, dead drunk, next to the infant Jesus. Father Multz was apoplectic and shouted, "Where is Tom Freely?" before closing the curtain and dismissing the congregation. I thought Tom had gone too far this time, but that afternoon I saw him carrying a case of wine to the rectory, and I knew that he had made up with Father Multz. Then I began to wonder how Tom had obtained the wine, and I figured he had won a big bet at the Aqueduct Racetrack, where he was known as "Longshot Freely."

Peg's dear friend Mary Guiheen married a retired merchant seaman named Maurice Kennelly. Maurice told me many interesting stories about life at sea and the interesting ports at which he had called, which gave me a very different picture than the tales of drunken brawls in foreign parts I had heard from my late uncle Tommy. I began checking out books at the public library about the foreign cities and countries I might visit when I went to sea. I started with Richard Halliburton's *Royal Road to Romance,* and went on to read his *New Worlds to Conquer* and *Seven League Boots.* That gave me the idea of being a travel writer, and I thought I would begin by exploring my own neighborhood and then go farther afield in Brooklyn and the other boroughs of New York, keeping a mental record of all the interesting people and places I came upon.

At the top of my mental record I put Mr. Thompson's shop on Evergreen Avenue between Covert and Eldert streets, next to the bakery where I sometimes bought a small pie for five cents if I had the money. While I ate my pie I looked at the pictures in Mr. Thompson's front window, which had a sign saying that he disguised black eyes with flesh-colored makeup. The pictures were of famous people—mostly movie stars, baseball players, and politicians—showing them before and after they had a black eye disguised by Mr. Thompson.

One day Mr. Thompson saw me looking through his window and invited me into the shop. He showed me letters from famous people thanking him for his good work, and I thought they wouldn't be too pleased if they knew he had put their picture in his front window, looking pretty terrible in the photo taken before he applied their makeup.

Mr. Thompson said his customers never came to his shop, but telephoned him to come to their home or hotel in Manhattan, where he was well known from his career in the Broadway theater world. He had rented this shop in the Bushwick district because the rent was much lower than in Manhattan, but also because it was near the Evergreens Cemetery, for he also made up the faces of wealthy people who were to be buried there, including the Schaefer and Trommer beer barons, before they were laid out in a funeral parlor. I was going to ask him why he didn't put before-and-after pictures of the corpses in his window, but on second thought I decided to keep my mouth shut.

My career as a writer started that fall when my school essay on the Blessed Virgin was published in *The Tablet,* the Roman Catholic newspaper that was distributed every Sunday in churches throughout the United States and the rest of the English-speaking world. My essay won first place in a national contest sponsored by the Holy Name Society, and my prize was a free trip to Washington, D.C. But Peg made me turn it down because I didn't have the proper clothes or underwear, she said, nor would I know how to behave in a hotel or restaurant, and she didn't want "the high and mighty" in Washington thinking I was a simple Irish immigrant. So my first published piece didn't get me very far, but at least it was a start, or so I thought at the time.

My essay on the Blessed Virgin made Peg think that I believed in God, which bothered her, since she thought all religion was ignorant superstition, as she told me many times. Every school day after mass we began our lessons with an hour of catechism, which I memorized, so I knew all the attributes of God, but I couldn't figure out how He (we were taught to write His name that way) could at the same time be the Father, the Son, and the Holy Ghost. What I liked most about religion was the sung liturgy, particularly in the solemn high mass and the requiem mass. I loved the aroma of incense and the sound of Latin, all the more so because I didn't understand a word of what was being said or sung. I liked the music, too, but our choir and organist were not very good, as I realized after hearing Beethoven's *Missa Solemnis* on the WNYC radio station one evening.

All of this made me want to become an altar boy, so one day after school I went to see Father Yander, Father Multz's assistant. He told me that they took in a new group of altar boys only every three or four years; it was too much trouble to train people every year, since they had to learn Latin and the liturgy for the various masses. When I said that I would teach myself he laughed and said he would see me in a couple of years.

But it took only a couple of months, and when I spoke to Father Yander again I told him that I had memorized the Latin and the liturgy for all of the masses. He looked very skeptical, but he told me to come to the church hall after school on Friday, when he would give the altar boys their assignments for the next week. I was assigned the six-thirty mass for the whole week, along with Joe Bausch, a classmate of mine who had been an altar boy for a year. Father Yander said that Joe would tell me what to do if I wasn't sure. I was terrified, particularly when I saw that Father Multz was going to say the mass, but I got through it without disgracing myself. When Father Multz was about to leave the sacristy after the mass he asked me where in God's name I had learned my Latin.

I said that I had taught myself, and he shook his head, as if in disbelief. Then he asked me my name, and when I told him he wondered if I was related to Tom Freely. When I told him that Tom was my uncle, he raised his eyes and said, "May heaven help you!"

That same year Richard Holtzman and I joined the Catholic Boys' Brigade—the Catholic version of the Boy Scouts, but on a much more humble scale. Our troop met every Monday evening in the church hall under the command of Major Smullens, a fat middle-aged man whom we called the "Field Marshal." Richard and I worked our way up to the rank of lance corporal, but then we were both court-martialed when Richard deliberately farted while we were doing a left oblique in a drill and I couldn't stop laughing. That cost each of us our stripe, and we were both reduced to the rank of private, with little hope of promotion, for Major Smullens had us labeled as "wise guys."

The only sport our troop did was boxing, which Major Smullens called "the manly art of self-defense," although he himself was anything but manly and didn't look as if he could defend himself in a pillow fight. He always put me up against bigger and older boys to teach me a lesson, but I was quick enough to escape without any damage other than one bloody nose.

Our troop marched up Fifth Avenue in the St. Patrick's Day parade on March 17, 1938. We wore old World War I uniforms, carrying plugged rifles and wearing puttees, long strips of khaki cloth wrapped around the leg from knee to ankle. My puttees came unraveled at the beginning of the parade and tripped up those in the ranks behind me, and I had to drop out of the line of march to wind them up again and then race back to catch up with the brigade, while the crowd along the avenue laughed at my predicament.

Our troop had only one out-of-tune bugler and two drummers who couldn't keep in time with each other, so we were all out of step when we passed the reviewing stand in front of St. Patrick's Cathedral. But no one paid any attention to our troop, because directly behind us was the marching band of the Ancient Order of Hibernians, and when their bagpipes began skirling the crowd cheered wildly and my heart filled with pride at being Irish. They were playing "The Wearing of the Green," and I sang the words with all of my might as I pulled up my unraveling puttees.

Oh I met with Napper Tandy
And he took me by the hand,
Saying how is dear old Ireland,
And how does she stand?

She's the most distressful country,
That ever yet was seen;
They are hanging men and women
For the wearing of the Green!

We had been very happy, but our world suddenly changed when
we returned home, for John had been laid off by the BMT, which had
decided to economize by cutting its workforce drastically. Peg was heartbroken, because for the first time in her married life she had been able
to raise her family in a nice apartment, and when John told her the news
she burst into tears and cried for hours. She finally stopped when Mrs.
Simmons came down to comfort her, telling her not to worry about the
rent until John found another job.

John went back to shaping up on the Hudson River docks, but
although he lined up every day for a week he wasn't once chosen for a
work gang, for he wasn't known to any of the foremen. Finally the little
money we had ran out and he didn't have enough for subway fare until
I found four empty beer bottles in the basement and returned them at
the Hellmans' grocery store for the deposit of twelve cents, which was
two cents more than we needed. But John found no work that day either,
and when Peg sent me to the grocery store to get something for supper
I had to ask Mr. Hellman to put it on the bill. Peg had told me to get
a bottle of milk but I ordered three, one of which we drank at supper,
after which I emptied the other two into a big pot. Peg asked me what
in God's name I was doing, and I explained to her that I would take the
three empty bottles out to the grocery store first thing in the morning for
the nine-cent deposit, which with the two cents I had left from today's
deposit would be enough for John's subway fare, with a penny to spare.

But John didn't find work the next day, either, and Peg had to borrow
money from her brother Mauris. Mauris also called on Paddy Burke,
a friend of the family who had connections with the Longshoremen's
Union. Paddy loaned John the money to join the union and introduced

him around to the foremen. He also loaned him the money to buy a bal-
ing hook, which he carried to and from work, and when he came home
with it Peg said he looked like Captain Hook. That was the first time I'd
heard her laugh in weeks, and from then on she was her usual self.

It was my job to read the shipping news in the *Journal-American*
every evening, to find out when a cargo ship was arriving in New York
Harbor and note the pier at which it would be docking. Usually it took
three or four days to unload a ship, and John earned five or six dollars
a day and sometimes a couple of dollars more if he worked overtime.
That was enough for Peg to run the household and to begin paying off
the back rent to Mrs. Simmons and the grocery bill to Mr. Hellman. But
I knew that John wasn't giving all of his pay to Peg, for once again he
began sending me out to buy bottles of beer to put in his hiding place in
the basement.

The New York World's Fair opened early in the summer of 1939 in
Flushing Meadows, Queens. Jimmy and I saved up the money we earned
by scavenging until we thought we had enough to spend a day at the fair,
for there was an admission charge for the fairgrounds and also for many
of the exhibits. The pavilions of all of the countries represented at the
fair were free and we saw them first, particularly those of places I hoped
to see on my travels. I was disappointed to find that China didn't have a
pavilion, but then I realized that the Chinese were fighting for their very
existence, which I knew from my collection of Japanese-atrocity cards
and from reading about the war in the *Journal-American.*

That following week Jimmy and I decided to visit the Museum of
Natural History in Manhattan, because I had read about the dinosaurs
exhibited there. We decided to go on a Saturday, when admission was
free. We had only a nickel each, for we had blown our savings going to
the World's Fair, so we decided that we would walk there and take the
subway back. I had measured the distance on the map and figured that
it was about a ten-mile walk, which should take us no more than three
hours, for I had paced off distances around the neighborhood and found
that I could walk a mile in less than fifteen minutes.

We started out at eight in the morning and arrived at the museum just
before noon, delayed because we stopped to take in the view from the
Williamsburg Bridge, and also to see how long it would take the stones
we had brought along to fall into the East River.

We went straight to see the dinosaurs, which were even bigger than I had imagined, particularly the Tyrannosaurus rex. After that we went through every single gallery in the museum, spending most of our time looking at the dioramas showing the wild animals of Africa, which seemed to be in better shape than the ones I had seen in the Brooklyn Zoo, or in the Tarzan films starring Johnny Weissmuller.

The last part of the museum we went to was the Hayden Planetarium, where we were too late for the last show in the Sky Theater. But we were able to visit the Copernican orrery, a huge working model of the solar system, where I was very pleased to see Pluto orbiting beyond all of the other planets. A lecturer was telling his audience that Pluto had been discovered only eight years before, and that the planet took nearly 250 years to complete one orbit around the sun, but I knew that already, which made me feel very superior.

We were very hungry when we left the museum because we hadn't eaten since breakfast, so instead of using our two nickels for subway fare we bought a bunch of bananas and ate them as we walked south through Central Park. Our route back to the Williamsburg Bridge took us through Times Square, where we stopped to look at the pictures outside Professor Heckler's Flea Circus. We thought of trying to sneak in, but the ticket taker at the entrance kept a close eye on us, and we moved on. At Herald Square we walked around the block to have a close look at the Empire State Building, where in my mind's eye I could see King Kong climbing up to the spire with Fay Wray in his hand as fighter planes fired at him with machine guns. Then we walked along the Bowery, where Peg told John he would wind up if he didn't stop drinking. We turned left on Delancey Street and walked through the Lower East Side to go across the Williamsburg Bridge and back into Brooklyn.

On the last stretch through Brooklyn we were so hungry we stole two apples from a fruit stand. I knew that I would have to tell this to the priest when I went to confession the following Saturday. But I couldn't do that at Fourteen Holy Martyrs because Father Multz and Father Yander would recognize my voice, so I went to Our Lady of Lourdes, where the priest told me to say ten Our Fathers and ten Hail Marys as my penance.

After that expedition I was determined to broaden my explorations of the city, starting with Brooklyn and Queens. I dreamed of getting a bike, but I knew that was impossible unless John won on the Irish Sweepstakes—only then Peg would use the money to pay our debts to Mrs. Simmons and Mr. Hellman. One Saturday evening we went to a bazaar at Fourteen Holy Martyrs where they were running a raffle to raise money for the African missions of the Little Sisters of the Poor. One of the top prizes was a Raleigh three-speed bike, the bicycle of my dreams, so I spent twenty-five cents I had saved up from cashing in the deposits on John's empty beer bottles to buy a chance. All the smaller prizes were picked first, until only the top two were left, the bicycle and a huge smoked ham, and the person who had the first of the last two lucky numbers could choose which of the two they wanted. Then the master of ceremonies called out the winning number, and it was mine! I ran up to grab the bicycle but Peg and Nell shouted out that I should take the ham, and when I hesitated they rushed forward to make sure I did what I was told. So we got the ham and someone else won the bike, which is as close as I ever came to owning one.

Bushwick Avenue led around the southern end of the Evergreens Cemetery to Highland Park, where Jimmy Anderson and I usually walked on Sunday afternoons during the summer. Once we climbed over the fence to go swimming in the reservoir at the far end of the park, but a park policeman saw us and we barely escaped by climbing over the fence into the cemetery.

After that we took our Sunday walks in the cemetery, bringing along two old watering cans that we had found in our scavenging expeditions, and earning a little money by watering graves. Sometimes we found pieces of ornamental ironwork that had fallen off around the older graves, and put them in the watering cans to get them past the guard at the gate so we could stash them in our hiding place in the abandoned ice house.

I spent some of the money I earned going to the movies, usually the Saturday matinee at the Colonial Theater, when there was a double feature along with a cartoon show and an episode of a ten-part thriller. After one of these matinees I bought the late-afternoon edition of the *Journal-American* and saw the headline NAZIS INVADE POLAND. The date was September 2, 1939, the beginning of World War II. That night we listened to Gabriel Heatter on the evening news, and he said that the Germans had invaded Poland at several points and were advancing rapidly. Mrs. Simmons was with us and she was very upset, for most of her family was still living in Poland. Two weeks later we learned on the evening news that the Russians had invaded Poland too, dividing up the country with the Germans. I had been following the news carefully, and I knew that all of Europe would soon be involved in the war, and that it was only a matter of time before the United States would be caught up in the conflict as well, in which case I would volunteer right away.

About a month later I came home from school to find Peg in tears. She said that a policeman had just been to the house to tell her that John had been badly injured in an accident on the docks and was in Bellevue Hospital. She told me to look after the other kids while she went to see him. When she came home she said he was out of danger, but that he had a broken leg and internal injuries that would keep him in the hospital for at least a couple of weeks. It seems that a crate of heavy machinery had fallen on him and another longshoreman, who had been killed instantly, and John was lucky to be alive.

It was three weeks before John came home, and Peg was told that it would be at least six months before he could go back to work. He was eligible for workers' compensation, which paid his hospital bills, but he received nothing to compensate him for his injury or to support him and his family while he was out of work.

So we went on the dole, which in those days was known as "relief" and is now called welfare. But it shamed Peg to wait in line at a government office to get coupons that entitled us to some free food, although not enough to live on, and so our bill at Hellman's once again began to rise, as did the amount of rent that we owed Mrs. Simmons. But Peg was determined not to despair, and one evening when she and I were talking she said to me that as bad as things were, at least her children had never gone to bed hungry. I have never forgotten that.

One Saturday a few weeks after we went on the dole, I walked with Peg to Friel's Pawn Shop, which was on the corner of Broadway and Jefferson Street. Friel's, with its three brass balls, was a neighborhood landmark, and it was a standing joke to ask someone "to meet me at the pawnshop and kiss me under the balls." I often stopped to look at the articles on display in the front window, things that had been pawned and gone unredeemed and were now on sale. There were musical instruments, watches, jewelry, a set of silverware, a gold-plated crucifix, works of art, radios, household appliances, and an Extreme Unction set that included all the items a priest would need to give the last rites to a dying Catholic in their home.

The main entrance to Friel's was on Broadway, but Peg and I used the family entrance on Jefferson Street. A bell tinkled and a clerk appeared behind the counter and very politely asked Peg if he could help her. Peg said nothing but took off her wedding ring and put it on the counter. The clerk placed on an eyepiece and examined the diamond on the ring, after which he said he would give her twenty dollars for it. She nodded and he rang up the cash register to give her a twenty-dollar bill, which she asked him to change into twenty singles. He did that and then gave her a pawn ticket, which had printed on it the interest, compounded weekly, that would have to be paid when the object was redeemed, the limit being one year, when it would be put up for sale. Peg held in her tears until we returned home, but then she began weeping, while John tried to comfort her by saying he'd redeem the ring as soon as he went back to work.

A few weeks later we pawned John's only suit, for ten dollars. That didn't seem so bad, since he wore the suit only when he went to church on Sunday, and now he couldn't go because he was laid up. He did ask Peg if he could have a bottle of beer out of the ten dollars, and she relented, for he hadn't taken a drink since his accident. I went out to buy the beer at Hellman's, and the next day I brought back the empty bottle for the three-cent deposit, which Peg let me keep, since I hadn't had any spending money since the accident.

Peg decided that she had to go to work, and after I had pored over the classified ads in the *Journal-American*, she finally took a night job as a cleaning woman at Rockefeller Center. She worked from six in the evening until two in the morning, five days a week, at a salary of twenty dollars a week, minus the Social Security tax and her subway fare. Once she went to work we no longer qualified for relief, but Peg said she didn't mind, since now she could hold her head high and not have people think we were "beggarly paupers on the dole."

Every day from Monday to Friday she left the house at five o'clock, after making supper for us, and didn't get back until three in the morning, when I would usually get up to talk with her while she had breakfast. Then we would talk for a while, usually about the lost world she had left behind in Ireland. "And I left all that for this," she would say bitterly, and I would try to cheer her up by saying that maybe we could go back to Ireland one day. But she would only say that things were worse there than they were here, and that would usually be the end of our "nocturnal dialogue," as she called it.

After a few weeks on the job Peg had put aside enough money to redeem her wedding ring from the pawnshop, so I went with her to Friel's one Saturday morning. She presented her pawn ticket, and the clerk brought out her ring, saying that she would have to pay thirty-five dollars, which included fifteen dollars in interest. Peg was devastated, for she hadn't anticipated that the interest would be so high and had brought along only twenty-five dollars. We had to come back again several weeks later, by which time the interest had gone up by another five dollars. But Peg had brought along enough to cover it, and she was able to hold up her head again, as she said to me on our way home.

After a few more weeks we went to redeem John's suit, for he was now able to walk on crutches and wanted to go to mass on Sunday. This time we were prepared, for I had taught myself how to compute compound interest, and I determined that we owed seven dollars extra on the ten dollars we had received for the suit. But when Peg presented the pawn ticket the clerk told her she owed twenty dollars, the extra three dollars being for dry cleaning and pressing and storing the suit. Peg didn't have enough money with her, so we came home without the suit and John missed mass that Sunday.

We went back two weeks later, by which time the interest had gone up by another dollar. This time Peg made sure she had enough money to reclaim John's suit. But she wouldn't let him wear it to mass the following day, for it smelled so strongly of camphor mothballs from being stored at Friel's that she was afraid everyone at church would know he had pawned his suit and we would be disgraced. She aired the suit on the clothesline for a week before she would let John wear it.

Later that fall I began looking for an after-school job, for I had dreams of saving up to buy a bicycle. Within a couple of weeks I found a job delivering newspapers for the *Brooklyn Daily Eagle.* I was very proud of this, for I knew that Walt Whitman had been editor of the newspaper. My route was in the Bedford-Stuyvesant district and most of my customers were black, though some were Jews from eastern Europe, all of whom spoke Yiddish. Many of my customers didn't answer the bell on Saturday morning when I came to collect the bill, nor when I rang it again the following week, so I sometimes ended up the week owing the newspaper money. I persevered for a whole winter, walking two or three miles in the snow and returning home long after supper without a penny to show for it. One of my customers, an old Jewish woman from Russia, always invited me in for a cup of tea, and if it wasn't for her I wouldn't have stuck it out as long as I did. But I finally quit when I paid back the money I owed the *Eagle* for the unpaid subscriptions I was stuck with, otherwise I would have forfeited the five-dollar deposit that I had borrowed from my aunt Nell.

I then used the five dollars to pay my deposit when I found a job delivering the *Long Island Press.* This time my route was in the Ridgewood district, about a mile from where we lived, in a neighborhood that was mostly German, which I could tell from the names of my customers, who numbered about fifty when I started. In the beginning I earned about two dollars a week, half of which I gave to Peg. I would have had twice as much if everyone had paid at the end of the week, but some of my customers said they would pay me next week or just didn't respond when I rang the bell on Saturday morning.

I thought I could earn twice as much money if I had a second route, so when one of the other newsboys left I asked our manager if I could replace him. He said yes, and I took over a route with about seventy customers not far from the one I already had. I relied almost entirely on my memory and didn't keep any records, so after a few weeks I had no idea of who owed me money and who did not. When I rang the bell on Saturday mornings, I had to rely on my customers to tell me what they owed. Eventually more and more of my customers stopped answering the bell, and I fell so far behind in my payments to the *Long Island Press* manager that he fired me and I lost my five-dollar deposit. When I told Peg about this she said that I wasn't meant to be a capitalist, and I went back to scavenging with Jimmy on Saturdays.

John was working on the docks again by then, though he earned much less than he had before because there was a different foreman on the pier where he usually shaped up, an Italian rather than an Irishman, and he was seldom picked for a work crew. This started him drinking again, as I learned when I saw him one afternoon in the Decatur Street Bar and Grill with his bailing hook hanging from his belt, looking as if he had given up hope. I said nothing to Peg, but she knew what was happening, and from then on there was silence at supper and John began sleeping on the old sofa in the basement.

One night on her way home from work Peg was mugged and beaten up outside the Wilson Avenue station at three in the morning. When she arrived home she was weeping hysterically and her face was covered with blood. I woke up John and then ran to the police station, which was just two blocks away, and I told the desk sergeant that my mother had been mugged. He sent a policeman back with me to the house and Peg told him what had happened, breaking down in tears as she described how the mugger had punched her in the face several times as he tore her pocketbook away from her. The policeman asked John what his wife was doing out on the street at three in the morning and Peg screamed that she was coming home after a long night's work. He laughed and said she was working on the streets, was she, and at that John raised his fist but the policeman hit him across the head with his nightstick and knocked him down. I tried to come between them and the policeman raised his stick as if to hit me, which made Peg start screaming. This woke up the other kids, and they started screaming too. By then Mrs. Simmons had come down to see what was going on, and she threatened to report the policeman to the captain at the station, which made him back off. As he left, he said that if we complained about him we'd regret it.

John didn't complain, because he knew it would do no good, and from then on he met Peg at the Wilson Avenue station when she came home from work. The good part of all of this was that John no longer had to sleep on the old sofa in the basement, and he cut his drinking back to the few bottles of beer he had me smuggle in from Hellman's, so I had a little money to spend from the deposit on the empties.

Things were just as bad all over the world, as Mrs. Simmons would say when we listened to Gabriel Heatter on the evening news, particularly on June 14, 1940, when he announced that France had surrendered to the Germans and that it would be only a matter of time before Hitler invaded England.

During that summer I began working for the *Long Island Press* again, once more borrowing money from my aunt Nell for the deposit. I was able to get the job because there was a new manager who didn't know how badly I had messed up my routes when I delivered newspapers for his predecessor. This time I took only one route, with about fifty sub-scribers, and I kept careful records so that on good weeks I earned as much as three dollars.

I gave half the money I earned to Peg and kept the rest for myself, spending most of it going to the beach on Sunday with my friends. Usu-ally we went to Coney Island or Rockaway Beach, but one Sunday we decided to go to Lake Ronkonkoma because the beach there had a raft in deep water with a diving board.

That September I started my last term at Fourteen Holy Martyrs School. We were an "in-between class," as they always told us, so we would graduate the following January—except those who might fail, like my friend Cliffy, who had been left back a half-dozen times and was now seventeen, earning his living as a professional boxer at the Broadway Arena.

We had a new teacher who had just arrived at the convent. Her name was Sister Jean Claire, and she had just graduated from St. John's University, then located in Brooklyn, the first time we'd had a teacher with a college degree. She was much more relaxed and friendly than the other nuns, and she talked to us about everything under the sun, not just the usual boring classroom subjects like the principal products of Peru.

She and I became very good friends and I often stayed after school to talk with her, something I had never done before with any other teacher. She advised me to take the entrance exam for St. John's Prep and to try to win a scholarship there. That would prepare me for St. John's University, where I could study science and mathematics, for she could see that I was interested in those subjects and did very well in them. I told her that I wasn't sure whether I wanted to be a scientist or a sailor or a travel writer, so I had decided to apply to Brooklyn Technical High School. I thought I might be able to study marine engineering there, so I could go to sea and then perhaps learn science on my own and maybe even begin writing books. She smiled and said that perhaps I should begin reading Joseph Conrad. So I went to the public library and checked out *Heart of Darkness*.

Every day after I finished my paper route I ran to the public school around the corner from Fourteen Holy Martyrs, because they had a playground where I played basketball until it was time to go home for supper. I became very good at basketball, and I was invited to join several club teams. One of them was the junior team of the Dux, whose senior team won the New York City club championship nearly every year. I was somewhat handicapped because I didn't have a jockstrap or proper sneakers. I couldn't afford to pay for the uniform, so I wore bathing trunks and a white T-shirt onto which I sewed my team number, though it kept falling off during games. One of the teams I played for happened to be made up of boys who were all interested in science, so we called ourselves the Molecules, and instead of wearing numbers we used chemical symbols. I chose H_2O, the symbol for water, which I said was appropriate because I was always dribbling down the floor.

I couldn't afford the carfare to and from the games, so I had to make my way on foot, usually by running to make up for lost time. I also ran to and from school, jumping over fire hydrants and grocery store milk boxes on the way. I ran partly to save time but also for the sheer exhilaration I felt when I was running, and sometimes in my dreams I would take off in a running jump and continue to soar a few feet above the ground like the cormorants I had seen skimming the sea in Dingle Bay.

I passed the exam for Brooklyn Tech and decided to go there rather than to St. John's Prep, for which I had won a scholarship. This upset my uncle Mauris; he thought St. John's was the most prestigious prep school in Brooklyn. It would prepare me for St. John's University and a career in business or law, and a scholarship to a place like that seemed beyond the dreams of someone from a family of poor Irish immigrants. I told him that Brooklyn Tech was a public school and charged no tuition, which was as good as having a scholarship, and that the school trained engineers, who could earn as much as businessmen or lawyers. But I didn't tell him that I wanted to be a marine engineer so I could go to sea, for he would have told me that I would end up six fathoms deep like his brother Tommy, for whom he and Peg still grieved.

Most of the rest of my classmates had decided to go to Bushwick High School, the local public secondary school, but Jimmy Anderson signed up for the Automotive Trades High School, because he wanted to be an auto mechanic. Uncle Mauris said trade schools had the worst students in Brooklyn and that many ended up in jail, like Billy De Witt, who had gone from Fourteen Holy Martyrs to Automotive Trades the previous year and was now in reform school serving a sentence for burglary; my uncle was afraid Brooklyn Tech would lead me down the same road.

I didn't tell Mauris that Jimmy and I might well have landed in reform school with Billy. The previous Christmas Day, Jimmy and I had been passing Woolworth's department store on the corner of Decatur Street and Broadway, when we looked through the window and saw that Billy had broken in and was in the process of looting the place. He waved to us to come join him, pointing to the freight entrance where he had broken in. Billy was wheeling a beautiful Raleigh three-speed bicycle that he had just stolen from the sports department, and I could see that there were several others just like it there for the taking. Jimmy and I looked at each other and wondered what to do, but just then we heard a police siren, and we ran off down Decatur Street and didn't stop until we reached our hiding place in the abandoned ice house. The next day we learned that the police had arrested Billy and that he would be sent to reform school, a bicycle thief caught in the act.

We graduated in mid-January 1941. I ranked first in the class and Jimmy was next to last, but at least he passed; our friend Cliffy was kept back once again. Neither Jimmy nor I were invited to the class party. Nor was Cliffy, but he wouldn't have been able to come anyway, since that evening he was fighting in one of the preliminary bouts at the Broadway Arena. Jimmy and I didn't let our unpopularity bother us, and on the evening of the party we went to a horror movie double feature at the Halsey Theatre, watching Boris Karlof as Frankenstein and Bela Lugosi as Dracula while we gorged ourselves on popcorn.

I started classes at Brooklyn Tech in early February. The school was in the Fort Greene section of Brooklyn, and it took nearly an hour to get there on the Halsey Street trolley. The school was enormous, an eight-story redbrick building that took up a whole block, with four thousand students from all over New York City, all boys.

I was very nervous, but so was everyone else, for it was freshman orientation day, and the only older students there were those who had volunteered to tell us about the school and show us around after we registered.

We went on a tour of the school, which our guide told us had been founded to train young men who wanted to be engineers but who would not necessarily go on to university. After a tour of the physics and chemistry laboratories, the forge, the machine shop, the woodworking and metalworking shops, and the mechanical drawing and applied art studios, we went on to see the two-story house that had been designed and built the previous year by the architectural students, its power and lights installed by the electrical engineers, its plumbing by the sanitary engineers, its furnishings and artworks by the students in applied art and interior design. We were also shown the chemical pilot plant designed by the chemical engineers and built by the mechanical engineers, as well as the materials testing laboratory of the civil engineers, the glider built by the aeronautical engineers, the radio station run by the electronic engineers, and the meteorological station operated by the students specializing in that field.

Another student told us about all of the clubs and other extracurricular activities, including the symphony orchestra, the string quartet, the glee club, the dramatic society, the gymnastics club, the chess club, the political discussion group, the school literary magazine, the yearbook, the school senate, and the Arasta, the society of honors students. All of this took my breath away, considering what had been available to us at Fourteen Holy Martyrs, which I now began to miss very much, particularly Sister Jean Claire.

When I looked over the class lists posted in the lobby I found very few Irish or Italian names; most of them seemed to be Jewish, German, and Scandinavian. One of the names listed in the freshman class was Patrick Irish, who turned out to be a very tall black boy with freckles and bright red hair. He and I quickly became good friends, and we signed up together to try out for the basketball team.

Another name I saw on the freshman list was William Shakespeare, and I thought it was a joke until I met him while signing up for the track team. So many of us signed up for track that they had us run against each other in pairs and the loser was eliminated. We ran on a highly banked track above the gym floor, and on the first trial I was matched with William Shakespeare. I was well ahead by the time we were halfway round the track, but then the knee-length underwear I had rolled up inside my bathing suit began to unroll and everyone watching burst out in laughter, which made me lose stride, and I lost the race and was eliminated. "Too bad, kid," said the track coach, "you've been beaten by the bard, try again next year."

I went to see the teacher who was listed as my adviser, and he shook his head when he saw that I came from a parochial school. He said that I probably had a weak background in math and science, which would put me at a great disadvantage, since most of the programs were highly technical. When I said I wanted to study marine engineering he told me that they didn't have a program in that field, and his advice was to take the college prep option, which emphasized the humanities. I had two years to make up my mind, he said, for all of the freshmen and sophomores took the same courses. I was very disappointed, but I didn't let on, because I could tell that my adviser wouldn't be interested in learning of my dream to spend my life sailing the seven seas.

I signed up for classes in humanities, history and civics, mathematics, chemistry, mechanical drawing, shop, and a course called Industrial

Processes, better known as IP, which involved a detailed study of all the industries in the world. We also had one period a week for physical education, in which half of the hour was spent taking attendance and the other half doing calisthenics. The PE teacher told us that each semester we would have to present a report from a dentist certifying that our teeth were okay—otherwise we would be given the minimum passing grade of 65. My heart sank when I heard this, for there was no way that I could afford to go to a dentist. I'd never been to a dentist in my life, nor had anyone in our family, but I knew that they charged five dollars a visit and a lot more if they had to fill up holes in your teeth, though there were probably none in mine, since I had never had a toothache.

I borrowed money from my aunt Nell to pay for my textbooks and the other things I needed for school, including a slide rule and the materials for my mechanical drawing course. I earned only about three dollars a week from my paper route, and after I gave half of it to Peg and paid fifty cents for carfare to and from school I had only a dollar left for everything else, including lunch, which I saved on by making my own sandwiches, although I sometimes splurged and bought a lemonade in the school cafeteria.

I wasn't given to despair or depression, though this constant struggle to get by was beginning to get me down. I felt that I was surrounded by an immensely high wall, with no hope of escaping. But I couldn't give up; as Peg always said to me, even during the most desperate of times, "All will be well."

I knew that I had to find a part-time job. The only experience I had was delivering newspapers and scavenging, so I went to the school employment office. The lady in charge said that there was an opening at the Willis Paint Company, and when I said I was interested she phoned to make an appointment for me that afternoon after school. She showed me where it was on a map, just behind the Brooklyn Edison powerhouse on the East River underneath the Brooklyn Bridge. I checked the scale on the map and saw that it was about a three-mile walk from school, which would take me less than an hour.

My route took me past the Brooklyn Navy Yard, which I could see was very busy outfitting ships for President Roosevelt's Lend-Lease program to send aid to Great Britain, which was in danger of being invaded by the Germans. Some of the sailors I saw going in and out of the Navy Yard seemed only a few years older than me, and I began to think about enlisting in the Navy, which would be a lot more exciting than going to work in a paint factory after a long day at school.

I had no trouble finding the paint factory—I just followed the approach to the Brooklyn Bridge, where I could see the huge power-house beneath it on the shore of the East River, its towering smokestack belching a cloud of black smoke, and there behind it was a three-story building with a large sign reading WILLIS PAINT.

I rang the bell, and the middle-aged man who answered it said, "You must be the boy from Brooklyn Tech." I said I was, and he said he was Herman Willis. He introduced me to his wife and said she was his office staff, and then he pointed to a man in paint-smeared overalls, identify-ing him as Saul Greenberg, his brother-in-law. "We're the Willis Paint Company," he said, "just the three of us, and if you join the firm you'll have to be a man of all work."

I said that I was willing, but that I had no experience. "Never mind," he said, "you'll learn on the job." He went on to say, "The pay is fifty cents an hour, and you'll work four to seven, Monday through Friday, and nine to six on Saturday, with a half hour off for lunch." I did a quick mental calculation to figure out that my pay would be twelve dollars a week, and said that would be fine.

Then he asked me how old I was, and I told him that I was fourteen and a half. "But then you don't have working papers," he said. "By law you have to be sixteen before you can work." I nodded, and he told me that he could pay me only forty cents an hour, because if the authorities found out he had hired an underage worker he would be fined, so he would have to withhold part of my salary to cover himself. I had no choice but to agree, though a lightning calculation determined that my salary was now only nine dollars and sixty cents a week, minus carfare, which would reduce it to exactly nine dollars, half of which I would give to Peg.

He threw me a pair of overalls and said I could start right away. Saul took me up to the top floor and handed me a bucket of white grease and told me that I should rub it into my hands and forearms to keep the paint from getting into my skin and bloodstream. Then he told me not to rub my eyes, for the paint might blind me, and he warned me not to breathe deeply when mixing the organic liquids, because some of them might scar my lungs.

He showed me how to mix the materials that went into the large conical vat on the top floor, after which I followed him down to the second floor, where he opened a valve to let the paint pour into one can after another. He showed me how to crimp tops on the cans, which we then loaded onto a freight elevator that carried them down to the first floor. There we put labels on the cans and stacked them in the warehouse, where I would load them onto a truck when the next order came in.

By the time we were finished I looked at the clock and saw that it was five to seven, so I began washing my hands and forearms to clean off the grease and paint. Mr. Willis shouted at me that I should wash up on my own time, for I was paid to work until seven o'clock and not a minute before. He handed me a broom, and I swept the floor for five minutes before I washed up and left.

It was past nine when I finally got home, and by the time I finished supper, which Peg had left on the stove for me before going to work, it was nearly ten. By then John and the kids were asleep, so I read the newspapers for a while before starting my homework. But I was so tired I gave up after half an hour and went to bed.

I overslept the next morning and was fifteen minutes late for school, where the door monitor told me to report to the discipline office. There I was told that for the next week I would have to report to Mr. Parker at morning detention at eight o'clock, an hour before school began. I already knew the strict rules of morning detention before I reported to Mr. Parker the next day. We weren't allowed to talk or move or look out the window or at one another, but had to sit up straight and stare straight ahead as Mr. Parker looked menacingly at us like the prison warden I had seen in a James Cagney film. I passed the hour daydreaming, thinking of the exotic places I would see when I finished school and went off to sea. The thoughts must have made me change my expression, for Mr. Parker shouted at me to wipe the smile off my face, which I did by thinking of the Willis paint factory instead of tropical islands in the Pacific.

I stuck it out at the factory for a year and a half. I tried to get all of my homework done on Sundays, which included not only reading literature and history and studying math and chemistry but also doing mechanical drawings and keeping a detailed notebook for the IP, where we had to draw complicated diagrams of every type of industrial process known to mankind, which I actually enjoyed doing.

I did well in all my courses except shopwork, for which I had absolutely no aptitude, and my low grade in that subject, as well as the mandatory 65 that I received in PE for not having a dentist's note, kept me off the honor roll. When Peg saw my report card she said I had been a big fish in a small pond at Fourteen Holy Martyrs, and clearly I wasn't up to competing with the very best at Brooklyn Tech, which she knew would get my goat and spur me to do better.

During the summer vacation I worked full time at the Willis paint factory, nine hours a day, Monday through Saturday. On Sunday I usually went swimming at Rockaway Beach with Jimmy Anderson, who worked after school in a local garage. The girls in our neighborhood usually went to Rockaway too, mostly with their boyfriends, which did not include me and Jimmy—we had been the odd men out even in grammar school. The boyfriends were better dressed than we were and had money to spend, or at least that's how we explained their success. They could afford to take their girlfriends to the Paramount Theatre to see a first-run movie and hear Frank Sinatra sing, and afterward they could go to a Chinese restaurant and eat chop suey, as I was told by one of my more fortunate friends, John Mione, who had ranked second to me in our final year at Fourteen Holy Martyrs and then gone on to St. John's Prep.

John was not only good-looking but also a sharp dresser, and I envied the sport coat he wore when he passed me with his girlfriend on the way to the movies. I started saving up for a sport coat, but by the time I had enough money, Peg made me use it to buy what was called a "convertible" winter coat—a white raincoat on one side and a green overcoat on the other. Uncle Mauris took me to buy it at a basement clothing store noted for its bargains, its motto being "Step down five, and save ten." The convertible was indeed a bargain, but after it was exposed to rain and snow the two sides shrank by different amounts so it curled up around the bottom, and the green dye of the overcoat ran into the white surface of the raincoat, giving it a mottled hue, somewhat like the skin of a frog.

I started saving up again to buy a sport coat. When I learned that there was a sale at Barneys clothing store I went and saw a great sport coat for twenty dollars. But I had saved only ten dollars, and I was sure the jacket would be sold before I could accumulate another ten. Then I suddenly remembered the suit that Nell had bought me for my first communion, which I had never worn again and was packed away in our trunk. The next Saturday, when Peg was out shopping, I took the suit to Friel's Pawn Shop, where the clerk told me that he couldn't do business with anyone under eighteen. Then he looked at the suit and said that in any event the suit had no resale value, since the knickers I had worn were now completely out of style; boys now always wore long pants for their first communion. I put the suit back in the trunk and continued saving up, but I never managed to accumulate enough to buy a sport coat. Thus my social life never measured up to that of John Mione.

Jimmy and I would usually meet in the evening in front of Otto's ice cream parlor on Broadway between Covert and Schaefer streets, where most of the kids in our neighborhood hung out. One evening I arrived to find several police cars parked outside the ice cream parlor with their lights flashing, and I saw that the front window was smashed and there was broken glass all over the sidewalk.

Jimmy and my other friends were being questioned by the police, and when I arrived a sergeant grabbed me by the arm and asked me if I knew Billy De Witt. I said that I did, and then he asked me when I had last seen him. I told him that it had been about a year before, but I didn't say that it had been when Jimmy and I saw Billy robbing Woolworth's. Then the policeman shoved me away and began questioning someone else.

I asked Jimmy what had happened, and he told me the whole story. Billy had escaped from reform school a few days before, after he learned that his girlfriend was going out with someone else. I didn't know the girl or her new boyfriend, but Jimmy said the two of them had been standing in front of the ice cream parlor half an hour before, when Dutch, the local cop on the beat, came to warn them that Billy had escaped and was looking for them.

At that moment, according to Jimmy, Billy suddenly appeared on the other side of Broadway with a pistol in his hand and began firing at them. Dutch drew his gun to fire back, but it went off too soon and he shot himself in the left hand. Dutch managed to get off another shot before he collapsed, and that frightened Billy into running away, while the girl and her boyfriend and everyone else took refuge in the ice cream parlor. Jimmy stayed outside to look after Dutch, while Otto, the owner of the ice cream parlor, called the police.

The next day I learned that the police had arrested Billy, who'd been hiding on the roof of his girlfriend's apartment house. He had surrendered quietly, but the police beat him up anyway, because Dutch had lost his left thumb in the shooting. We never saw Billy again, because he was sentenced to twenty years in prison, but he became immortal in our neighborhood folklore for his spectacular shootout with Dutch the cop.

That September everyone's attention was focused on baseball; the Brooklyn Dodgers, affectionately known as "Dem Bums" because they were usually down at the bottom of the National League, were making a run for the pennant. On my way home from work after school every day I checked the baseball scores, which were posted on the side wall of the Macon Street Bar and Grill, where two bartenders climbed ladders to chalk up the scores inning by inning in both the National and American leagues. On Sundays I listened to the radio broadcast of the Brooklyn game by Red Barber, who had started announcing for the Dodgers two years before.

The Dodgers won the pennant, their first in twenty-one years, and all of the students in Brooklyn walked out of school, even at Brooklyn Tech, the first relaxation of their strict rules that anyone there could remember. But I still had to show up for work that afternoon at the Willis paint factory, where no one even mentioned the Dodgers, for everything was strictly business there.

Baseball fever continued through the World Series, with the Dodgers playing the New York Yankees in what the sportswriters called a "subway series." There was no way I could get to the games, but I tried to follow them through Red Barber's radio broadcasts. The school radio station was following the games, and students who worked there were passing along the results every half inning, using as couriers anyone who left class with the wooden pass that you took from beside the classroom door when you went to the toilet. The couriers then passed the news to their classmates by hand signals, indicating the number of runs scored by each team, all in absolute silence behind the teacher's back for fear of a week in morning detention.

The Dodgers finally lost to the Yankees, four games to one, breaking the hearts of everyone in Brooklyn. But then the Brooklyn fans began saying "Wait till next year!" and the season ended in a mood of optimism for the future.

Two months later the Japanese bombed Pearl Harbor. We heard the news midafternoon on Sunday, December 7, when an announcer interrupted the regular program to say that Japanese planes had attacked the U.S. Navy base in Hawaii, and later we learned that they had destroyed much of America's Pacific fleet.

On Monday we listened to President Roosevelt's speech to Congress in which he called for a declaration of war against Japan, and on Friday evening Gabriel Heatter told us that Hitler had declared war on the United States. Then on Saturday night I was listening to the *Green Hornet* mystery program, where the hero, Britt Reid, was always assisted by his "faithful Japanese companion Kato." But now Kato had suddenly become Britt's "faithful Filipino companion," and I knew that our world would never be the same again.

The Sunday after Pearl Harbor I went to the ice cream parlor and met Jimmy, who told me that he had just enlisted in the Marine Corps. He was six months older than I was and had recently turned sixteen, a year younger than the minimum age at which you could enlist with parental consent, but he had altered his birth certificate to make it appear that he was a year older. He said that Phil Gould, one of our former classmates at Fourteen Holy Martyrs, who was almost exactly my age, had done the same, and that both of them were waiting for their orders to report for duty.

Jimmy and Phil received their orders early in February 1942, when they left for the Marine Corps training camp at Parris Island, South Carolina. Three months later they came home on a week's furlough before taking the train to San Pedro, California, where they were to board a troopship that would take them to some unknown destination in the Pacific. They figured that they were probably going with the 1st Marine Division to Hawaii, where the United States was beginning to group its forces to mount a counterattack against the Japanese, who had taken the Philippines, Malaya, and Burma.

After I said goodbye to Jimmy and Phil I decided that I would try to enlist too. Peg must have read my mind, for she put my birth certificate out of reach. On the way to the paint factory one afternoon I stopped off at the recruiting station by the entrance to the Brooklyn Navy Yard, and was told that there was no way they would let me enlist without a birth certificate proving that I was eighteen, or seventeen with the written consent of my parents.

So I had to wait, and meanwhile I followed the progress of the war, reading the morning and evening newspapers, listening to the radio, and watching the newsreels. The first good news came with the American victory over the Japanese fleet at the Battle of Midway on June 3–5, 1942. Then came the news that the 1st Marine Division had landed on Guadalcanal in the Solomon Islands on August 7, 1942, and I wondered if Jimmy and Phil were among them.

All of this made it difficult for me to keep my mind on schoolwork, and at the end of the first half of the spring term my marks had fallen so much that I was put on probation and assigned to compulsory study hall every afternoon and all day on Saturdays. The good part of this was that I had to quit my job at Willis Paint, which I was happy to leave forever. By the end of the semester my marks had improved so much that I would have made the honor roll were it not for PE, where my failure to turn in a dentist's note lowered my grade to a 65 yet again.

My only close friend at Brooklyn Tech at that time was a classmate named Dick Ward, who wanted to go to college to study geology, a subject that wasn't offered at Brooklyn Tech. We were taking a chemistry class together, and since we were both doing well in the course we had time to goof off a bit in the laboratory section. He made fun of my literary ambitions, and to get back at him I wrote some doggerel poetry and submitted it in his name to the school literary magazine, which rejected it with a snide comment. Many years later Dick sent me my handwritten copies of these poems, including my "Verses in Praise of Monosyllables," which began with the lines "Give me the simple 'How' of the Sioux / A monosyllabic 'Ugh' or 'Ha' will do."

As soon as I turned sixteen, on June 26, 1942, I applied for working papers, because my experience with Mr. Willis had taught me that I had to do this to get a full-time job that I could continue with after school in the fall. I needed my birth certificate, and I thought that now was my chance to change the 6 in 1926 into a 4 so I could enlist in the Navy. But Peg, as usual, read my mind, and she went with me to the State Employment Bureau when I applied for my working papers, producing my birth certificate and then locking it away again that evening in the metal box where she kept all of the family documents.

I pored over the want ads in the *Daily News* and the *Journal-American,* looking for an opening as a stock clerk or delivery boy, for those were the only jobs I could think of that I could do without experience. There were a number of openings, but by the time I appeared they were taken, and after a couple of weeks I began to get very discouraged.

But then my friend Ed Casey, who had graduated from Fourteen Holy Martyrs a year ahead of me, told me how I could get a head start on applying for a job. He worked as an apprentice pressman at the *Journal-American,* and he said that if I came to the paper he would give me a copy of the want-ad pages as soon as they came off the press. We made a date, and I met him at the employees' entrance during his mid-morning break; he handed me the freshly printed want-ads and wished me good luck. I went through the pages quickly and checked them against the previous day's edition to see which ads were appearing for the first time. I circled the first new ad I found, which was for a part-time stock clerk at the Allied Art Company at 123 West Twenty-third Street.

I ran across town to Broadway and Fifth Avenue, where I turned onto West Twenty-third Street and found number 123 on the south side of the street near Sixth Avenue. I looked at the directory in the lobby and saw that the Allied Art Company was on the sixth floor; with great trepidation I entered the elevator, the first one I had ever used, and pressed the button marked 6, feeling that there was no way to turn back now.

The elevator was enclosed with an ironwork grille, and as we passed the successive floors I could see the names of the firms that did business there: an industrial printer on the second floor, a book supply firm on the third, children's clothing on the fourth, and the Eagle Druggist Supply Company on the fifth.

I was surprised when the elevator came to a stop on the fifth floor, where a rather distinguished-looking gentleman in a black suit opened the elevator door as if he had been expecting me. He asked me if I was answering the ad for a stock clerk at the Allied Art Company, and when I said yes he invited me to come in.

He introduced himself as Mr. Mendoza, president of the Eagle Druggist Supply Company, and he said that he had an opening for a stock clerk. He explained that he had been about to put an ad in the *Journal-American* when he learned that the Allied Art Company was going to advertise for one in that day's paper. He thought he would save himself the trouble by intercepting the first applicant to appear, though he was surprised at how early I had come. I told him how I had beaten the gun and he smiled appreciatively, saying that he admired my initiative and that the job was mine if I wanted it.

I said that I wanted to work full-time for the rest of the summer and then part-time after school began in the fall. He said that would be fine, and that during the summer I would work from nine to six, Monday through Saturday, with half an hour off for lunch. My salary would be fifty cents an hour, minus a 2 percent deduction for Social Security. I agreed and presented my brand-new working papers, which he returned to me after his secretary recorded my name, address, and Social Security number. He told me I could start right away, and that he would introduce me to the people with whom I would be working.

He explained that the Eagle Druggist Supply Company packaged and distributed everything you would find in a pharmacy except the actual medical drugs themselves; their main items were condoms, finger cots, nipple guards, and plastic combs, as well as their own brands of septic powder and smelling salts, the manufacture of which would be right up my alley, since I was a chemistry student at Brooklyn Tech.

He took me out onto the main production floor, where about fifty young women were working at a series of long wooden tables. There I was introduced to the forelady, Nan MacDowell, a little Scotswoman of about forty with a mop of carrot-red hair, who told Mr. Mendoza that she would take good care of me.

As soon as Mr. Mendoza left Nan told the girls to stop working so she could introduce the new stock clerk. Then, when she had their full attention, she smiled and grabbed me by the testicles, and I jumped and let out a yell. After the girls stopped laughing, Nan patted me on the behind and said that she just wanted to break the ice and make me feel at home.

Nan then took me to the stock room to meet Harry Epstein, whom I would help when he needed me. Then she brought me to meet the chief shipping clerk, Abe Cohen, and his assistant, Nathan Jefferson, a giant black man who put his arm around my shoulder and said I'd be working with him most of the time.

Nathan showed me how to make up a big cardboard carton, which we filled with boxes of condoms. When the carton was filled he showed me how to seal it, write the address with a black marker, weigh it and figure out the postage, and then stack it in the rope-operated freight elevator. After we packed about twenty cartons, Nathan showed me how to operate the ropes of the elevator to take us down to the ground floor. There we carried the cartons out the back entrance of the building on Twenty-second Street and loaded them onto a big truck. When we were finished Nathan smiled and said that now we would take a little sweet-assed time on our own, which I thought was a great idea. When he offered me a cigarette I said I didn't smoke, but I enjoyed the heady aroma all the same, though I had the feeling that it was something other than tobacco.

Most days I worked with Nathan and Isaac in the shipping room, but if there wasn't enough for me to do there I reported to Harry, helping him unload cartons from trucks on Twenty-second Street and then bringing them up in the freight elevator to put away in the stock room. Harry also showed me how to mix the materials for the septic powder and smelling salts, which I worked on in a little room that I called my laboratory, where I could see a patch of sky through a tiny window near the ceiling. As I worked there on hot summer afternoons, running with sweat, choking on septic powder, and half blinded by ammonia fumes, I would occasionally see a cloud passing in the blue sky and longed to be at Coney Island or Rockaway, where most of the boys I knew were swimming and sunning themselves with their girlfriends.

If there was nothing else to do I was sent out to find used cardboard boxes, in which we stored the materials from our incoming shipments that would be packaged by the girls in the main room. These scavenging expeditions were the high point of my working day, for I was able to escape from my prison and explore the surrounding neighborhoods, prowling through warehouses and subterranean storage areas. I was also sent off to mail packages of condoms at the post office opposite Penn Station, or to deliver special orders to wholesalers throughout Midtown Manhattan, constantly adding to my knowledge of what I imagined was the secret labyrinth at the heart of the metropolis.

On Sundays, my only day off, I went to the beach at Coney Island or Rockaway with my friends, most of whom I knew from Fourteen Holy Martyrs. After swimming at Coney Island we would go to Luna Park or Steeplechase, which charged no admission fee other than a general ticket that could be used for all of the rides, the most popular of which were the parachute jump and the Cyclone roller coaster. The tickets were circular, with numbers around the periphery for each of the rides, which were punched by the clerk as you entered. We hung around the exit of the park and picked up the discarded tickets of those who had left, going on the rides that hadn't been punched, though these were never the parachute jump or the Cyclone, which now and then we paid to go on ourselves.

We preferred the beach at Rockaway, though it was more expensive to get there, since we had to use both the subway and the Long Island Rail Road, where we often got away without paying the fare by running from car to car to avoid the conductor. The girls in our neighborhood usually went to Rockaway too, although not with us.

I continued at the Eagle Druggist Supply Company after school began in the fall, working from four to six, Monday through Friday, and nine to six on Saturday. It took me an hour to get home by subway, and after supper I was able to begin my homework by eight o'clock, two hours earlier than I had when I was working at the Willis Paint Company. As a result, I was able to keep my grades up, and I would again have been on the honor roll were it not for the automatic 65 in PE because of my unexamined teeth.

Our family fortunes changed early in 1943, when John was hired as a gravedigger in the Evergreens Cemetery, replacing a young unmarried man who had been drafted into the Army. Peg was beside herself with joy, because John had been getting only irregular work shaping up as a longshoreman on the docks, and at times when he was not chosen for the work gang by a foreman he became terribly discouraged, having wasted ten cents on subway fare and coming home at the end of the day without a penny to show for it. Now he could walk to and from work, for the cemetery was only a mile away, and he would have a steady job that didn't depend on the whims of a corrupt foreman.

But the situation at the cemetery turned out to be no better than on the docks, at least as far as salary was concerned, because the gravediggers were paid only when there was a funeral. And even then they were paid only for the time they were actually digging the grave and filling it in again after the funeral, so John found himself taking in little more money than he had been earning on the docks.

The gravediggers and other employees of the cemetery talked about forming a union to get better pay and working conditions. Some of them contacted the local representatives of the two most powerful groups in organized labor, the American Federation of Labor (AFL) and the Congress of Industrial Organizations (CIO), but neither union was interested in obscure workers such as gravediggers. And besides, the AFL and CIO had their own troubles; in June 1943 the U.S. Congress passed a law, the Smith-Connally Act, which imposed severe penalties on anyone encouraging strikes in plants involved in the war effort. But then John L. Lewis, head of the United Mine Workers, reached an agreement with the government in what was known as the "portal to portal" pact, whereby coal miners would be paid for the entire time they were within their place of employment, and not just when they were mining coal.

I had been closely following these developments in the newspapers, and when the portal-to-portal agreement was approved by the War Labor Board I could see that it should also apply to gravediggers as well. I mentioned this at supper, but John said that if any of the gravediggers were heard to even mention "portal to portal" they would be fired on the spot. I would have said that they should form a union, but I knew what his response would be—that they would be fired if they even attempted to organize.

The gravediggers and other cemetery workers did manage to form a union, which they organized under the aegis of the Food, Tobacco and Agricultural Workers of America, an affiliate of the AFL. When the union presented its demands, which included the portal-to-portal pact, the cemeteries in New York City united to reject them, so all the grave-diggers and other cemetery workers went on strike. This caused a crisis in the city, as the dead piled up in morgues and funeral parlors, with editorials in the *Daily News* and the *Journal-American* condemning the strikers and warning of an epidemic.

Archbishop Spellman, later to be a cardinal, head of the Roman Catholic diocese of New York, took to his pulpit in St. Patrick's Cathedral and warned the Catholic gravediggers that it was their Christian duty to bury the dead, threatening to excommunicate them if they didn't end their strike immediately. When the strike continued, he ordered the students in the seminaries in the New York area to begin burying the dead in Catholic cemeteries (Evergreens was nonsectarian). But it was a fiasco, for the seminarian scabs were physically incapable of digging graves; they could be as much as nine feet deep for a fresh burial, which John and his partner could dig in less than four hours.

The strike went on for seven weeks before the cemetery owners finally gave in, agreeing to all the union demands, including portal-to-portal pay and a scale of wages that gave the gravediggers seventy-five cents an hour (they had been earning fifty) for a workweek of eight hours a day, Monday through Friday, with time and a half for Saturday, and two weeks of paid vacation a year for those who had been employed for more than five years.

All of this and my own experience as an underpaid, underage worker had made me very radical. I went to the public library and checked out the Modern Library English translation of Karl Marx's *Das Kapital,* and at a newsstand in Times Square I bought a copy of the *Daily Worker,* the newspaper of the American Communist Party. When Peg saw what I was reading she laughed and called me "Class-Struggle Freely," saying that I'd have us all arrested as communists, and wouldn't that be a fine thing.

I read only that single issue of the *Daily Worker,* but it gave me a different slant on the Eastern Front, where earlier that year the Russians had defeated the Germans at the Battle of Stalingrad. Stalin was calling for a second front in western Europe, where only Great Britain was holding out against the Nazis, although the Allies had landed in North Africa.

I was paying far more attention to the war in the South Pacific, where fighting was continuing on the Solomon Islands. The newspaper reports indicated that the U.S. Marines were suffering heavy casualties, but no one had received any news about Jimmy Anderson or Phil Gould. As I walked around the neighborhood I occasionally saw an apartment with drawn shades and a small American flag with a gold star displayed in the window, indicating that someone in the family had died for their country. Every saloon in the neighborhood had an honor roll on the wall above the bar, with gold stars next to the names of those who had been killed and silver for the wounded or missing. My uncle Tom reassured me that neither Jimmy nor Phil had gold or silver stars next to their names in the honor rolls of the many saloons that he frequented.

As soon as I turned seventeen, on June 26, 1943, I asked Peg if she would give me permission to join the Navy, but she refused and said I should wait until I was drafted, which would be at least another year, by which time the war might be over, which is exactly what I was afraid of.

That fall I began to lose interest in my studies, particularly in the technical courses, for they would be of no use to me in the seagoing career I had in mind, and I longed to be off in the Navy. The only class that interested me was Humanities, in which we were reading Homer's *Odyssey*. We were using a prose translation, which our teacher, Mrs. Jacobs, said did not do justice to the poetry of Homer's epic, but she said it was the textbook assigned by the Board of Education, which we called the "Bored of Education." She said that the *Odyssey* told the story of the homecoming of the hero Odysseus after the Trojan War, which was the subject of Homer's *Iliad,* the first of his epics. I asked her why we didn't read the *Iliad* first and then the *Odyssey*. She explained that we only had time to go through one of the two books, and that the Board of Education had chosen the *Odyssey* because it was easier to read than the *Iliad,* which was very intense and violent. Then I asked her why we were reading the *Odyssey* in prose and not in poetry, and she said that I asked too many questions, but if I wanted to read it in poetic form I could go to the main branch of the New York Public Library at Fifth Avenue and Forty-second Street and look for a version I liked.

When I did so I was astonished to see how many English translations there were of both the *Iliad* and the *Odyssey,* all of them in poetic form. The earliest was by George Chapman in the years 1599–1607, so

I decided that I would ask for his translation of the *Odyssey*, though I could only look at the book in the reading room and not check it out. The first lines were so different from anything I had read before that I had to put the book down after a few minutes and reflect upon them.

The man, O Muse, inform, that many a way
Wound with his wisdom to his wished stay;
That wandered wondrous far, when he the town
Of sacred Troy had sack'd and shivered down.

I asked Mrs. Jacobs why Chapman's language was so different from our own, and she told me that it was the English of Elizabethan times, the same as that of Shakespeare. I said that I had read some Shakespeare in the Modern Library edition, but that it hadn't been like Chapman's Homer. She explained that editions such as the Modern Library were in modern English, and for the present I should stick with them; she advised me to read Robert Fitzgerald's translation of Homer, though she had to admit that Chapman's translation sometimes took her breath away. She also advised me to read the poetry of John Keats, which would give me some idea of Chapman's influence on later poets. I was able to find the collected poems of Keats at the Hopkinson branch of the Brooklyn Public Library, and I read some of them that evening, starting with one that Mrs. Jacobs had particularly recommended, "On First Looking into Chapman's Homer." Reading this poem made me realize that when I had looked into Chapman's Homer, I had had the same feeling that Keats said he had felt, and I repeated six lines of it till I had them by heart.

Then felt I like some watcher of the skies
When a new planet swims into his ken;
Or like stout Cortez, when with eagle eyes
He stared at the Pacific—and all his men
Look'd at each other with a wild surmise—
Silent, upon a peak in Darien.

Later that night I talked about these things with Peg in one of our nocturnal dialogues. I asked her if she had read Homer or Keats or

Shakespeare. She said she had never read Homer, but she knew the stories of the *Iliad* and the *Odyssey* from her mother. She had read some poems by Keats, but all she remembered was a line from his *Endymion,* "a thing of beauty is a joy forever." And the only Shakespeare she knew was a film version of *Romeo and Juliet.* I had seen this film with Peg some years before at the Colonial, and I recalled that Romeo and Juliet were played by Leslie Howard and Norma Shearer, who seemed much too old for the parts, while John Barrymore was perfect as Mercutio. I reminded Peg that we had laughed when we saw the credit line at the beginning of the film: "*Romeo and Juliet,* by William Shakespeare, with additional dialogue by Sam Taylor." We laughed again at it now, and then she recited what I knew to be her favorite Shakespearean lines: "This above all,—to thine own self be true, and it shall follow as the night the day, thou cannot then be false to any man." That was her advice, she said to me that night, and I remember telling her that I would always keep it to heart.

My report card in January 1944 showed that I had flunked all of my courses except Humanities, in which I received a perfect grade of 100, and PE, where I was once again given the mandatory 65. The "Remarks" entry at the bottom of my card said that I was being expelled from school because of my unsatisfactory academic record, and I was required to report to my adviser along with at least one of my parents.

Peg was devastated when I showed her my report card. When she went with me to see my adviser she said not a word but just signed the forms that he put in front of her. I hadn't seen my adviser since the day I entered school, and now as I left he offered no advice, nor did I need any, for I knew what I was going to do, and that was join the Navy.

Peg finally agreed to let me enlist, although she wasn't happy about it. Early in February I went to the main Navy recruitment headquarters in Manhattan and asked for the parental permission form. After Peg and John signed the form I returned it and began the process of enlistment, which involved a series of medical, dental, and psychological examinations and the filling out of endless forms and questionnaires.

The doctors and dentists who examined us were all recent graduates who were serving as Navy ensigns. At the start of my medical exam I was asked if I had any medical problems, and I said I didn't think so, though I had never before been examined by a doctor, at least so far as

I knew. The doctor, whose ID card identified him as Ensign Harrison, began by examining my penis, and I knew from my older friends that he was checking for signs of syphilis and gonorrhea, which they referred to as "syph" and "the clap." He found no signs of venereal disease but said that I should have been circumcised, and that if I had to have it done while I was in the Navy it could be very painful at my age.

At my dental exam I was told that my teeth were perfect, which made me think of all the 65s I'd been given in PE for not having a dentist's report. Then the dentist ensign told me to sit in the chair while he read a magazine, getting up now and then in a pretense of examining me whenever one of his superior officers appeared. I tried to talk to him, but he told me to be quiet, so I started daydreaming, wondering where my Navy career would take me. I hoped it would be the Pacific, for that's where all the action was. The Marines had landed on Tarawa the previous November, and fighting continued on New Britain, New Guinea, and the Solomon Islands. There was still no word from Jimmy Anderson or Phil Gould, but my uncle Tom assured me that there were still no gold or silver stars next to their names on the saloon honor rolls.

One of the psychological examinations was in the form of a questionnaire, which I had been told was designed to eliminate obvious lunatics, although if you wanted to stay out of the service by pretending to be crazy you could do that by giving contrary answers. I thought of that as I tried to answer one of the questions, which asked whether I wanted to be a poet or a motorcycle racer, and I wondered which choice I should make if I wanted to be considered sane. And so I filled in the circle for "poet," which was probably the wrong answer.

I'd also been told that another purpose of the psychological examinations was to weed out homosexuals. But the tests didn't seem to be too successful, for many of the pharmacist's mates were "queer" and were called "pecker checkers," or so said my older friends who had enlisted in the Navy. I saw no evidence of that during my own enlistment process, although Ensign Harrison seemed to have taken longer in examining my private parts than I thought necessary.

I filled out the questionnaires together with at least a hundred other applicants in a large hall, where a chief petty officer took us through the questions one by one, assuming that we were brainless and leaving no room for ambiguity, with all entries to be made in block capital letters.

When it came to "Color of Skin," he said that if we were Caucasians we should write "White," whereas Negroes were "Black," Latin Americans, Hawaiians, Samoans, and American Indians "Brown," Chinese and other Asians "Yellow." This caused a lot of confusion, particularly among those I could identify as Latins, many of whom seemed to know hardly any English, and their skin color covered the whole spectrum from pale white to jet black. So far as my own skin color was concerned, I decided to write "Ruddy," which got me in trouble when my form was checked by a chief petty officer, who called me a "goddamn wise ass."

We were then shown a film to inform us about the schools and training centers that were open to us in the Navy, and then I knew why they wanted us to write down the color of our skin. All of those who were in the Cooks and Bakers School were BLACK and BROWN and YELLOW, and everyone in all of the other schools was WHITE. I wondered what my black friend Patrick Irish would think about this when he enlisted, as I knew he would be doing soon, for his skin was lighter in color than that of some of my Italian friends and his hair was as red as my father's.

One of the orientation lectures informed us about the financial benefits of a Navy career. As recruits we would have the rank of apprentice seaman and would be paid fifty dollars a month. When we completed basic training we would be promoted, to either seaman second class or fireman second class, the latter being for those who were assigned to engine room ratings, in both cases at a salary of fifty-four dollars a month. Those who then went on to graduate from an advanced training school would be promoted to seaman or fireman first class at sixty-six dollars a month. The lecturer then smiled and said that those who served in a combat zone would receive a 20 percent bonus, which even for a seaman second class would be an extra ten dollars and eighty cents. This brought a big cheer from the crowd. He said that it was highly recommended that we sign over as much as 90 percent of our pay to be withheld and sent home to our parents, which I knew Peg would appreciate when I told her about it, for then she would have more than I had been giving her from my salary at the Eagle Druggist Supply Company. The lecturer finished by telling us about the $100,000 life insurance policy that we could have for an extremely low premium, with our next of kin as beneficiary. I did a quick calculation and figured out that at fifty cents an hour it would take me nearly a hundred years to earn that much money, so I would be worth much more dead than alive—though I didn't tell that to Peg.

After several days of tests, interviews, and orientation films and lectures, I was told that I would be informed by mail whether or not I was accepted as a Navy recruit. I was very disappointed by the delay, for I had thought I would be going into the service right away, as Jimmy and Phil had when they enlisted in the Marines. When I asked a petty officer at the recruitment center about this, he said that the Navy was much more particular than the Marines, whom he referred to cynically as "dummies" and "cannon fodder," and I thought that I'd like him to say that in front of Jimmy and Phil.

Two months later I received an official letter informing me that my application to join the U.S. Navy had been accepted, and that I should report to the recruitment center to be sworn in. I did so, expecting to go into the Navy right away, but again I was told that I would be informed by mail as to when and where I should report to be sent off to training camp.

In the meantime I had continued working at the Eagle Druggist Supply Company, where, after flunking out of Brooklyn Tech, I spent eight hours a day, six days a week. Because I would soon be going off to the Navy I decided I would quit my job, for there were things I wanted to do before I left. Peg was agreeable to this, because I was able to pay for my board out of the money I had saved up in my second attempt to buy a sport coat, which I would now no longer be needing. I informed Mr. Mendoza, who graciously thanked me for my services and told me that I could have my job back after the war, and I had to make an effort not to laugh. Then I said goodbye to Nan and Harry and Abe and Nathan, who told me he had just been drafted into the Army and expected to be going off soon himself. I left on the rope-operated elevator with him and he walked me out to Twenty-second Street. He gave me a big hug and said, "Goodbye, little buddy, maybe I'll see you in the Pacific," but that was the last I ever saw of him.

By then it was mid-April, and on sunny days I took the train to Rockaway, where I swam for a while and then walked for hours along the empty beach, daydreaming as I had when I strolled along the strand on the Dingle Peninsula, which I now remembered with some sadness, wondering if I would ever see Ireland again. But I cheered up when I thought of all the other places in the world I'd soon be seeing, and when I returned home in the late afternoon I anxiously checked the mailbox, only to be disappointed day after day when there was no letter from the Navy.

On cloudy or rainy days I went to the New York Public Library on Fifth Avenue and Forty-second Street, for there were far more books there than in our local branch on Hopkinson Avenue. My course with Mrs. Jacobs had given me a deep interest in Homer, and I had managed to find a cheap paperback edition of the *Odyssey* in a secondhand bookstore, the first book I had ever bought. But once again it was in prose, in a translation done in 1879 by S. H. Butcher and A. Lang. I was curious to see how it compared with Chapman's Homer, which I once more consulted at the New York Public Library, where just sitting in the main reading room gave me the feeling of being a scholar.

I found that Chapman's translation was very different from that of Butcher and Lang, not just in the language, or in being poetry rather than prose; he also called the hero Ulysses rather than Odysseus, using the Latin version of the name rather than the Greek, and even the descriptive terms were different. One difference that particularly struck me was that Butcher and Lang always wrote of the "wine-dark sea" while Chapman usually described it as the "sable sea," as in one passage that literally, as Mrs. Jacobs had said, "took my breath away." This was in Book 19, where the disguised Odysseus describes to Penelope a false version of his voyage through the eastern Mediterranean, where he first lays eyes on Crete:

In the middle of the sable sea there lies
An isle called Crete, a ravisher of eyes,
Fruitful and mann'd with many an infinite store
Where ninety cities crown the famous shore,
Mix'd with all-languag'd men. There Greeks survive,
There the great-minded Eteocretans live,
There the Dorensians never out of war,
The Cydons there, and there the singular
Pelasgian people. There doth Gnossus stand . . .

Those lines gave me a lot to think about, beginning with the color of the sea, for the seas that I had seen ranged through many shades of blue and green but were never wine dark or sable. I guessed that "wine-dark" and "sable" were poetic ways of saying that the blue of the sea is sometimes so deep that it seems bottomless and dark, as I remembered it from our trips across the Atlantic, when I used to stare into it for hours, losing myself in its depths.

I was also curious about the route that Odysseus had followed on his long journey home from Troy to Ithaca, for although most of the place names in the eastern Mediterranean were familiar to me, I had no idea where the Land of the Lotus-eaters or the Land of the Cyclops, or Siren Land, or the Land of the Phaceaeans, were. I guessed that Scylla and Charybdis were in the Strait of Messina, between Sicily and the toe of Italy, but the others were a mystery.

Then I found a four-volume work by Victor Bérard entitled *Les navigations d'Ulysse.* I couldn't read it because it was in French, but the maps enabled me to follow the wanderings of Odysseus. Parts of these made sense, but some of the places were so strange and far out of the way that I began to think that Homer had just made them up. Anyway, I now had at least a general idea of where Odysseus had sailed; if my Navy career took me through the Mediterranean, I would know when I crossed his wake.

But it was more likely that I would be sent to the Pacific, for most of my friends who had enlisted in the Navy during the past year were now serving there. I thought I should find some books about the Pacific, and a librarian at the New York Public Library recommended that I look for works about Ferdinand Magellan and other early explorers.

The first book I found was a biography of Magellan, which described his circumnavigation of the world in the years 1519–22, during the course of which he became the first Western navigator to cross the Pacific. I checked the track of his voyage in the *National Geographic Atlas of the World,* and I was able to identify his first landing place, the Ladrones, or Isles of Thieves—now known as the Marianas—which the Japanese had occupied at the beginning of the war, and which I knew the United States would be trying to regain in its island-hopping campaign.

I found other books about the voyages of Sir Frances Drake and Captain James Cook, both of which I followed in the *National Geographic*

Atlas, particularly their journeys across the Pacific, which I now felt I knew as well as I did the Atlantic, at least as far as maps were concerned.

While I waited for my letter from the Navy I also revisited the Museum of Natural History and the Hayden Planetarium, only this time I took the subway rather than walking, as Jimmy and I had done four years before. At the Museum of Natural History I looked at the dioramas devoted to the Pacific islands, Australia, and Asia, places I might see when I was in the Navy. At the planetarium I saw projections of the night sky in the Southern Hemisphere, and I checked the celestial coordinates of the Southern Cross and other constellations I would see in the South Pacific, as well as the Magellanic Clouds, which I had learned were two dwarf galaxies 160,000 and 200,000 light-years distant. I also took a look at the planetary orrery, where I could see that Pluto had hardly moved along its orbit since I had last visited the planetarium.

I also visited the Metropolitan Museum of Art for the first time. I spent the whole day there, trying to see every one of the galleries, pleased when now and then I came upon a painting that I recognized from my reading, such as Emanuel Leutze's *Washington Crossing the Delaware.* The last galleries I visited were devoted to Greek and Roman art, which I had become interested in through my reading of Homer, and I saw several vase paintings depicting scenes from the *Iliad* and the *Odyssey.*

The work that caught my attention in the gallery of classical Greek sculpture was a marble statue of a wounded Amazon, one of the women warriors I had read about in a book on Greek mythology. Peg sometimes talked about the Amazons, saying that women were braver and fiercer than men, and if they could shake off male bondage to restore the matriarchal society of old the world would be a better place. But the wounded Amazon in the Metropolitan Museum looked defeated and forlorn, though I didn't mention this to Peg when I told her about my visit to the museum in our next nocturnal dialogue.

The letter from the Navy finally arrived at the beginning of May. I was informed that on May 26 I should report to the officer on duty at Penn Station at eight p.m. sharp, when I would be mustered along with other recruits who would be sent off on a troop train to Sampson Naval Training Center in upstate New York. Peg sighed when I told her, and she said that I would be going into the service at almost exactly the same age, seventeen years and eleven months, that her maternal grandfather, Thomas

Ashe, had been when he went off in the British Army to fight in the Crimean War. She said that he came back alive, though badly wounded, and otherwise none of us would be here today, and I should take good care of myself, for there were unborn generations depending upon me.

A week later my uncle Mike Freely received a notice from his draft board, informing him that he would be inducted into the Army early in June. Mike was thirty-nine years old and was married and had three small children, but his wife had left him because he was out of work and never sober. Married men with children were usually exempt from induction, but Peg figured that Mike's wife had informed the draft board that he was unemployed, and if he was in the Army she would at least have most of his pay sent to her.

A few days after that my aunt Mary Freely's boyfriend, a French Canadian named Phil Pelletier, received a notice from his draft board that he too would be inducted into the Army early in June, despite the fact that he was forty and had only one eye. He and Mary decided that they would get married right away, just a civil wedding, for there wasn't time to do one in the Catholic Church, where the banns had to be posted for three weeks.

On the last Sunday before I left I went to Rockaway Beach with my friend Martin Kaiser, along with his younger brother Francis and their mother. Martin had turned eighteen a few weeks before, but he had a heart murmur and had received a medical exemption from the draft. Francis was approaching seventeen and wanted to join the Navy, so he kept trying to talk to me about enlisting. His mother wanted no part of it, so she kept changing the subject, which was easy enough to do on a warm spring day at the beach, where Martin and Francis and I swam and tumbled in the waves until we were exhausted and then had a picnic that Mrs. Kaiser had prepared for us.

On the way home, as we crossed the marsh that separates Rockaway Beach from the mainland, we sang some of the songs that were in the top ten of the Hit Parade, beginning with "Sleepy Lagoon," which had been number one for months: "a tropical moon, a sleepy lagoon, and two on an island . . ." I thought the song was very sappy, particularly because my friends Jimmy and Phil were probably now fighting the Japanese on one of these tropical islands. Then we began singing a new song, whose refrain caught the mood of that beautiful spring day literally on the wing.

Skylark, have you anything to say to me?
Won't you tell me where my love can be?
Is there a meadow in the mist
Where someone's waiting to be kissed?

The war seemed very far away at that moment, but its clouds returned when I heard the evening news with Gabriel Heatter, who began with his usual opening line, "There's good news tonight." Then he announced that the U.S. Navy's amphibious forces had landed an Army division near Hollandia on the island of New Guinea, north of Australia, the start of the newest phase of General Douglas MacArthur's "island-hopping" campaign across the Pacific against Japan, which I hoped to be part of in the near future.

The day before I left I said goodbye to all of my relatives and friends. That evening I took one last stroll around the neighborhood, and on the way home I passed the park on Wilson Avenue and Halsey Street where some of my pals went to go "necking" with their girlfriends. When I passed the entrance to the park a girl whose voice I didn't recognize called out to me, but then she laughed and I just kept walking, figuring that one of my friends had put her up to it just to make fun of me. Then I remembered the episode in the *Odyssey* where Odysseus puts wax in his ears and has his men tie him to the mast of his ship so he will be able to resist the call of the Sirens. To buoy up my feelings, I thought of the Halsey Street park as Siren Land.

I went to bed and set the alarm for three a.m., so that I could get up for one last nocturnal dialogue with Peg when she came home from work. But the alarm must have failed to go off, for I woke to find that Peg was holding me in her arms, and she told me that when she came home she heard me crying in my sleep. When she asked me what was wrong I couldn't tell her, for I didn't know, and she said not to worry, for all would be well, as the Irish say. She told me she would take the next night off from work so she and John could go with me to Penn Station, and then she kissed me good night and I went back to sleep.

The next evening I kissed Dorothy and Nancy and Jimmy goodbye, and we left for Penn Station, taking the subway at Wilson Avenue. When we arrived at the station I saw a sign directing Navy recruits to gate 8, where an ensign and a chief petty officer were waiting, along with two sailors wearing leather leggings and carrying billy clubs, identified by their armbands as SP, Shore Patrol. I saluted the ensign, for I had been trained to do this in the Catholic Boys' Brigade, though he seemed surprised. He told me to give my name to the chief, who ticked it off on the list and told me to stand by the entrance to gate 8. Then other recruits began arriving, none of them accompanied by family, and I kissed John and Peg goodbye, watching them until they reached the entrance to the subway. They turned and waved goodbye to me there, and I could see that they were trying not to cry. I did my best not to cry too, for I was in the Navy now.

Part Two

War

By eight o'clock about fifty recruits had assembled at gate 8, all of them around my age. Some of them seemed to know one another, though there was no one I recognized from my neighborhood. A few minutes after eight the ensign ordered all of us to line up in front of the gate, in the order that the chief petty officer called off our names. The chief then went down the line to check our papers, and at the end he turned to the ensign and said we were all present and accounted for. One of the SPs took his place at the front of the line and the other at the rear, and when the ensign said "Forward march!" we followed him and the chief as we entered the gate and walked down the stairs to track 8.

The train waiting for us on track 8 was marked LEHIGH VALLEY RAILWAY, a name that I had never seen before in my explorations of the freight yards of Brooklyn. The passenger cars were completely empty, and we were herded aboard the first of them by the SPs. After we took our seats the chief checked off our names again, and then he told us to stay in our seats except when we went to the head, which I already knew was the Navy term for the toilet. Then he took his seat at the front of the car with the ensign, while the two SPs sat at the back. A few minutes later the train whistle blew and we were enveloped in a cloud of steam as the engine began puffing away faster and faster. One of the black porters waved goodbye as our car passed, but otherwise there was no one on the platform to notice our departure, as we entered the tunnel under the Hudson River.

When we emerged from the tunnel I could see the gently glowing skyline of Manhattan across the Hudson, and I knew that all of those lights were on because the offices in the skyscrapers of New York City were being cleaned by women like Peg, who at least had the night off because she and John had come with me to say goodbye at Penn Station.

We stopped in Newark and another group of recruits boarded the train, and I noticed that they were filing into the car behind ours. Then we started up again, and as the train chugged along I could see the familiar names of towns in the New Jersey suburbs of New York City as we passed them in the night. I had a seat to myself, so as soon as the lights in our car were turned off I stretched out and tried to sleep, but it was difficult to do so because every half hour or so we came to a screeching halt as our troop train was shunted aside to make way for high-speed expresses between New York and Philadelphia.

Other groups of recruits boarded our train in Trenton and Philadelphia, where I could see from a clock on the platform that it was past midnight when we finally left. I fell asleep soon afterward, but I was jolted awake when we were shunted off the main line in Mauch Chunk, Pennsylvania, the birthplace of the great Native American athlete Jim Thorpe.

It was dawn by then, so I stayed awake to enjoy the scenery, as our route took us along the Lehigh River as far as Wilkes-Barre, where we went along the Susquehanna. After crossing into New York State we headed north along the west side of Lake Seneca, which I knew from my study of geography was the longest of the Finger Lakes. At the northern end of the lake we stopped at Geneva, where a crowd of U.S. Navy personnel boarded the train, including a number of WAVES, the women's branch of the Navy. I heard one of the SPs saying that the new arrivals were returning from "liberty," the Navy term for shore leave. The other SP said that Geneva was a "one-horse hick town" and that he preferred Syracuse and Rochester, where there was a better chance of "getting laid."

We were shunted onto a branch line that took us around the northern end of the lake and down the eastern shore to the Sampson Naval Training Base, one of the Navy's two largest boot camps, or recruit training centers, the other being Great Lakes, near Chicago. It occupied four and a half miles of lakefront, and it was operated by about 5,000 Navy personnel who at any given time were training some 25,000 recruits.

As soon as we were herded off the train we boarded trucks that took us into the base to a huge building identified by its sign as the reception center, where the chief checked us off on his list once again as we entered. Once inside the reception room we filed past a desk where each of us was given a canvas bag, into which we were to put all of our clothing and belongings, which would be mailed back to our homes. We stripped down, put our things into the bag, filled out the address on the label, and handed it in as we filed out of the reception room into an enormous drill hall.

We were among the first to arrive, but within a half hour the hall filled up with what I estimated to be a thousand recruits, all of us stark naked, and I was sure that they all felt as defenseless and apprehensive as I did, though everyone tried to act nonchalant. The clock on the front wall read eight o'clock when a voice on the public address system told us to line up at desks alphabetically. This seemed to puzzle some of the Spanish-speaking recruits, but eventually we were all checked in. They gave each of us our dog tag, the metal medallion inscribed with our name, serial number, and blood type, which we were to wear around our neck day and night. We were also handed a baloney sandwich and an apple, which we ate while milling around waiting for further instructions, still naked, except for our dog tags.

When we finished eating we filed through into a shower room where we washed ourselves with a strong-smelling soap that we were told would kill any lice and crabs; then we were given haircuts that were virtually a clean shave.

We filed through a storeroom where we were issued uniforms and other clothing, which we put in our seabag and a smaller sack called a ditty bag. We were also issued a mattress and mattress cover—known in Navy slang as a "fart sack"—as well as a hammock, although we were told that we wouldn't use that until we went to sea. The last thing we received was a thick book called *The Bluejacket's Manual,* which we were expected to read from cover to cover while we were in boot camp, for it contained everything we needed to know while we were in the Navy.

We then put on our GI underwear, socks, dungarees, white canvas hat, and boots, wound our hammock around our mattress and seabag, and carried that and our ditty bag as we were marched out of the reception center to our barracks. It was pouring rain and the paths were churned up into slippery mud, and as we trudged along we were jeered by the recruits in the barracks that we passed; they referred to us contemptuously as "boots," even though they themselves had been in the Navy only a few weeks at most.

Sampson was divided into five units, each with 1,000 ship's company, or permanent personnel, and 5,000 recruits, who were housed in barracks that accommodated 228 men each. Each of the units was named for a famous admiral; ours was Dewey, and our barracks was D-20. The bunks were stacked five high, and I was lucky to be assigned a top bunk— the lower ones were claustrophobic and airless. After I put my mattress in its fart sack I laid back to rest for a few minutes before I stowed my belongings in my locker, putting everything in the order described in *The Bluejacket's Manual.*

We were then called out to muster outside the barracks, lined up in ranks six deep by our company commander, a fat brute who must have been about forty, although he was only a seaman first class and didn't have any hash marks, the diagonal arm stripes that each indicate four years of service. He reminded me of Charles Laughton playing Captain Bligh in *Mutiny on the Bounty,* particularly when he gave us a tongue-lashing for our disorderly appearance and told us that he was going to whip us into shape before we went off to sea. I mentioned the resemblance in a whisper to the person on my right, and the word spread through the ranks; from then, on our company commander was known to us as Captain Bligh.

Captain Bligh lined us up four abreast, and for the next two hours he marched us around and around the circular drill track that we came to know as the "Grinder" because it was designed to grind us down. At around six o'clock he marched us to the mess hall, where we lined up for our food with five thousand other recruits, and when we were finished we made our own way back to our barracks. At eight o'clock we were mustered by Captain Bligh, who told us that lights out would be at nine o'clock, and that reveille would be at five thirty in the morning.

Since I had a top bunk I could read by the overhead lights, and so until nine o'clock I paged through *The Bluejacket's Manual,* beginning with the section on the Navy terminology I'd been hearing all day. "Floor" was "deck," "ceiling" was "overhead," "wall" was "bulkhead," "toilet" was "head," "underwear" was "skivvies," "downstairs" was "below," "upstairs" was "above," "left side" was "port," "right side" was "starboard," "medical center" was "sick bay," "cafeteria" was "mess hall," and "food" was "chow." The word for "drinking fountain" was "scuttlebutt," which was also slang for gossip and rumor. I had already learned some Navy slang, for in the mess hall I heard someone referring to our evening meal of stew on cold burned toast as SOS, "shit on a shingle."

I could see the clock on the front wall of the barracks, and as nine o'clock approached I climbed down from my bunk to kneel and say my prayers, as I had done every evening of my life since I was a boy. I had been hesitant to do this, because I didn't want to call attention to myself, but I could see that others were doing the same without anything being said about it. I got back to my bunk just before the lights went out, thinking that in the future I would stay put while I said my prayers; those in the bunks below me didn't seem too happy about being disturbed by me on my way down and up.

Then I lay awake for a while thinking of my family. This was the first time in my life that I had gone to bed without them around me. I thought particularly of Peg, because when she came home at three in the morning I wouldn't be there for our usual nocturnal dialogue. So I had the dialogue in my mind, telling her all that had happened during my first day in the Navy.

We were awakened at five thirty by a recorded bugle call on the PA, followed by an announcement that we should fall in for muster outside the barracks at six.

There was barely time to go to the head and wash up; there were long lines at the showers, washbasins, urinals, and commodes—although there was no one lined up to use the toilet seat that was painted red, with a sign above saying it was reserved for VENEREAL PATIENTS.

After we were mustered in, Captain Bligh announced that we would have a "short arm inspection," and we all looked at one another, wondering what he meant. He then said we should drop our pants and take out our "little friend" and "skin it back" so that the "pecker checker" (pharmacist's mate) could check to see if we had caught the clap or "the old Joe," by which I assume he meant syphilis.

When the short-arm inspection was over he said we would spend the day at the sick bay, where we would be given the first of our inoculations as well as dental and psychological exams. He said that if the dentist found that our teeth were rotten they would all be yanked out and we would then be classified as "gummer's mates." And if the psychologist thought that we were "nuts" or "queers" we would be assigned to barracks L-16, where they would either straighten us out or get rid of us; in the U.S. Navy it was either "shape up or ship out." With that he spat a big oyster, picked his nose, scratched his behind, and dismissed us for the moment, saying that we would muster again at seven to march to the mess hall.

After we broke ranks the person to my right introduced himself to me as Dave Zuloff, a Russian Jew from New York City. We laughed about Captain Bligh, and then Zuloff said he couldn't take "this kind of shit," and that he would try to escape from the camp. I tried to talk him out of it, but at the next morning muster he was missing and Captain Bligh blew his stack, hauling me in for questioning and telling me that if I didn't reveal where Zuloff was I'd be put in the brig. But I said I had no idea where Zuloff had gone, and he let me go.

Dave was absent from evening muster, too, but when I was sitting outside before lights-out I saw him beckoning to me from behind one of the concrete pillars that held up the barracks. I crawled in and talked to him, and he said that he was reconnoitering the boundary fences to see if there was an unguarded stretch where he could escape, but in the meantime he would appreciate it if I could bring him some food from the mess hall. I said that I would, and in the days that followed I brought him whatever food I could smuggle out of the mess hall as well as candy and drinks that I bought in the ship's service canteen with money we had been advanced from our salary, leaving it under the barracks behind the pillar where we had talked.

After the first two weeks of training our barracks was scheduled for inspection by the commander of Dewey Unit, a full lieutenant, the equivalent of an Army captain. I could see that Captain Bligh was nervous about the upcoming inspection, because the disappearance of Dave Zuloff had focused attention on our boot company, and teams of SPs had searched our barracks and the surrounding woods looking for him. I was nervous myself, for I had neglected to write my name on the clothing that had been issued to me, as prescribed in *The Bluejacket's Manual,* and some of it had gone missing. As a result, the neatly folded pile of belongings in my locker was noticeably lower than those on either side, which the lieutenant was bound to notice. He skipped my line of lockers during the inspection, but I knew that I would surely get nailed the next time.

Most of the recruits in my barracks were from New York, New Jersey, and Pennsylvania, the largest contingent being from Philadelphia, easily identified because they always said "Yo!" instead of "Hey!" or "Hi!"

The first friends I made were Pete Hansen, from Teaneck, New Jersey, and Charles Shelmerdine, from Philadelphia. But Pete soon fell in with another group from New Jersey and I found myself spending most of my time with Charles. His parents were from England, and the other recruits called him "Limey." Like me, he had joined the Navy to see the world, and much of our conversation was about the places we might go after we left boot camp and went to sea.

Everyone thought we would be sent to the southwest Pacific, where the Navy was involved in the fighting that was going on in the Solomon Islands, the Bismarck Archipelago, and Papua New Guinea. Then on June 6 we heard that the Allies had landed at Normandy to begin the long-awaited second front that I had first read about in the *Daily Worker*. For the next few days scuttlebutt had it that our training would be cut from eight weeks to six, and that we would be sent as replacements to the Navy amphibious forces in action on the beaches in Normandy. But then on June 14 the Marines landed on the island of Saipan and four days later the Battle of the Philippines began, so the scuttlebutt shifted the focus back to the Pacific.

Most days we spent several hours drilling on the Grinder and the rest of the time in orientation films and lectures, aptitude tests, and training classes in things nautical. One of the orientation films concerned the various branches of the Navy for which we could volunteer, including submarines, Naval aviation, underwater demolition, and commando units such as Scouts and Raiders. I signed up for all of these and took several aptitude tests, including one for aerial gunner, which scuttlebutt said had many openings because of the buildup of Naval aviation in the southwest Pacific.

I scored very high on aptitude tests involving general knowledge and mathematical ability, but extremely low on those involving technical subjects—probably because I had no interest in them, but also because I didn't want to be assigned to a school for further training, since that would delay my being shipped out.

The training classes I enjoyed most were those in plane spotting and simulated antiaircraft gunnery. We learned to identify silhouettes of various German and Japanese warplanes and to fire at them when their images popped up on the screen. We were told to pay particular attention to the Japanese carrier-based fighter plane, the Zero, and to their land-based fighter-bomber, the Betty, for our instructor said we would be seeing many of these in the Pacific. We were also shown the silhouette of a typical kamikaze dive bomber, but our teacher said that there was little chance of hitting one once it began its dive. Our simulated firing at these planes was great fun, as was listening to the war stories of our instructors, some of whom had seen action in the Battles of Midway and the Coral Sea. The latter name intrigued me since it reminded me of Homer's "wine-dark sea" and "sable sea," and I hoped my assignment would take me there.

Other training classes involved signaling with flags, which I had already learned in the Catholic Boys' Brigade, and knot tying, at which I was hopeless. In knot-tying class I just looked out the window and daydreamed, which annoyed the instructor and led him to put me on report. I was called before the lieutenant who commanded Dewey Unit and given a week's extra duty, to be served in the evenings after supper. The discipline report was also entered in my service report, and the lieutenant told me that it could influence my assignment after boot camp, because no ship's captain would want a "goof-off" like me in his crew.

We spent one whole afternoon in the gymnasium taking a strength test, where we were scored on our performance in rope climbing, two-handed and one-handed chinning, push-ups, and sit-ups. I did well above the average in the first four tests, without undue effort, and when it came to the sit-ups I just kept going since I wasn't in the least tired. The instructor finally stopped me because the gym was closing, and he told me that I had done 748 sit-ups, and that the Navy record was 950. I was very proud of this, but for several days afterward I could hardly straighten up, and Charles Shelmerdine said that I walked around like Groucho Marx.

A week later we spent an entire day being tested in the swimming pool, where everyone was required to swim two laps and then jump into the water from a thirty-foot tower. I could only do a dog paddle and a sidestroke, but I could hold my breath for a long time so I decided I could make better time if I swam underwater. I dove in and didn't come up until I reached the other end of the pool, where I took a deep breath and then swam back underwater. My instructor said, "Well, I'll be a son of a bitch!" and he shook his head in disbelief as he checked off my name.

Then I climbed the ladder to the top of the tower, where two instructors were struggling with a recruit who was too terrified to jump and was hanging on to the railing. They finally pried him loose and threw him into the pool. His scream was still echoing when I jumped in myself, spreading my arms like the wings of a seagull and then folding them to my sides as I plunged into the pool, coiling myself at the bottom so I could surge up out of the water like a dolphin. My instructor called me a "goddamn show-off" and ordered me to "get the hell out of the pool." I did get out, but only after swimming the length of the pool underwater once again, which made him threaten to put me on report.

Most evenings Charles and I went to the ship's service canteen to have a Coke and listen to the jukebox. "Sleepy Lagoon" was still number one on the Hit Parade, but a new song by Bing Crosby, "Don't Fence Me In," was now moving up the list, and it became our favorite because its lyrics expressed our frustration at being confined to boot camp when we wanted to be off at sea.

> *Give me land, lots of land,*
> *Under starry skies above,*
> *Don't fence me in!*

A letter from Peg arrived on June 26, 1944, my eighteenth birthday. She listed the names of everyone in our extended family who sent their love, and she said they all missed me and were looking forward to seeing me when I came home on leave. She said that my uncle Mike had been taken into the Army and was now in training camp too, and that my uncle Tom had put up both of our names on the honor rolls of all the saloons in our neighborhood, although she was embarrassed by this, since it might lead people to think that I drank in those places like my father and his brothers.

Peg also said that she had sent me a fruitcake for my birthday. Since I hadn't received it in mail call that day, I asked the recruit assigned to mail duty in our barracks if he had seen it. He said that he had, but that Captain Bligh had taken it for himself and was probably having it now for his dessert. I headed toward the door of his quarters to confront him about this, but Charles persuaded me not to, saying that Captain Bligh would only make life difficult for me and might put me on report and delay my being shipped out to sea. So I let it pass, and when I wrote back to Peg I thanked her for the fruitcake and said that we, my friends and I, had really enjoyed eating it, though as I wrote those words a bitter feeling of suppressed rage rose up within me.

Our boot company was assigned to mess-hall duty for the first two weeks in July. We had to get up at four thirty in the morning and didn't get back to our barracks until well after supper. Charles and I served together in the mess line, where our pranks got us into trouble with our supervisor, a black chief petty officer. One of the things we did to have fun and pass the time was to invent a new way to dispense pats of butter, spearing them on the bent tine of a fork and flipping them in the air onto the trays of the recruits in the mess line. This amused everyone except our chief, who was so provoked that he assigned us to the scullery, which was very filthy work. When we continued fooling around in the scullery, he put us on the garbage detail, which was even more disgusting, but even there we managed to have some fun, figuring there was nothing worse the chief could do to us. But there was: in addition to the garbage detail, he assigned us to the crew that swept up and swabbed the mess hall after everyone else had left, so we were the last to leave and barely made it back to our barracks for evening muster. In any event I always brought back food for Dave Zuloff, for though I hadn't seen him for several weeks the food was always gone when I returned the following morning.

After our mess duty was over we began what was called Hell Week, which involved twelve-hour days on an obstacle course simulating combat conditions, followed by all-night marches. Charles and I enjoyed this immensely, but a number of people in our boot company broke down under the strain and were assigned to the L16 barracks, known as "the Loony Bin," whose inmates were usually released from the service with a medical discharge, which labeled you for life as a mental case.

The Sunday after Hell Week we were scheduled to have a day off, which I greatly appreciated, for I was dead tired. I went to the Catholic chapel for mass after breakfast and then decided I would spend the rest of the morning dozing in a shady spot I had found in the woods beside our barracks. I thought I might spot Dave Zuloff there, for I had a feeling that he was hiding in the woods, but he was nowhere to be seen.

When I returned to the barracks I was told that after lunch we were all going to be marched to the main athletic field to watch a baseball game. The Boston Braves of the National League were playing the Sampson team, which I thought was a joke until I saw that our team included some of the most famous stars in the big leagues, all of whom had enlisted in the Navy to avoid being drafted, on the promise that they could continue to play ball, which was better than being blown away on the battlefields of Europe or the South Pacific. The game was indeed a joke: Sampson beat the Braves 24–0. The stands were almost empty by the time the game was over, but I stuck it out till the end. I hadn't had a chance to see big-league baseball all through high school because of my odd jobs and our penury.

After Hell Week we were told that we would finish boot camp at the end of July, and that lists would be posted on the barracks' notice board informing us where we would report after our week's leave. On the first day of that week Pete Hansen found his name on a list of those assigned to a destroyer in San Francisco, while other lists appeared for submarine service, Naval aviation, the amphibious forces, and various battleships, aircraft carriers, heavy and light cruisers, destroyers, destroyer escorts, gunboats, and patrol boats, most of them on the West Coast. On the second day, Charles and many others I knew were on a long list assigned to the USS *Dickerson,* an attack transport docked in San Pedro, California. I was very disappointed that my name was not on this list, and could only think that it was the discipline report I had received for not paying attention in the knot-tying class that prevented me from being assigned to the same ship as my friends.

The next day I was dismayed to find my name on a list of those assigned to the electrician's mate school at Sampson, which meant I would be stuck ashore for a couple of months while all of my friends went off to sea. I was afraid that the war would end before I was shipped out; the Allied forces were now beginning to break out of the beachheads in Normandy, while the Navy had defeated the Japanese in the Battle of the Philippines and the Marines had taken Saipan as well as Tinian and Guam.

At the end of July we packed our seabags and mustered for the last time outside our barracks, wearing our dress white uniforms. Captain Bligh inspected our company and then bid us farewell, telling us to "keep our peckers up." He then told us to stand at ease, while we waited to be taken off in trucks to board the troop trains that would be taking us home on leave. Charles and I said goodbye to each other then; we had been assigned to different trains, his going to Philadelphia and mine to New York City. He said that he would write to me once he had a Fleet Post Office, or FPO, address, so we could keep in touch, and maybe we'd meet up in the Pacific.

After Charles left I waited for the next truck, and just as I was about to board it I saw a white handkerchief being waved at me from under the barracks. It was Dave Zuloff, wrapped in a khaki blanket, his unkempt hair and beard giving him the appearance of a medieval hermit. He smiled as soon as he saw that I recognized him; then, with a last wave, he disappeared under the barracks, and that's the last I ever saw of him.

Our troop train pulled into Penn Station at eleven o'clock on Sunday morning, and I arrived home at 225 Cornelia Street just before noon. Peg was waiting for me with Dorothy and Nancy and Jimmy, and shortly afterward John came back from eleven o'clock mass.

Peg had cooked a leg of lamb for my homecoming dinner and the six of us ate together for the first time in a long while. Her night job put her on a different schedule than the rest of the family, even on Sunday, when she was usually so exhausted that she slept through the day. But not this Sunday, which she said she had looked forward to since I had gone away, and so had I.

While we ate we talked about all that had happened since we had last been together. Or, rather, Peg and I talked, as I told her about life in the Navy, while she brought me up to date on news of our family and our "Gaelic ghetto." I told them all about my experiences in boot camp, leaving out "short-arm inspection" and some of my misadventures. Peg was pleased to hear that I would be going to electrician's mate school rather than being shipped out right away, and she said that my uncle Mike had already been sent overseas with the U.S. Army infantry and was probably fighting in France. I felt ashamed at this, for my uncle Mike was more than twice my age and had a wife and children, and now he was off in the war while I would be stuck in school for months.

Peg told me that Dorothy had just finished her sophomore year at Bushwick High, where she was on the honor roll for the second year in a row. I could see that Peg took great pride in this, particularly since I hadn't made the grade at Brooklyn Tech, although she didn't say this, to spare my feelings.

Dorothy and I had been very close when we lived in Ireland, and in photographs taken during those years I am always holding her by the hand, as if I were protecting her. But in the years since then, when our family life had been so difficult, we'd had little to do with each other and had drifted apart, even though we were living under the same roof. She had always been quiet and self-contained, perhaps as a reaction to the turbulent way of life in our Gaelic ghetto. I realized she had developed into a dignified and quite beautiful young woman, and as I looked at her across the dinner table it was almost as if I were in the company of a stranger.

Nancy was a different matter altogether. She was nine years younger than I was, and the years of her early childhood had been the most difficult period in our family life, when John was unemployed and we were evicted from one apartment after another before the Morans took us in. I hardly knew her; when she was a toddler I was out on the streets scavenging and delivering newspapers, and for the four years before I went into the Navy I had been working after school, first at the Willis Paint Company and then at the Eagle Druggist Supply Company, and by the time I came home from work she and Jimmy were in bed.

Now she had just finished the third grade at Fourteen Holy Martyrs, where she was barely passing; she seemed to have little interest in schoolwork, and preferred to be out on the streets having fun with her friends, who were predominately boys. Peg was working nights and wasn't around to look after her in the evenings, so Nancy was pretty much on her own. She was an imp, and everyone liked her so much that she got away with things that would have brought down Peg's wrath on me. But I was very fond of Nancy, and I felt bad that I wouldn't be around to look after her, for she was my baby sister.

And Jimmy was my baby brother. He was eleven years younger than I was, almost half a generation, and I felt almost like an uncle to him, although I had just turned eighteen myself. During what little spare time I'd had these past four years I'd looked after him as best I could, rocking his carriage when Peg put him out in the backyard in good weather, and wheeling him around the neighborhood whenever I was running errands. Then, when he was old enough to walk, I took him with me wherever I went, though during the past four years I had been able to do that only on Sundays, because I worked every afternoon and on Saturday.

Jimmy looked very much like John, with the same red hair and very fair complexion. When John sat in the Morris chair after supper, Jimmy would climb up on his shoulders to peel away the sunburned skin from his back. The two of them were very much alike, sweet-natured and soft of speech, though Peg gave John very little time to talk. This seemed fine with him, for after a hard day's work all he wanted to do was to eat his supper and then sit in the Morris chair and read the *Journal-American*. Afterward he would go down to the basement to tend the furnace and drink the two or three bottles of beer that I'd smuggled in for him from Mr. Hellman's grocery. I was pleased to see that Jimmy had taken over that job from me; when Peg wasn't looking he showed me the nine cents he'd earned from the deposits on the three bottles of beer that John had drunk the evening before.

That night, my uncle Tom threw a party at his apartment on Central Avenue to welcome me back, and all of our extended family members were there. He had brought a barrel of beer in the Collins Brothers hearse, several quarts of whiskey he had stolen from the rectory at Fourteen Holy Martyrs, and a bottle of sherry from the convent, because most of my aunts preferred sweet wine to "the hard stuff."

Mary Guiheen's brother Mauris had brought his accordion, and played a number of jigs and stack-of-barleys so Peg and my aunts could dance. Then he accompanied himself while he sang one of Peg's favorites, "She Moved Thro' the Fair," which made her cry.

She stepp'd away from me, and she went thro' the fair,
And fondly I watched her move here and move there,
And then she went homeward with one star awake —
As the swan in the evening moves over the lake.

The next morning John went off to work without the sandwiches that Peg had made for his lunch, so I brought them to him at the Evergreens Cemetery before his noon break, taking Jimmy along with me. We arrived at exactly noon, just as John's lunch hour began, and when he came out from the workmen's quarters I gave him the big bag of sandwiches, which pleased him no end. Then, just as he left, a car drove out through the cemetery gate and stopped beside us. The driver, a distinguished-looking white-haired gentleman, smiled at me and introduced himself as Mr. Dwight, the director of the cemetery. He had seen me giving my father his lunch and asked me if I was John Freely's son. When I said that I was indeed, he told me of his high regard for John, whom he considered to be a cut above all of the other men who worked at the cemetery, a true gentleman. And with that he bade me good day, leaving me pleased beyond measure.

Later that day I took Jimmy to the local public school at the corner of Cornelia Street and Wilson Avenue, and I registered him so he could begin first-grade classes in the fall semester. Peg was taking a nap before she went off to work at five in the afternoon.

After Peg left I took a walk around the neighborhood, noticing that there were more gold stars in the windows than there had been before I left. From what my relatives had told me the previous evening I learned that boys I knew had been killed both in the Pacific and in Europe, where the Allies were now advancing deep into the continent. No one had any news about Jimmy Anderson and Phil Gould, but my uncle Tom said he had not seen gold stars next to their names on the honor rolls of the saloons he frequented.

I met Tom when I visited Fourteen Holy Martyrs, and he took me to Paul Hesse's bar. He showed me my name on the honor roll, as well as those of Jimmy, Phil, and my uncle Mike, which was three names below mine. He wanted to buy me a beer, but I had a Coke instead, for I had promised Peg that I wouldn't drink—at least until I was twenty-one—and I didn't want her to smell alcohol on my breath when I came home. As I sipped my Coke I looked around the saloon, and there on the wall above the bar was the framed front page from the *Daily News* of December 20, 1927, with the headline STORK SNARLS TRAFFIC.

During the week I looked up those of my friends who were not in the service, either because they were waiting to be called up or, like Martin Kaiser and Billy Decker, because they had not passed the medical exam and thus been classified 4F. I read in the papers that Frank Sinatra had been classified 4F because he had a punctured eardrum, a condition that seemed to be endemic among famous singers and actors.

I spent one afternoon with Jean Caputo, who told me that she was "going steady" with a Jewish boy named Artie Spielman, whom I didn't particularly like, but I didn't tell her that. She said that most of the other girls we knew were going steady too, although some of their boyfriends had enlisted in the Navy or been drafted into the Army. She asked me if

I'd like to go on a double date with her and Artie, but I said that I didn't know any girls who might be willing to go out with me. Jean said she knew several girls who would love to go on a date with me. I told her not to bother because I was tied up with my family, but the real reason was that I was too shy.

Every night that week I got up at two in the morning to meet Peg at the Wilson Avenue subway stop when she returned from work, and we stayed up for hours engaged in our nocturnal dialogues. Her talk was very spirited early in the week, for she was so happy to have me home again. As my departure drew near, though, she became increasingly sad, and on the last night she said that if we had stayed in Ireland then I wouldn't have had to go off to war. Then she brightened up and said, "All will be well, Jackie, all will be well."

I was due back in Sampson before noon on Monday, so I had to catch a train at Penn Station on Sunday afternoon. I told John and Peg there was no need to come with me to the station this time, so I kissed everyone goodbye at home, walking to the Wilson Avenue subway stop with my seabag on my shoulder and my ditty bag in my hand, wondering when I'd see my family and my old neighborhood again.

When I returned to Sampson I was assigned to a barracks in Edwards Unit, where all of my shipmates (that was the word we used, even though we weren't on a ship) were assigned to one or another of the advanced training schools, in my case the one for electrician's mates. The electrician's mates and motor machinist's mates were engineering ratings, since on a ship most of them worked in the engine room, while others such as the signalmen, radiomen, yeomen, pharmacist's mates, gunner's mates, and boatswain's (pronounced *bosun's*) mates were deck ratings. Those of us in training for the engineering ratings had the rank of fireman second class, while the deck ratings were seamen second class. I was a fireman second class, electrician's mate striker, and if I passed the course I would be promoted to fireman first class, and then, I hoped, through the successive ranks of petty officer—third, second, first, and chief—with the almost unattainable rank of warrant officer being the ultimate promotion for enlisted men.

The classes were even less interesting to me than the technical courses at Brooklyn Tech, which were at least scientific, but those at Sampson were totally devoted to electrical work that we would do aboard a ship—principally electrical motors, generators, electrical machines, and wiring in general—so I soon tuned out the lectures and spent my time day-dreaming. This got me in trouble with one of my instructors, who put me on report. After a second warning, he had me brought up on a "captain's mast," the lowest form of court-martial.

My trial was held in mid-October, when I was taken before the commanding officer of Sampson Naval Training Base, a commodore who in civilian life had been a florist and looked the part. The chief in charge of our barracks had instructed me in the protocol to be followed, and I had turned my white Navy cap inside out so I was immediately identifiable as "the accused." When the commodore and his entourage arrived, the chief in charge called everyone to attention, and when the officers took their seats he ordered that "the accused step forward!" I strode forward two steps, whereupon a pair of armed SPs grasped my elbows and brought me before the commodore, who looked at me disdainfully, as if I were some lower form of insect life on one of his flowers. The instructor who had turned me in was called up to read the charge he had made against me, which was that I was "inattentive in class and disrespectful to a superior officer." The chief asked, "How does the accused plead?" as if he had any doubt—and I managed to speak with a firm voice as I answered, "Guilty, sir."

I saluted and was led away by the two SPs into the waiting room, where I was dismissed and told that my sentence would be posted on the bulletin board of my barracks by the end of the day. So it was, and I learned that I was sentenced to one hundred hours of hard labor, to be served in the evenings and on weekends. I started my sentence after supper the following evening, serving on a work detail assigned to repair the roads within the base and to clear out brush from the woods that surrounded it on all sides except the lakefront. As I worked I kept an eye out for Dave Zuloff, although I hoped that by now he had made good his escape from Sampson.

On October 20 we learned that the U.S. Army under General Douglas MacArthur had landed at Leyte in the Philippines. Then a week later we heard that an American fleet commanded by Admiral William Halsey had been victorious in a three-day battle in Leyte Gulf that effectively destroyed the Japanese navy. This was a cause for celebration in the canteens of Sampson, but I began to worry anew that the war would end before I got into action, though I was careful to keep this to myself.

It took me more than a month to work off my sentence, and by the end of that time the first blizzard of the coming winter had begun, and our labor gang was ordered to shovel snow off the roads and paths around the base. Working in the snow was great fun, and I took every opportunity to throw snowballs at my friends who were going to and from the canteen, though I stopped after the chief in charge of our work detail threatened to put me on report.

My best friend at electrician's mate school was Bernard Coopersmith, a Jewish boy from Newark, New Jersey. Bernard was a couple of years older than I was and had finished his freshman year at Newark College of Engineering before he enlisted in the Navy. He was the only one of my class with whom I could have a serious conversation, and I learned a lot from him, including Jewish history, sparking my lifelong interest in that subject. Bernard advised me to go to college after the war, but I told him there was little likelihood that I would, since I didn't have a high school diploma, and in any event I intended to be a merchant seaman. This led him to shake his head in evident disapproval, saying, "Do think about it."

Our classes finished at the end of November, and we were given a forty-eight-hour liberty before graduating and being reassigned. The leave wasn't long enough to go anywhere except Rochester, where we all checked into a cheap hotel that catered to the Navy—which meant that they had few amenities and were battened down when mobs of sailors blew in on leave from Sampson.

The minimum drinking age in Rochester was twenty-one, and most of us were well under that limit, which was enforced by SPs checking ID cards at the entrance of every bar in town. One of our gang had just turned twenty-one, so he bought a fifth of cheap rye whiskey at a liquor store, which four of us drank in a park, oblivious to the bitter cold and the blizzard howling around us. I spent the rest of my short liberty recovering from a colossal hangover, wracked with guilt that I had broken the promise I had made to Peg not to drink until I was at least twenty-one. Bernard was not with us on our bender, but he sat next to me in the train on the way back to Sampson, and when he saw my condition he shook his head in disapproval, saying, "Freely, you're heading for trouble."

My captain's mast meant that I would not be promoted to fireman first class, and, in addition to that, I also received the lowest grade in the class. This gave me some satisfaction, since now there was no way

I would be assigned to an advanced school; only the very best students such as Bernard Coopersmith went on to further studies in radio, radar, and sonar. Scuttlebutt had it that the worst graduates were assigned to the amphibious forces, which our chief said were manned by the "scum of the Navy," and he assured me that I was headed that way. He was absolutely right, and the next day I found my name on a list of those assigned to the amphibious training base at Little Creek, Virginia, where I was ordered to report on December 15, 1944.

My orders gave me time for a week's leave at home, where Peg was very disappointed because she had hoped I would be there for Christmas. We celebrated Christmas early, though with some sadness, for John had learned that his brother Mike had been badly wounded in France. Before I left we received word that Mike had been shipped back to a hospital in New York City, and that there was hope he would recover.

I left early the next morning, taking a regular passenger train from Penn Station to Norfolk, Virginia. There I boarded a Navy bus that took me out to the amphibious training base at Little Creek, on the coast near the North Carolina border. When I checked in at the base I was given a short-arm inspection, and I saw that several of the sailors who arrived with me were taken aside after the exam. The pharmacist's mate who had examined me told me that the amphibious forces had a higher incidence of venereal disease than any other branch of the service, and this seemed to corroborate what our chief at Sampson had said about the kind of people who ended up in the "amphibs."

The men in my barracks were for the most part somewhat older than I was, many of them having already served overseas, as I could tell from the campaign ribbons they wore on their dress blues, some with several battle stars. The oldest of those I got to know was a yeoman first class known as "Seagoing Baker," who told me that he had been in the amphibious forces since the beginning of the war, and had served in half a dozen campaigns. But now he had had enough, and he said that if he was assigned to sea duty again he was going to head for the hills. He advised me to do the same, saying that the landing craft in the "amphibs" were "sand-scrapers" and would take me to an early grave.

Little Creek was the largest amphibious base in the United States. The largest and most numerous of the ships at the base were of the type known as LSTs, landing ship, tank, which were designed to land infantry and tanks on invasion beachheads, as they had at Omaha Beach in Normandy. The LSM (landing ship, medium) was smaller and could carry fewer men and vehicles than the LST. Some of these had been converted to form a type known as LSM(R), landing ship, medium (rocket), so called because they were armed with rocket launchers as well as a five-inch naval gun and several antiaircraft machine guns. Only a dozen LSM(R)s had been launched by the time I arrived in Little Creek, and when I looked at the bulletin board in our barracks I saw that I would be in the first crew assigned to one of them as soon as they were ready for us. It seems that there had been an unexpected delay, for one of the LSM(R)s had sunk on its shakedown voyage in Chesapeake Bay, having sprung a huge leak when its five-inch gun was fired. Luckily, none of the crew drowned, but from then on the LSM(R) was referred to as a floating coffin, and Seagoing Baker told me I might as well have been given a death sentence by being assigned to one.

After morning chow each day we assembled on an enormous drill field, lining up according to our rank and rating. I represented a unique case, for among the several thousand men assembled on the field I was the only fireman second class, electrician's mate striker, a distinction I had achieved because of my captain's mast and my failure at electrician's mate school. Thus I formed a group all by myself, and when the duty officer of the day checked the various formations he paused in surprise when he came to me, and he tried not to smile when I saluted him and said, "All present and accounted for, sir," as I had been trained to do in the Catholic Boys' Brigade.

The Saturday muster was held on a special drill field down by the docks, where all the LSTs, LSMs, and LSM(R)s were tied up, along with smaller vessels such as LCTs (landing craft, tank) and LCVPs (landing craft, vehicle, personnel). We all saluted when the commanding admiral of the base and his staff arrived, accompanied by a chief gunner's mate carrying a shotgun. I wondered why the chief was carrying a shotgun, but then I saw him fire both barrels to disperse a flock of seagulls hovering overhead, and I realized that he was making sure the admiral and his staff wouldn't be shat upon by the birds—though some of the other officers and men at the muster weren't so lucky.

Later I mustered with the crew of the LSM(R) to which I had been assigned, with a ship's company of five officers and seventy-six enlisted men. Our captain, a lieutenant senior grade, informed us that our ship would make its shakedown cruise in mid-January 1945, and that we would be going aboard a week or so before she sailed in order to get her ready. Scuttlebutt had it that we would be going to the Pacific via the Panama Canal, and that we would be part of an invasion force landing on the Ryuku Islands in the East China Sea, the largest of which was Okinawa.

We spent several days checking out our LSM(R), which looked more like a gunboat than a mere landing ship, for it was bristling with weapons. There was a five-inch naval gun just forward of the bridge, a twin 40mm antiaircraft gun at the bow, three 20mm machine guns on the fantail and the flying bridges, four 4.2-inch mortars in a guntub above the bridge, and 156 rocket launchers arrayed on the tank deck. Our captain told us that all of us, regardless of our rating and regular duties, would be manning the various guns and rocket launchers. He said that our gunnery training would begin on our shakedown cruise, which was good news for me, since I hadn't wanted to go into combat just looking after electric motors and generators, which in any event I knew little about. I was relieved to learn that I would be serving under an experienced electrician's mate first class.

Shortly after New Year's a notice was posted on the bulletin board in our barracks calling for volunteers for a top-secret commando unit. I immediately signed up, because it seemed more exciting than serving as an apprentice electrician aboard an LSM(R). Two days later I found my name on a list of those who had signed up for the unit, with orders to muster the following day outside the base headquarters. I informed the captain of my LSM(R), and spent the following day being examined and interviewed. Two days later I found my name on a list of those who would report the following week for shipment to the amphibious training base at Fort Pierce, Florida.

We were given a twelve-hour liberty in Norfolk before we shipped out, from noon to midnight on Saturday. Norfolk was the home port for the Navy's Atlantic Fleet, with battleships, cruisers, destroyers, and troopships constantly crossing from there to the European theater. The war seemed much closer in dockside Norfolk than it had in New York, for the piers on Chesapeake Bay were lined with warships and the streets were full of sailors streaming in and out of the bars and nightclubs (which were open in the daytime as well) that I'd heard so much about in Sampson. I had been told that there were signs that said NO DOGS OR SAILORS ALLOWED, but I didn't see any during the twelve hours or so that I spent in Norfolk. The bars were far rougher than those I knew in Brooklyn, and the only patrons seemed to be drunken sailors and the women whom historians of earlier wars had called "camp followers." I saw several drunken brawls, one of which was ended only by a flying squad of SPs, who carried off some of the sailors in their paddywagons, leaving their girlfriends to the local police. Around midnight I hitched a ride aboard a Navy truck headed back to Little Creek. I helped the driver and two SPs load dead-drunk sailors aboard the truck if their liberty passes showed they were from the amphibious base. Then I helped them unload the drunks when we reached the base, after which I checked in with the duty officer and was given a short-arm inspection before going off to my barracks. Such was my one and only liberty in Norfolk, which otherwise I saw only from the trains that brought me in and out of the city.

On Sunday afternoon I wrote a short letter to Peg, telling her that I was fine and that I was being transferred to Florida, though I didn't tell her what I would be doing there. Then I began packing my seabag, wondering about the secret commando unit I had joined and where it would be taking me.

It was bitterly cold when we left Little Creek early Monday afternoon, traveling in trucks that brought us to the train station in Norfolk. The troop train that we boarded in Norfolk was unheated, so I bundled up in my peacoat to keep warm, gratefully accepting a swig of whiskey from the sailor sitting next to me, who handed me the bottle as he drifted off to sleep. After a few more swallows I began to doze off myself, thinking of my father and his brother Willie leaving Ballyhaunis on Easter Sunday 1916, sharing bottles of whiskey with shipwrecked Irish sailors on the train that took them to Dublin. We Freelys had come a long way in one generation.

When I awoke the next morning I could see from the stations we passed that we were in Florida, whose palm trees and orange groves seemed like paradise after the grim winter landscapes we had left behind. By the time our train reached Fort Pierce the weather was as warm as if it were late spring, and the air was heady with the aroma of the flowers and fruit trees that were just beginning to blossom in the garden around the station.

There were several hundred of us aboard the train, and after we got off we were herded aboard trucks to take us out to the base, which was on South Hutchinson Island, one of the string of barrier islands separated from the mainland by the Indian River, part of the inland waterway along the east coast of Florida.

The entrance to the base was at the far end of the causeway across the Indian River, where a sign said U.S. NAVY AMPHIBIOUS FORCES—UNDERWATER DEMOLITION TEAMS—SCOUTS AND RAIDERS. We got out of the trucks and filed into the administration building, where we checked in and were given our assignments. About half of the group was marched off to the barracks of the Underwater Demolition Teams (UDT), which were on the inner side of the island, facing the Indian River. The rest of us were put back on the trucks and taken out to the seaward side of the island, where the entrance to a separate tent city bore a sign reading SCOUTS AND RAIDERS. I was very excited, for this seemed to promise the adventure I had sought when I'd enlisted in the Navy. But when we checked in at that administration center I found from my orders that I was not going into the Scouts and Raiders after all, but into a commando unit called Amphibious Roger Three.

Later that day, when we went to a briefing after evening mess, we learned that we would be the third contingent of the commando unit to train at Fort Pierce, Roger One and Two having completed their program and now gone overseas. We were the last contingent of Roger Three to arrive, we were told. Our training program would begin tomorrow morning and would combine those of the UDTs and the Scouts and Raiders. There were about a thousand of us, but by the time our training was over our number would be winnowed down to one hundred and fifty, the chief said, because "the men would be separated from the boys."

And with that we were sent off to our various barracks, laid out at the north end of a beach that stretched the whole length of South Hutchinson Island, which was separated from North Hutchinson Island, the barrier islet to its north, by the Fort Pierce Inlet. During the hour that was left before lights-out I walked along the beach to the breakwater on our side of the inlet, where pelicans, cormorants, and myriad other seabirds were skimming the water in their hunt for fish, occasionally plunging in like kamikazes, the Japanese suicide dive-bombers I had seen in training films. This was the tropical setting I had imagined in my daydreams, and the war seemed very far away, until a deafening explosion sent up an enormous plume of smoke across the inlet on North Hutchinson, where I later learned that the UDTs were conducting a night exercise.

The next morning after breakfast we mustered and were organized into platoons, each with ten enlisted men and an ensign. All of the ensigns were "ninety-day wonders," college boys who had been commissioned after three months of intensive training. This made them less experienced than any of us, but most of them were smart enough to make up for it. Some of them were very good athletes as well and had played football and other varsity sports, as I learned from listening to their conversations. The senior officers for the most part had been in combat, and one of them had commanded a UDT unit in the Normandy invasion. But our commanding officer, a lieutenant commander who had been a lawyer in civilian life, had never been to sea and seemed completely unsuited to be the CO of an outfit like ours, or so I thought when I sized him up during our first muster.

After the muster we were issued U.S. Marine Corps fatigues and combat boots, which were more suitable for the kind of training we would be doing, which in the beginning included strenuous and prolonged calisthenics, weight lifting, boxing, and long-distance marching and swimming, designed to toughen us up for our subsequent training in underwater demolition, scouting, gunnery, and hand-to-hand combat, as well as infantry tactics under simulated combat conditions.

There were also evening orientation films and lectures, as well as classes for those who were qualified in fields such as radio and telegraphy. One of the classes was very hush-hush, but I learned from a friend who was enrolled in it that it was an intensive course in Chinese. I would love to have taken it, but I figured I had been left out because I was a high school dropout and had failed my course in electrician's mate school. But at least I now knew that our outfit would be going to China, which led me to begin asking questions of the ensign who headed our platoon. That, together with the scuttlebutt I gathered from my shipmates, eventually gave me some idea of what our unit was all about.

I learned first of all that we were involved in a top-secret operation run by the U.S. Naval Group China, which was the core of a clandestine organization known as SACO (pronounced *socko*), an acronym for the Sino-American Cooperative Organization. The Loyal and Patriotic Army (LPA) of China, an elite force of Chinese commandos, would be trained and led into battle by members of SACO.

SACO had been founded in 1942 through an agreement between President Roosevelt and Generalissimo Chiang Kai-shek, under which the United States and the Kuomintang Nationalist government would create a joint intelligence-gathering organization against the Japanese.

The commander of Naval Group China was Captain (later Rear Admiral) Milton Miles, an Annapolis graduate who had been director of the Office of Strategic Services in the Far East. Miles was also deputy director of SACO, whose director was General Tai Li, Chiang Kai-shek's right-hand man and spymaster. The activities of Naval Group China included the collection of meteorological data for the U.S. Army Air Forces, gathering Japanese shipping information and other intelligence for both the U.S. Navy and Army, and the training of Tai Li's guerrilla force, the LPA, which had been very effective fighting against the Japanese in China.

The Roger Amphibious Unit was established in 1943, when Miles decided that the U.S. Navy should train its own commandos to go into action with the LPA. Roger One had been trained and sent to China in 1943, followed by Roger Two in 1944, and then our Roger Three, which was scheduled to be shipped out in the spring of 1945. All of this was very exciting for me, and as soon as I became fully aware of the great adventure involved I did everything I possibly could to survive the winnowing-out process that began on the first day of our training.

Our physical training included boxing, and every day each one of us had to box three two-minute rounds against a different opponent, with no consideration given to differences in height, weight, strength, or pugilistic experience. I had learned how to box in the Catholic Boys' Brigade, and since I was in excellent physical condition I more than held my own against my opponents, defending myself against the bigger ones and sometimes clobbering those who were my own size or smaller.

The toughest guy in our outfit was a Mexican American man named Pete Echeverry who had boxed professionally. He took it easy on his opponents, since otherwise he might easily have killed them, but once our commander made the mistake of challenging Echeverry and was knocked out cold with one punch. Echeverry and I became good friends, and when I had to go into the ring with him our bout was essentially a boxing lesson for me, which I used to good advantage in my later fights.

The enlisted men in our outfit were mostly country boys from the South and Southwest, including Pete Echeverry and a Navaho named Joe Jackson, who also became a good friend of mine. But one day a couple of SPs came and took Joe away, for what reason we never learned, and that was the last I ever saw of him.

The only other New Yorker in the outfit was Bill Glennon, an Irish American man from the Bronx who had already done a tour of duty in the Caribbean. Bill and I became good friends, for we had a lot in common, particularly because our parents were Irish immigrants. Another good friend was Tunney King, who was from Greenville, Maine, on Moosehead Lake. I asked him about his curious first name, and he said that his godfather was the famous boxer Gene Tunney, former world heavyweight champion, who had trained for his fights at the King family's farm on Moosehead. Another of my good friends was Ron Fuller, from Waterville, New York, who told me that he had girlfriends who were identical twins, and he was never certain which one he was with at any time, and though he seemed to be keeping both of them happy, he wasn't quite sure which sister he would end up with after the war.

Underwater demolition training started in the third week, when we learned to handle dynamite, TNT, plastic shaped charges, and other types of explosives including Bangalore torpedoes, which were long tubes packed with TNT that were set off to the create trenches in beaches so that LCVPs could come in close to land troops. Mostly we worked with half-pound blocks of TNT, which we carried in pouches around our waist. We became so used to TNT that we lost all fear of it, though we were told that a half-pound block could cost us a hand or our "dangling participles," which were particularly exposed when we set off charges in water.

During the fourth week we were taken in trucks every day to the gunnery school at the southern end of South Hutchinson Island, where we learned to fire virtually every weapon in the U.S. arsenal, starting on the rifle range. I was a very poor marksman, and I was afraid that this would get me eliminated from the outfit, but I did much better with the other weapons we fired, including the .45-caliber pistol and the Thompson submachine gun. I also did very well on aerial gunnery, particularly on a 20mm antiaircraft gun, where I was the only one in our outfit to hit a target drone pulled by a Navy seaplane. It was all great fun, particularly learning to fire a bazooka and a trench mortar, although I found hand grenades a little scary, particularly when we had to pick up a live grenade and throw it out of range before it exploded. Another perilous exercise involved crawling through barbed wire under live machine gun fire, which caused several of our outfit to chicken out, but I kept my nerve and made it through without "marking my laundry," GI slang for shitting your pants from visceral fear.

At the start of our second month of training we went on a five-day exercise, the first day of which took us along the whole length of North Hutchinson. We marched thirty miles from the Fort Pierce Inlet to the Sebastian Inlet, carrying a forty-pound pack with a rifle and hand grenades and wearing a belt with a dozen half-pound blocks of TNT, accompanied by trucks loaded with a ton of dynamite and TNT.

We were supposed to pitch our tents on the beach at Sebastian, but when we reached the inlet just before sunset we were amazed to find the abandoned cars of a circus wagon train among the dunes. Our ensign said that we might just as well unroll our sleeping bags in the circus cars, some of which had barred sides, indicating that they had been used as cages for lions and tigers. Other platoons did the same, and as we sat around our campfires that evening we laughed as we tried to imagine how a circus wagon train might have ended up abandoned on the dunes on an island off the Florida coast. It still tickles me to think that I spent a night in a lion's cage.

We spent the next three days setting off explosives in various exercises, some of them underwater charges off the beach by the Sebastian Inlet, others in the junglelike interior of the island. At one point I was having a fungus on my right ankle treated by a pharmacist's mate when a large piece of shrapnel from the end of a Bangalore torpedo smashed the box on which my foot was resting. Another time a charge that I had set failed to go off, and our ensign sent me back to see what was wrong. I found that the fuse had only burned halfway, and when I reset it I had barely enough time to take shelter behind a dune before the charge went off, showering me with sand and fragments of palmetto trees.

At the end of our last day at Sebastian we gathered all of the explosives we hadn't used—several hundred pounds of dynamite and TNT—and after we piled up the charges we set fuses connected with explosive primer cord so they would all go off at the same time. I volunteered to set off the final fuse, trying to make up for having bungled my earlier assignment, while everyone else took cover behind the dunes farther down the beach. I just made it to the dunes before the charge went off with a tremendous blast, which we later learned blew out many of the windows in the town of Sebastian on the Indian River.

The following week we practiced amphibious landings on South Hutchinson, some of us setting underwater explosives off the beach and others landing in LCVPs as the charges exploded. One of my friends had picked up a stray dog in Fort Pierce and it became our mascot, and in our amphibious landings it was always the first to run ashore, barking loudly while we shouted "Gung ho!," the rallying cry of the Marines, which we had been taught to do by one of our instructors, a Marine master sergeant. When I later looked up "gung ho" in *Merriam-Webster's Collegiate Dictionary,* tenth edition, I found that it was an abbreviation for "Zhongguo Gongye Hezuo She," meaning "Chinese Industrial Cooperative Society," first used in 1942. This made me think that the term was associated with the name of our outfit, SACO, the Sino-American Cooperative Organization, which was founded the same year.

Another of our exercises took us out for a week into the swampy land around Lake Okeechobee in the Everglades. The expedition was led by Lieutenant Ross Allen, who in civilian life ran what he called a "gator farm" in the Everglades, a game farm with alligators, water snakes, and other creatures of the swamp in their natural environment. We made our way through the swamp in inflatable seven-man rubber boats, complementing our K rations with palmetto hearts that we carved out of the swamp trees and rattlesnakes that we caught, skinned, and grilled, as well as eggs that we bought in a Seminole village. One of our officers, Ensign Bosco, was bitten by a water moccasin, which, we were told, was even more poisonous than a rattlesnake. We thought he was a goner, but he was given first aid and rushed back to Fort Pierce for treatment, after which he was able to resume training.

Meanwhile, I followed the progress of the war on our camp radio and through news bulletins posted in our headquarters building. First came news that the Marines had landed on Iwo Jima on February 16,

1945, beginning a battle that lasted two weeks before the Japanese were defeated. Then, on April 2, U.S. forces landed on Okinawa, while the Battle of the Philippines continued. The bulletins gave no details of these battles, but we knew for sure that the Navy's amphibious forces were involved in both the Iwo Jima and Okinawa landings, and I wondered if the LSM(R) to which I had initially been assigned had taken part in either landing. I wondered also about Jimmy Anderson, Phil Gould, and Charles Shelmerdine. I hadn't expected to hear from Jimmy or Phil, but Charles had promised to write as soon as he had an FPO number, and I hadn't had a word from him.

I also followed the progress of the fighting in Europe, where the Allies had penetrated deep into Germany on both the Eastern and Western fronts, and the Far East, where American and British forces were slowly retaking Burma from the Japanese, who had launched a new offensive in China. I was particularly interested in news from Asia, for, according to scuttlebutt, SACO had bases all over the China-Burma-India theater, and our senior officers had said that some of our units were operating behind enemy lines.

Then, on April 12, the devastating news came that Franklin Roosevelt had passed away and that Harry Truman had succeeded him as president. All activity was suspended at Fort Pierce, and during Roosevelt's funeral three days later the only sound came from the PA speaker, which played a recording of Bing Crosby singing the president's favorite song, "Home on the Range."

Oh give me a home
Where the buffalo roam,
And the deer and the antelope play.
And seldom is heard
A discouraging word,
And the skies are not cloudy all day.

At the moment of his burial a bugler played taps, and many broke into tears, as did I, for Roosevelt had first been inaugurated just after we came back to the United States from Ireland for the second time, and he was the only president I had ever known.

Two weeks later we learned that Hitler was dead, and then on May 8 the news came that Germany had surrendered. The war in Europe was over, but fighting continued unabated in the Pacific and the Far East. Scuttlebutt said that our outfit would take part in the invasion of Japan along with General Tai Li's LPA, crossing over from China to attack one of the main Japanese islands.

Scuttlebutt also had it that our training would now be terminated so that we could be sent to China as soon as possible, and for once rumor turned out to be true. A few days later we were informed that we would finish our program almost immediately, after which we would have a week of home leave before being shipped out.

I did a quick check of the roster at the next muster and saw that we were now down to 160 enlisted men, 10 over the limit that had been set for Roger Three. Five of the 10 were eliminated in the last of our endurance tests, when we had to swim a mile parallel to the beach, beginning from the end of the breakwater at the Fort Pierce Inlet. Time was not a factor, but endurance was, and I had no difficulty—though I was one of the last to finish, as I had to drag along a friend, a Puerto Rican boy named Juan who otherwise would have been eliminated.

Scuttlebutt said that the last cut would be made at the beginning of our final week, and once again rumor turned out to be true. When the final roster was posted, I was relieved to find that my name was on the list, along with my friends Bill Glennon, Tunney King, Pete Echeverry, and Ronald Fuller, though Juan didn't make it. We received our individual leave papers and orders the following day, and I learned that after my home leave I would report at Penn Station to be sent by train to the naval base at San Pedro, California, the main port for troopships leaving for the Pacific and the Far East.

I was sorry to leave Fort Pierce, which I had enjoyed more than any other part of my Navy training. But I had been in the Navy for a year and was anxious to go overseas; the war was reaching a climax, and I wanted to get into action as soon as possible.

Our training had ended so abruptly that I hadn't had time to write home and tell my family I was coming. So my homecoming was a complete surprise for them, and because I arrived on a Sunday afternoon they were all gathered around the table having dinner.

That evening all of my relatives came by to welcome me home. Mary Guiheen (we still called her that even though her married name was

Kennelly) came with her brother Mauris. Mauris brought along his accordion and played for us, reminding me once again of Ireland.

Only when the party was over did Peg tell me the bad news about my uncle Mike. He had been recuperating from the wounds he had suffered fighting in France, where he had been machine-gunned in the stomach. But he had managed to get friends to smuggle bottles of whiskey into the hospital, and because of his heavy drinking he had just suffered a hemorrhage and was in critical condition. All of the extended family would be going to visit him the next day, and I said that I would go along too.

John took off from work, and on Monday morning we all went to Bellevue, where we gave blood and then went to see Mike, who was in intensive care. He was sitting up in bed and cheerfully greeted each of us as we arrived, though he was deathly pale from loss of blood, and he said that all he needed was a good stiff drink. The Catholic chaplain came in and administered Extreme Unction, and we all laughed when Mike asked the priest for some communion wine, saying that he had need of a last drink to speed his way to the next world, which he didn't think would be heaven.

We were then asked to leave so they could give Mike a blood transfusion, and we all kissed him and wished him well, though I remember thinking I would never see him again. It was raining heavily when we emerged from the hospital, and we waited under the awning at the entrance, hoping that it would clear so we could walk to the subway. We were there for about half an hour before the rain diminished enough for us to make a run for it. Just at that moment I heard a clatter above us, and I looked up to see Mike climbing down the fire escape in his pajamas, bathrobe, and slippers. My aunt Mary screamed when she saw him, but Mike said that he was just going out for a drink, since they wouldn't let him have any in the hospital. John and my uncle Tom went up the fire escape and managed to get Mike back into his bed, promising they would buy him a bottle of whiskey, but Peg and my aunts would have none of that.

I spent most of the rest of the week at home, walking to the Evergreens Cemetery at noon with my brother, Jimmy, to bring John the sandwiches Peg had made for his lunch, and after supper I sat and talked with John, Dorothy, Nancy, and Jimmy until they went to bed. Then I read until two in the morning, when I left to meet Peg at the Wilson

Avenue station to walk her home, after which we ate together and then talked for hours before we went to sleep, a peaceful routine that I found blissful after the constant hyperactivity at Fort Pierce, though I knew it was just the calm before the storm.

On the final day of my leave I went out after supper and made one last round of the neighborhood, stopping at Otto's ice cream parlor to say goodbye to any of my friends who might be gathered there. Many of the boys I knew were now off in the service, but some of those who were not were hanging around outside Otto's with a group of girls, a few of whom I knew. We talked for a while, until one of my friends said they were all going up to Highland Park, but I declined, saying I had to go home since I was catching a train at Penn Station at eight in the morning. One of the girls, someone I hadn't seen before, asked me if I would come along for a little while, which caught me in the heart because the jukebox was playing "Linger Awhile," and the vocalist was singing "Whisper I love you, oh linger awhile." I told her that I was very sorry, but that I simply had to go, and then I said goodbye and started home, listening to the fading sound of their laughter as they headed toward the park, my heart aching.

When I got home I slept for a few hours and then got up to meet Peg at the Wilson Avenue station. We ate together, and then we had a nocturnal dialogue that lasted until the first light of false dawn. It was time to go, and Peg woke up the rest of the family so they could all kiss me goodbye. Then I slung my seabag and ditty bag over my shoulder and left, walking along Wilson Avenue to the subway station just as the sun was rising over the hills in the Evergreens Cemetery.

I arrived at Penn Station well before eight a.m. and checked in with the Navy duty officer. Then I waited at the gate for the train to Chicago, where I was soon joined by Bill Glennon and other people in my outfit who had been on leave in the New York area. I fell asleep soon after we went aboard, for I had been up half the night before, and by the time I woke up we were chugging across Pennsylvania.

We changed trains in Chicago at Union Station, and while we waited for the train to Los Angeles, Bill and I stowed our bags in lockers and went out to get a drink at a bar with an Irish name. An old man at the end of the bar bought us beers and introduced himself as "a retired small-time Chicago gangster." He offered to take us on a tour of the drinking places around the Loop, in the course of which he introduced us to a number of other retired Chicago gangsters.

We barely made it aboard the train to Los Angeles, where the only seats we could find were in a smoking lounge near the dining car. A number of others from our outfit ended up in the lounge too, and since most of them had brought along bottles of rye whiskey we began drinking. This developed into a wild party when four more men from our outfit joined the train in Des Moines, Iowa, accompanied by girls they had picked up while waiting on the platform.

One of our newly arrived shipmates, an Iowan named Clem Barbee, took out a half-pound block of TNT that he had retained as a souvenir from Fort Pierce, and when our train was stopped at a siding outside of Grand Island, Nebraska, he set the fuse and threw it out the window onto the prairie, where it exploded with a tremendous bang. A conductor rushed into our lounge, where Clem, who was very drunk, readily admitted that it was he who had thrown the TNT. When the train reached Grand Island the conductor called the local police, who came to arrest Clem, but one of our petty officers explained to them that we were catching a troopship in California. The police relented and let Clem go, but only after they searched his seabag and ditty bag to make sure he had no more TNT. Then they confiscated all of the alcohol they could find in our lounge and ordered the women to leave—which they did willingly, for the TNT had scared the hell out of them.

The party started up again after the train left Grand Island; some of our shipmates had stashed away bottles that the police failed to find. When we reached Des Moines, Clem and a couple of his friends went out to buy a new supply, which they came running back with just as the train was pulling out of the station. But the party was quieter from then on, for most everyone was so drunk that they were in a stupor or slept the rest of the way.

I stayed awake to take in the magnificent scenery as we passed through the Rocky Mountains. The landscape reminded me of a gravure I had seen in *A Pictorial Journey Around the World,* where in the chapter on "A Railway Journey Across the American West" there had been an engraving of a train crossing an enormously high wooden bridge. And now here I was amid the same scenery myself, on what I hoped was the first leg of my own journey around the world.

When we got off the train at Union Station in Los Angeles we checked in with the Navy duty officer, who herded us aboard the Pacific Electric Railroad for the short ride south to San Pedro. At San Pedro we were taken in trucks to the Navy base and put up in an enormous barracks. We mustered there and were informed that we would be given evening liberty in San Pedro before being shipped out on the following day.

That evening we went into San Pedro, where the bars were packed with men and women in uniform, most of them having one last bash before going overseas. Bill and I had a few drinks with two Army nurses who said they too were being shipped out the following day. But a couple of MPs, a corporal and a sergeant, came along and told us to break it up, because the nurses were lieutenants, and they said there was a strict rule against enlisted men fraternizing with officers, particularly if the officers were women. So Bill and I backed off, only to see the MPs sit down at the bar with the two nurses, who seemed quite happy to drink with them.

By that time Bill was so drunk that I took him back to the base and sacked in. I got little sleep, for the lights in the barracks were kept on through the night so new arrivals could find their bunks. I got up at five thirty, half an hour before reveille, so I could use the head and wash up before the mob poured in, for there were several hundred sailors in the barracks.

Half an hour after reveille we were ordered to proceed to the mess hall, and after eating we returned to the barracks to await further orders. About an hour later there was an announcement on the PA that the Naval Group China should muster outside the barracks, which surprised all of us, since until then we'd only heard that name in scuttlebutt and never in public. Now we knew we really would be going to China, though at the moment I couldn't figure out how we would get there by sea, for the Japanese were occupying all the seaports of China and had penetrated deep into the hinterland. This added to the sense of adventure I felt as we mustered outside the barracks.

We were marched out onto the docks, which were lined with troop-ships, all of them being loaded with supplies and ammunition, some already beginning to take troops aboard. We stopped at the main gang-way of a troopship identified as AP-147, USS *General E. T. Collins,* where a long line of soldiers was waiting on the dock. An announcement came over the PA on the dock that the Naval Group China should come aboard, so we began to file up the gangway, each of us with our seabag over our left shoulder and our ditty bag in our right hand, as specified in *The Bluejacket's Manual.*

When I reached the top of the gangway I put down my ditty bag and saluted the officer of the day, an ensign, saying, "Request permission to come aboard, sir." He returned my salute and indicated that I should follow those of my outfit who were gathering on the quarterdeck. As I did so a chief boatswain's mate who was standing beside the gangway with two of his men laughed at me and said, "Come here, kid, we're gonna put you to work." Without thinking about my reply I said, "I'm sorry, sir, but my doctor advised me to take this voyage as a rest cure," and this so astonished the chief that he said not another word as I passed him and his men, who were trying not to laugh.

When all of our unit were gathered on the quarterdeck, our com-manding officer reported to the captain of the *Collins,* who welcomed him aboard. Then our commander and our other officers left us and went off to their cabins in "officer's country," while we were led off to one of the troop compartments, of which there were four, each holding five hundred men. We were the first troops aboard, since we were Navy and the rest Army, so we had our pick of the berths, which were stacked five high. All of us chose a top berth, for we knew that it would be as hot as hell and there would be more air circulating above than below.

Announcements were being made over the ship's PA system, each preceded by a hiss of air rushing through a pneumatic hose, followed by the shrill piping of a boatswain's whistle, then the speaker saying, "Now hear this, now hear this!" The first call that I heard was "Sweepers, man your brooms, clean sweepdown fore and aft!" Then I heard an announcement ordering enlisted men of the Naval Group China to report to the quarterdeck for work details.

This came as a surprise to me; I thought we would be treated like the other troops on the ship and could just take it easy until we arrived at our destination, enjoying the voyage through the South Seas that I had always daydreamed about. But it turned out that the *Collins* was shorthanded, and since our outfit included men who were qualified in virtually every deck and engine room rating we could fill in any vacancies in the regular ship's company, which normally had a crew of about 450. What is more, since all of us were also qualified in gunnery because of our training at Fort Pierce, we could fill in on the gun crews of the *Collins,* which had four five-inch naval guns, two twin 40mm antiaircraft guns, and fifteen 20mm machine guns.

I was originally assigned to one of the twin forties, each of which had a crew of four men, one to "train" the gun, a second to "point" and fire it, and the other two to load the ammunition, which came in clips of five shells each. But when the chief gunner's mate of the *Collins* put us through a practice drill I dropped a clip of shells, which sometimes go off when that happens, so I was chewed out and assigned to a 20mm machine gun instead, a one-man job.

My machine gun was on the starboard side of the flying bridge, the outward extension of the superstructure on either side of the ship's bridge. I took my place in the swiveling seat attached to the gun, which was mounted within a guntub on a platform at the outer end of the flying bridge, one of the most exposed positions on the ship. The chief checked me out on the gun, which I had already learned to operate at Fort Pierce, where I had fired it to shoot down a target, the only one of my unit to do so. The chief said I couldn't do any damage to the ship with the gun, since it had blocks that prevented its fire from hitting any part of the superstructure. I was to man the gun whenever GQ (General Quarters) was sounded over the PA system, which would be for drills early on our voyage, but when we reached the war zone it would be the real thing, either an air raid or a submarine alert. He said that the 20mm gun didn't have a long enough range to be used against high-flying Japanese aircraft, but would be effective against kamikazes or fighter-bombers of the Betty type, which were designed for strafing or dropping torpedoes. I remembered what this plane looked like from seeing its silhouettes, head on and sideways, in our aerial gunnery course at Sampson.

The chief told me that he had been on the *Collins* since its launching at the Kaiser shipyard in Richmond, California, on January 22, 1944. He said that troopships of the "General" class were known as "Kaiser coffins," because they had no armor plating or double hulls; if they were hit by a torpedo or a kamikaze they would go straight to the bottom in minutes. They had been lucky so far, he said—although the *Collins* had transported troops in the amphibious landings at Saipan and Guam they had not come under air attack, though there had been several sonar detections of Japanese submarines when they were in the southwest Pacific.

I asked the chief where we were going and how long it would take, and he said that we were headed for Calcutta via Fremantle, near Perth on the western coast of Australia, and that it would take thirty-seven days. I wondered why it would take so long, and he said that during most of the voyage, both in the southwest Pacific and in the Indian Ocean, we would be continually zigzagging during the day to avoid Japanese submarines. We would also be stopping for three days in Fremantle, where we would replenish our fuel and water supplies, and would pick up an escort of two Australian destroyers to accompany us through the Indian Ocean. By then we would be within range of Japanese air and naval bases, particularly when we passed between the Burmese coast and the Andaman and Nicobar Islands.

After the chief left I sat in the gunner's seat for a while, swiveling myself around so I could survey the ship, which was taking on supplies that were being loaded into cargo hatches amidships, while GIs were making their way up the gangway and filing aboard. I could see the ship's officers on the bridge, and beyond them on the port side of the flying bridge was another 20mm antiaircraft gun manned by someone from my outfit. Below me on the foredeck I could see the crew of the forward five-inch gun going through their drill, all of them ship's company, as were those manning the two five-inch guns amidships and the one on the fantail behind the aft superstructure, which was bristling with anti-aircraft guns, both 20mm and 40mm, most of them operated by men from our outfit.

After I left my guntub I returned to our compartment, which was now filling up with GIs. From their conversations I learned that some of them had served on the Aleutian Islands and others in Europe. Many of them were infantrymen who had fought in France and Germany, and they weren't too happy about being sent to the Far East to fight against the Japanese. When they saw my Navy dungarees and hat they asked me what I was doing in their troop compartment, and when I said that I was in a Navy commando unit being sent to China they seemed skeptical, although some of them had seen our Underwater Demolition Teams and Scouts and Raiders in the Normandy landings.

The bunk below mine was occupied by a Japanese American sergeant, who told me that he had served in the Nisei regiment that had been one of the most highly decorated U.S. units in the European theater. After the German surrender he and many of his comrades had volunteered to serve in the Far East, even though they would be fighting their own people, for they wanted to prove that they were loyal Americans. He said this with some bitterness, for while he had been fighting for his adopted country, his family and thousands of other Japanese Americans had been confined in U.S. internment camps because of the fear that they might be enemy agents.

I was stowing my gear in my footlocker when I heard my name on the PA system, ordering me to report to the engine room. I went back to the main deck, which was swarming with GIs getting from the gangway to their compartments, and I forced my way through the crowd, trying to locate the engine room, whose hatch I finally found on the aft deck. I descended by a series of almost vertical metal ladders, hardly using my feet but sliding down the handrails to the engine room, where I reported to the officer in charge. He checked my name on his list and turned me over to the chief electrician's mate, who told me that I would report to him every day with the other electrician's mates, eight hours on and eight hours off, which meant that every other day I would be on duty for sixteen of the twenty-four hours.

My main duty on watch would be to monitor the twin generators that powered the *Collins,* making sure they remained in balance so neither of them drew too much power and tripped the main circuit breaker, which would leave the ship dead in the water. I would also be given other jobs, which I knew would be "shit details," because as a fireman second class I was the lowest-ranking man in the engine room, and not even ship's company at that. I was dead right, for the chief said that my first job would be to clean the bilges, the crawl space beneath the deck plates of the engine room. When I was finished with that, I would be given a pot of red lead to paint the interior of the ship's hull where it enclosed the main boilers. He showed me the rope harness in which I would be suspended from pulleys between the hull and the boilers, and he said with sadistic pleasure that if the ship was hit by a torpedo it was a toss-up as to whether I would be drowned or scalded to death by high-pressure steam.

After the chief dismissed me I returned to my compartment, where I finished stowing my gear. One of the engine room crew had told me that the ship was still filling its tanks with fresh water, and if I wanted to take a shower I should do so right away, for once the tanks were full there would be only salt water in the shower heads for the rest of the voyage. So I rushed to the head and took a shower, and not a moment too soon, for as soon as I finished the fresh water was turned off and replaced with salt water, to the consternation of the GIs who had arrived too late.

I then set out to explore the ship, figuring that I was wearing dungarees and could pass myself off as ship's company, which seemed easy, since I had already been assigned to a gun crew and would be standing watches in the engine room. But I wouldn't try to get into officer's country, because our own officers would spot me there.

I concentrated on finding an alternative place to sleep at night, since I knew it would be stifling in the troop compartment, particularly as we headed into the South Pacific. I finally found a small platform high up on the mast amidships where the searchlight was located, approached by a metal ladder. I knew from *The Bluejacket's Manual* that the searchlight was the responsibility of an electrician's mate, so if anyone challenged me I could justify being there by saying that I was checking it out. I decided I would bring my sleeping bag up to the searchlight platform on nights when the troop compartment was too hot and airless. I sat up there for a while watching the GIs filing up the gangway of the *Collins* and another troopship tied up at the next dock.

Then I heard the PA system announce that it was chow time, and I rushed down to the main deck, for there would be two thousand GIs lined up outside the hatch leading down to the mess hall. I was among the first in line, and I had to wait for only a few minutes before we went down into the mess hall. All of the mess cooks who served us on the chow line were black, which didn't surprise me, since I knew that those who identified themselves as black on their questionnaires at the Navy recruitment centers ended up in Cooks and Bakers School or as ship's stewards in officer's country.

We ate standing up at metal tables, the main course for the evening being cold "shit on a shingle," which I ate only because I was so hungry. I was still hungry when I left the mess hall, but I couldn't go back for seconds because my meal ticket had been punched when I entered the hall, and besides, the line stretched all the way around the main deck several times. An electrician's mate whom I had met in the engine room told me that we would be fed only twice a day during the voyage, but he said, I think cynically, that once the sea became rough many of the GIs would be so seasick they wouldn't be interested in eating, so I might be able to borrow a meal ticket from one of them so I could get seconds. He suggested that I talk with the chief electrician's mate about getting a ship's company ID card so that I could eat in the crew's mess hall. I thought this was a good idea, because then I would also have free run of the ship.

I went down to the engine room, where the twin diesel engines were being fired up; now it was much hotter than before, and I wondered what it would be like when we got to the South Pacific. The chief electrician's mate spotted me and put me to work for a while monitoring the twin generators, and when he let me go I asked him if I could be given a ship's company ID card. He wrote me out a chit and said I should present it to the chief yeoman in the ship's office. The chief yeoman turned out to be a New Yorker, as I could tell from his accent, and when I told him I was from Brooklyn he asked me how the Dodgers were doing. I said they had a chance to win the pennant, and he smiled and made arrangements for me to obtain a ship's company ID card, which I could pick up in a couple of days. He then wrote me out a chit that I could use as a temporary ID. I thanked him and left, looking for the crew's mess hall.

When I found the ship's company mess I was told that it was open twenty-four hours a day for those going on and off watches and for those on watch who wanted a cup of "joe," strong black coffee. When I presented my chit I was served baked beans and "horse cock," a shriveled frankfurter with a dab of what the mess cook called "baby shit," which I recognized as mustard. When I finished I went back for a cup of joe, which I laced with enough sugar to make it drinkable.

The coffee gave me enough of a buzz to restore my vitality, and I went up on deck to see what was going on. The cargo hatches were all closed and covered with canvas, the gangway had been pulled up, the longshoremen on the dock were standing ready to release the ropes that held us to the bollards, and the chief boatswain's mate was working the engine on the foredeck to lift the anchor. I could see the same preparations under way on and around the troopship at the next pier, which was probably going to leave at the same time as the *Collins*.

The deck was now swarming with GIs, so I climbed up to my refuge on the searchlight platform, from which I could see the whole of San Pedro Harbor. Then I heard the sound of music, and I saw that a local high school band and girls' chorus had come to give us a send-off, which brought a tremendous cheer from the GIs on the two troopships. The band first played a couple of Army songs and then, just as the anchor was hauled into place and the mooring ropes let go, they began playing "Anchors Aweigh," and the *Collins* slipped away as two tugboats pulled it into position to head out into the harbor. The other troopship was going through the same procedure, and it moved into position just astern of the *Collins*. As we moved away from the pier, the band played a farewell song and the girls in the chorus waved to us as they sang "I'll see you again, whenever skies are blue again," which were the last words I heard before the *Collins* and the other troopship sounded their horns to signal their departure.

It was dusk by then, and from my perch on the searchlight platform I watched as the *Collins* and the other troopship steamed out of San Pedro Harbor and on into the Pacific, where the two wakes began to diverge as our ship headed more to the southwest. Looking back, I could see the lights of San Pedro flickering in the gathering darkness, and then after they faded away there was nothing in view except the boundless ocean and the stars as they began to appear one by one in the celestial sphere. The next phase of my odyssey had just begun, less than three weeks before my nineteenth birthday, and I let myself imagine that I was Odysseus in the middle of the sable sea.

On our first night aboard the *Collins* I slept below in the troop compartment where I had been assigned, but it was so hot and airless that I decided from then on I would take my sleeping bag up to the searchlight platform and sleep there. The last sound I heard was the boatswain's whistle over the PA signaling that dusk had fallen, an elegiac tune that told me that the long day was over and the long night was about to begin.

I knew that reveille would be sounded at six o'clock, which in Navy terms was at four bells on the four to eight a.m watch. But I got up half an hour before reveille so I could get to the head and wash before the other 499 men in our compartment crowded in. The facilities were very basic. A row of taps supplied cold salt water for washing at a long sink; the urinal was a trough on the deck, and the toilet seats were holes cut in a wooden plank over another trough. Both troughs were continually flushed with seawater, which sometimes came up in geysers through the toilet seats on the ends when the ship rolled.

The sun had already risen before I came out on deck, and I could see that we were heading southwest. The horizon formed a perfect circle between the blues of sky and sea, whose mirroring surface was marked only by our churning wake.

Chow was cold scrambled eggs made from powdered eggs and powdered milk served on a slab of cold and almost black toast. But since it was the crew's mess, I was able to wash it down with two cups of sweet joe, which wired me up enough to face my first full day in the engine room.

I spent the eight-to-four watch monitoring the twin generators, which was tricky, since one or another of the generators was always drawing a little more current, and if I didn't correct it the imbalance could quickly get out of hand and blow the main circuit breaker. But I learned how to keep an eye on the two current meters while I kept part of my mind free for daydreaming and thinking about other things, mostly about the unknown world into which I was now heading.

After an hour or so the chief told me to start cleaning the bilges, handing me a rag, a wire brush, and a can of carbon tetrachloride solvent. He had me lift up the grated metal deck plates in front of the generators and said I should begin there and work my way around the engine room. I was to clear away any rust that might have accumulated on the inner surface of the hull and the underside of the deck plates by wiping the surface with carbon tet and then scrubbing it off with the wire brush. He handed me a flashlight as I crawled into the bilges, where I spent the rest of my watch, sweating like a pig and gagging on the fumes of the carbon tet.

When I came up on deck I was temporarily blinded by the blaze of day, and I had to pick my way through the GIs who occupied every inch of deck space. I took a salt water shower and then lay in my bunk until evening mess, which was shit on a shingle, with a green apple for dessert.

As soon as it was dark the PA announced that a movie would be shown on a screen set up on the cargo hold amidships. I went up to my gun station on the flying bridge for a better view of the film, which starred John Wayne in *Tall in the Saddle*. The projector was mounted on the aft superstructure and a huge sheet served as the screen. Those of us on the forward side of the ship thus saw the film on the rear side of the screen, making the images left-right inverted. High winds began howling near the climax of the movie, and the screen started to undulate, so as John Wayne went riding off into the sunset I thought I was looking at the film in the big funhouse mirror at Steeplechase Park in Coney Island. But no one minded in the least because it was such a relief not to be cooped up down below in the troop compartments.

After the film I took my sleeping bag and climbed up to the searchlight platform, where I lashed myself to the mast so I wouldn't fall out during the night. Before I fell asleep I ticked off the constellations that I could identify, because I knew I would be seeing new ones as we approached the Southern Hemisphere. I was particularly anxious to spot the Southern Cross and the Magellanic Clouds.

The next day was much the same. I spent the day hung in a rope harness from pulleys between the hull and the boiler. The heat was intense, and I burned myself several times when the ship rolled and brought me up against the surface of the boiler.

On the third day I was again hung from my harness, but my ordeal was cut short after about an hour when the PA speaker gave the alarm for General Quarters, ordering everyone to man their battle stations. I worked the ropes to return to the main deck of the engine room, reporting to the officer in charge that I was going to man my gun. By the time I got up to the main deck all of the GIs were down below and all of the ship's company were at their posts except me, or so it seemed, so I raced to my antiaircraft gun on the flying bridge. I put on my helmet and earphones and strapped myself in, waiting for instructions on the intercom. The chief gunner's mate checked me in over the intercom, chewing me out for having taken so long to get to my gun.

I took the opportunity to enjoy the fresh air and sunshine, as the PA announced that this was a drill and then called up the troops in the various compartments to proceed to the lifeboats to which they had been assigned. After half an hour or so the PA announced that the drill was over and we should all return to our posts. I took my time getting back to the engine room, for which I was chewed out by the chief in charge. I didn't really care; there was nothing worse that he could do than put me back in my rope harness between the hull and the boiler, which he did. General Quarters had at least given me a break, and I knew there would be more of them as we approached the war zone.

Two days later there was another General Quarters in the midafternoon, and this time all of us manning the antiaircraft guns fired a few rounds from our weapons to make sure they were working properly. Everything went smoothly, and I felt very proud of myself: it was the first time I had fired a weapon other than in our training camp at Fort Pierce, and this was more like the real thing.

Three days after that, in the midafternoon the PA announced, "Now hear this! All hands on deck!" without the General Quarters alert, and as I emerged from the engine room I wondered what was up. Everyone was on deck, so I went up to my guntub on the flying bridge to see what was going on. I could see that everyone's attention was focused amidships on the starboard side, where the chief boatswain's mate and his men were lowering a Jacob's ladder over the side. The PA announced that we had just crossed the equator, and that Neptune, King of the Sea, was about to come on board to welcome us to his kingdom. At that moment an almost naked figure carrying a trident climbed up the ladder and jumped down on the deck, shaking the sea water from his long beard, which almost fell off in the process. We were all invited to file by Neptune and receive a certificate welcoming us to his kingdom. I was among the last to go, for I wanted to spin out my absence from the engine room as long as possible, and after I received the paper from an Army major standing beside Neptune I sat out on deck long enough to read it.

TO ALL BROTHER SHELLBACKS, SEA SERPENTS, MERMAIDS AND OTHER DENIZENS OF THE DEEP, GREETINGS: By these tokens be you so advised that the most worthy _____ has this day been admitted, initiated and inducted into our ANCIENT ORDER OF THE BRINY DEEP, in Latitude ooo and Longitude CENSORED, given under my hand this _____ day of _____ in the year Nineteen Hundred and Forty Five.

(Signed) Neptunus Rex & Max Fisher, Major, U.S. Army
Transportation Corps, U.S.S. *General E. T. Collins.*

Because we had now crossed the equator I knew that I should be able to see all of the constellations in the southern celestial hemisphere, or at least those visible in mid-June. When I climbed up to the crow's nest that evening I scanned the sky until I identified the constellation Centaurus, and then south of that I finally spotted the Southern Cross, distinguished by the pale red star Gamma Crucis at its top. Then I looked still farther to the south until I found the Greater and Lesser Magellanic Clouds just above the southern horizon, reminding me of the day that Jimmy Anderson and I missed the show at the Hayden Planetarium. I realized what a long way I had come since then, and I wondered where Jimmy was at that moment and if he too was looking at the Southern Cross and the Magellanic Clouds.

The next day, after yet another General Quarters, I plucked up my courage and entered the wheelhouse on the bridge. I wanted to look at the charts and find out where we were, for we hadn't seen land since leaving San Pedro. The enlisted men on duty recognized me from having seen me at my antiaircraft gun, and none of them challenged me when I went over to examine the charts. I saw that we had crossed the equator just south of the Kiritimati Atoll, better known as Christmas Island, and that we would soon pass through the Samoa Islands.

Two days later the PA announced that we had just crossed the International Date Line, and that the date should be advanced from June 18 to June 19. I had completely lost track of the date till then, and I realized that it was just a week till my nineteenth birthday. I resolved to keep track of the days during the next week, so I would at least know when I turned nineteen.

The next day the *Collins* ceased steaming straight ahead and began zigzagging, for we were now in the war zone and within the range of Japanese submarines, which would be waiting for troopships heading toward Australia. We were told that General Quarters would no longer be drills, and when the PA gave the GQ alarm that afternoon we stayed at our posts for several hours. I watched our radar dish as it scanned the horizon, now and then locking in when it spotted something suspicious. I could also hear the resonant pings from the sonar scope on the bridge, where the two helmsmen were continuously turning the steering wheel clockwise and counterclockwise as we zigzagged, our wake forming a sinuous curve behind us.

The continual turning made many of the GIs even more seasick, and I saw one of them puking into his helmet liner, which he then put on to shield his head from the sun, oblivious to the vomit that trickled down his face. The troop compartments were unbearable, and I went down to ours only to get a change of skivvies and socks whenever I took a shower, and then only when everyone else was out on deck. There was only one scuttlebutt in every compartment, and it was guarded by an armed Marine day and night so that no water was wasted. When I used it I drank like a camel setting out on a long journey across the desert.

After passing through the Samoa Islands, without seeing any of them, I could tell from the charts that our route would take us between the Fiji and Tonga islands, but though I scanned the horizon whenever I was manning my antiaircraft gun I saw not a trace of them. Nothing was in view other than the eternal sea. But at least it was beginning to get a bit cooler, and when I next checked the charts I saw that we had crossed the Tropic of Cancer, less than two weeks after crossing the Tropic of

Capricorn, or so I estimated, having once again lost track of the passing days.

The following morning I must have dozed off while I was on watch in the engine room monitoring the main switchboard, for when I looked up at the two ammeters, the one on the starboard side was beginning to draw more current than the other one. I got up to adjust the voltage to correct the imbalance, but before I could do so the current in the starboard generator suddenly surged and the pointer on the ammeter went over the red danger mark, tripping the main circuit breaker and plunging the engine room into darkness.

There was chaos all around me, as the head engineering officer and the chief in charge struggled to get the emergency generator started, but in the interim the ship drifted in the water, and in a combat zone, at that. Even after the emergency generator kicked in it took the better part of an hour to get the diesel engines relit and up to full power again. In the meantime frantic messages were coming over the intercom from the captain to the head engineering officer, who looked as if he was going to blow a valve.

It was all my fault, and I anticipated that I would spend the rest of the voyage in the brig, which I thought would be preferable to working in the engine room. But by the time power was fully restored my watch ended and someone else came on duty to monitor the generators. In the confusion the engineering officer and the chief seemed to have forgotten all about me. So I left the engine room and went up on deck, where I remained until a GQ sounded and I hurried to my battle station on the flying bridge.

The only time I had off was Sunday morning, when I went to mass in the chapel, given by the Catholic chaplain, Father Ryan. I stayed after mass to talk with him, and our conversation turned to books. He apologized for having none to lend me, and asked me what I had been reading before I went into the Navy. I told him that I had just finished the *Odyssey.* He said that I should go on and read the *Iliad,* and after that I should continue with Herodotus and the other classics of Greek and Roman literature.

I asked Father Ryan for advice on what I might read to educate myself after I got out of the Navy, for there was little chance that I would go back to school. He looked through his desk and handed me the catalog for the Great Books program at St. John's College in Annapolis, Maryland, which he had attended before going into the seminary. The curriculum began with Homer's *Iliad* and *Odyssey* and ended with James Joyce's *Ulysses;* it included not only the Great Books but also works about the authors themselves and the times in which they lived. I asked him if I could borrow the catalog and he said I could keep it, for he had used it to the fullest in his own self-education, and now it should be passed on to someone else who would benefit from it. I thanked him and took the catalog back to my compartment, where I tucked it away in the bottom of my seabag, with the thought that sometime in the unforeseeable future I might have a chance to read through the Great Books, which at the moment seemed like an impossible dream.

It was now becoming perceptibly colder, and when I checked the charts I saw that we were nearly forty degrees south of the equator in the Tasman Sea, off the southeastern tip of Australia. The following day, on what I figured was June 26, 1945, my birthday, we passed through the Bass Strait between Australia and Tasmania. I was on duty at my antiaircraft gun, because it was possible that Japanese submarines might be lurking in the strait, through which all U.S. troopships bound for Calcutta had to pass.

I was sitting in the swivel seat of my gun, looking ahead toward the strait, when we were suddenly hit by a blizzard that drove all the GIs below, leaving only the deck crews and the antiaircraft gunners above deck. The storm cleared as we passed through the strait, with the Australian coast clearly visible to starboard and Tasmania with its satellite isles in view to port, the first land we had seen since leaving San Pedro.

The weather stayed clear and cold as we rounded the southern coast of Australia. The ship's company put on their foul-weather gear, but the GIs and those of us in SACO had no protection against the cold, so I froze as I manned my gun. Still, it was better than slaving away in the heat of the engine room. I continued to sleep up on the searchlight platform despite the cold, since I had my sleeping bag to keep me warm, and I kept up my observation of the constellations in the southern celestial sphere, which shone brilliantly in the clear moonless nights that followed.

Our next landfall was Cape Leeuwin, the southwesternmost promontory of Australia, where we changed course to head north. The following day we made our way into the harbor of Fremantle, the port of Perth, where we were to stop for three days to take on supplies and refill our fuel and water tanks. All the ships in the harbor sounded their horns as we approached our berth, and the GIs crowding the deck cheered in response, as did I from my perch on the searchlight platform.

The next morning after mess the PA announced that all of the troops on the ship would be given a few hours of shore leave, and we should go to our muster stations and prepare to debark. I was due to stand watch in the engine room, but the engineering officer gave me permission to go ashore. After going down the gangway we assembled on the dock, staggering, after nearly a month continually at sea, from the unaccustomed feel of terra firma under our feet instead of a rolling deck.

We then proceeded to march into town four abreast, with our outfit leading the way, since we were U.S. Navy, with the Marine detachment from the *Collins* riding herd on us to make sure no one escaped. We marched along what appeared to be the main street leading in from the port, and everyone in town seemed to have turned out to cheer us as we passed. Most of the shop signs along the way had Irish names, and when I passed a Duggan's Pub I began singing a song about a lad from the Dingle Peninsula who became a highwayman in Australia. "There was a wild colonial boy, Jack Duggan was his name . . . ," which brought a cheer from the crowd, and they cheered again when I shouted "Up Kerry!" and "Up Mayo!," honoring my parents' home counties in Ireland.

The parade ended at the football stadium, where we were turned loose for a couple of hours, to run around or walk or just talk with the locals, as we pleased, with most of the GIs heading for the girls, who were all chaperoned. The townspeople had provided free sandwiches, cakes, candy, and soft drinks, though the GIs would have preferred beer or booze.

The next day we continued to take on supplies and to top up our fuel and water tanks. I managed to get myself assigned to a work detail supervising the filling of our fuel tanks, and I took the opportunity to walk around the dock and talk to the longshoremen, most of whom were of Irish origin, men who were too old for military service or had medical disabilities. They were all sorry not to be in the service, and they wished us luck in the forthcoming invasion of Japan; everyone in Australia thought that would be the last phase of the war in the Pacific, since the fighting in the Philippines and Okinawa was winding down and the Allies were pushing the Japanese back in Burma.

A Dutch submarine was tied up next to the *Collins,* and when I walked over to take a look at it one of the crew invited me aboard. He told me that theirs was one of the few surviving ships of the Dutch navy, most of which had been destroyed in the Second Battle of the Java Sea in February/March 1942, when the American heavy cruiser *Houston* and the Australian light cruiser *Perth* had also gone down. Their submarine was preparing to go on patrol again in the Java Sea, where my friend thought the Allies would soon be launching an amphibious landing on Borneo and Sumatra, which we would be passing on our voyage from Fremantle to Calcutta. North of Sumatra we would go through the Andaman Sea between Burma and the Andaman and Nicobar Islands. The Japanese had air bases on the Burmese side of the strait, and if my Dutch friend was right in his prediction, we would be directly in their path if they decided to attack the Allied forces landing on Sumatra.

We weighed anchor the following morning, with a crowd of towns-people waving farewell, along with a detachment of Australian veterans of World War I, while the town band played "Waltzing Mathilda." I realized that Australians were much closer to the war than we Americans, particularly here in Fremantle, where ships like ours and the Dutch submarine were constantly sailing off into the combat zone.

We were followed out of the harbor by another American troopship, the *General D. E. Aultman,* together with two Australian corvettes, which would protect our little convoy on its way through the Indian Ocean. A GQ sounded when we reached the open sea, and soon after I reached my gun station I was informed on the intercom that I should be prepared for aerial target practice and that I should load the ammunition belt of my gun with tracer bullets.

A few minutes later a light plane appeared, towing far behind it a long sleeve that looked like a windsock, which was to be our target. The tow-plane turned to fly across our path, and at that moment an order came over the intercom to "Fire at will!," which I did along with every other antiaircraft gunner on the two troopships, our tracer bullets making a spectacular display, though hardly any of them hit the target. We did better the second time the towplane flew by, and I felt sure that some of my bullets hit the sleeve. On the third and final pass, nearly all of us were on target, which earned us a tremendous cheer from the GIs on the two troopships.

After the towplane flew away our convoy formed up, with the *Collins* leading the way and the *Aultman* following, both troopships zigzagging, while the two corvettes threaded their way between and around us. Soon afterward a fighter plane buzzed us and then wagged its wings as it flew back to the mainland, and I was told by a sailor on the bridge that this was part of the air cover that the Australians would provide for our convoy as long as we were in range of their airfields.

I was informed on the intercom that until further notice I was to remain at my gun station throughout the day, and that the crew mess hall would be open before sunrise and after sunset to feed the gun crews. I was very pleased to hear this, for it meant that I would be freed from my slavery in the engine room on our voyage through the Indian Ocean, and that I would enjoy the fresh air and sunshine as we headed back toward summer in the Northern Hemisphere.

I figured we would be crossing the equator about a week after we left Fremantle, and at that point we would be off the western coast of Sumatra. I was hesitant about checking our position on the charts in the bridge, for the ship's captain was now there all day long and the atmosphere was very tense, because the Allied invasion of Sumatra was now imminent, if my Dutch friend was to be believed.

We had left behind our Australian air cover, and as far as I knew the only air bases along our route would be those of the Japanese on the Burmese coast opposite the Andaman and Nicobar Islands, which extended northward from Sumatra for some seven hundred miles into the Bay of Bengal. I knew that any aircraft I spotted for the next three or four days were sure to be Japanese, and that brought to mind the plane-spotting course I had taken in boot camp, although it would probably be of little use to me in action.

Two days after crossing the equator, according to my reckoning, we changed course to head due north, as I could tell from checking the direction of the noon shadow. I figured, from having looked at the charts on the bridge, that we would then be passing on our port side the so-called Ten-Degree Channel, which separated the Nicobar Islands, on the south, from the Andaman Islands, to the north.

I looked at our radar dish and saw that it was revolving steadily, with no pausing to indicate that it had spotted anything, so I sat back and relaxed.

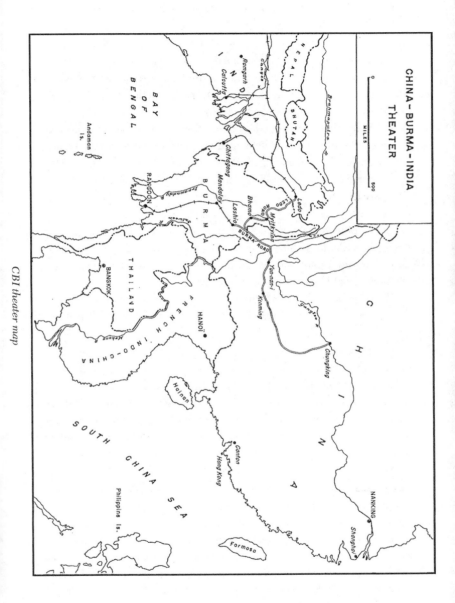

CBI theater map

The heightened alert lasted till we were well clear of the Andaman and Nicobar Islands, after which the two Australian corvettes split off from our convoy, presumably heading back to Fremantle. Nevertheless, we manned our guns throughout the day, and our two troopships continued to zigzag. There was still a danger from Japanese submarines, which had sunk Allied ships in the Bay of Bengal earlier in the war, as I was told by a petty officer I spoke to on the bridge.

A few days later I emerged on deck after morning mess and noticed that the color of the sea had changed from clear blue to muddy brown, with clumps of vegetation and other flotsam forming a scum on the surface of the water, reminding me of a lithograph I had seen of the Sargasso Sea, the legendary graveyard of ships in the Atlantic Ocean. I asked one of the ship's company about this, and he said that we were looking at effluents of the Hooghly River, the branch of the Ganges that flows past Calcutta into the Bay of Bengal. He said that we would soon be picking up a pilot who would take us up the Hooghly to Calcutta, where we would be docking before nightfall.

The pilot came aboard about an hour later, and with him were half a dozen barefoot "natives," as the old travelogues I had read called them, all of them carrying beads and other trinkets, which were quickly bought up by the GIs. I reported to my gun post, but I was soon informed over the intercom that I should secure my weapon and its ammunition. After I did that I remained on the flying bridge while the *Collins* made its way up the Hooghly, the *Aultman* following closely behind. Then an announcement came over the PA for all troops to go below and pack up their gear and prepare to disembark. I went up to the searchlight platform that had been my aerie for more than a month to retrieve my sleeping bag, after which I went below to my troop compartment, which was now packed with GIs getting ready to leave. I emptied my footlocker and stowed my gear, making sure that the catalog for the Great Books program was safely tucked away in the bottom of my seabag.

It took me the better part of an hour to make my way up on deck, for the passageways were jammed with GIs struggling under the weight of forty-pound packs. At least they were strapped to their backs—I had to balance my equally heavy seabag on my left shoulder while I held my ditty bag in my right hand, which made it difficult to climb the almost vertical ladders that led up from the troop compartment.

The PA announced that Naval Group China would muster on the quarterdeck, so I headed that way and saw our commanding officer for the first time since we had left San Pedro. After we were mustered he told us that we would be the first to disembark, but still it took another hour before we made our way down the gangway and lined up on the dock. We were told to stand at ease while we waited for trucks to take us wherever we were going, though no one seemed to know where that was.

I had again lost track of the passing days, so I asked Bill Glennon if he knew the date; he said he thought it was July 17, give or take a day or two, for he wasn't sure whether we had gained or lost a day when we crossed the International Date Line. Either way, it had taken us about six weeks to go from New York to San Pedro to Calcutta, which was not bad for traveling halfway around the world by land and sea in wartime, particularly when we were forced to zigzag through a large part of our voyage. I remembered that Odysseus hadn't taken a direct route either, and I wondered where the next stage of my own odyssey would take me.

The dock where we landed was on the east bank of the Hooghly, downstream from the center of Calcutta. The river was teeming with traffic, including freighters, lighters, barges, and junks, as well as marigold-covered rafts carrying what I was told were corpses to be cremated at the burning ghats along the river upstream from our dock. The coolies loading and unloading the ships in the docks were barefoot and clad only in loincloths, and when I saw them I thought of John doing the same kind of work in New York when he could find it. I wondered if these long-shoremen supported families on their earnings as my father had done, or at least had tried to do.

It was dusk by the time we were herded onto Indian army trucks, about a dozen of us sitting on planks on either side of the open back, our seabags and ditty bags piled between us on the floor. No one told us where we were going, but from watching the road signs, which were in both English and Bengali, I figured we were heading for an airport with the funny name of Dum Dum. Our progress was very slow, for we had to make our way through swarms of humanity, halting every time a sacred cow crossed the road.

We eventually stopped near the airport at a base called Camp Knox, which turned out to be the Calcutta headquarters of Naval Group China.

We were taken to our barracks there, which were luxurious compared to anything I had seen before in the Navy, with individual beds rather than five-high bunks, hot-water showers, and a lounge with sofas where we could relax when we were not on duty. The mess hall was run by the Indian army, as was everything else at Camp Knox. The food they gave us was the same as what they served their officers, one of them told me, and at our first meal that evening we had a delicious curry, the first Indian food I had ever eaten.

The recreational facilities included a basketball court, and after supper that evening a bunch of us organized a pickup game and played for an hour or so, the only physical exercise we had had in the past six weeks other than our afternoon in Fremantle. Then I went back to the barracks and took a hot shower, something I hadn't had since we left Fort Pierce. We didn't have a shower at home, and I recalled Peg saying that we were lucky we had a tub, not to mention a bathroom and toilet.

There were newspapers available in the lounge, both the English-language *Calcutta Times* and the *CBI Roundup*, a U.S. Army paper. I learned that the Australians had launched an amphibious invasion of Borneo on July 1, just when we were in Fremantle, so my Dutch friend had been partially correct, and the fighting would have been going on while we were passing Sumatra and the Andaman and Nicobar Islands.

The papers also reported on the progress of the war in Burma, where the Japanese had been in full retreat since the capture of Rangoon by the Allies in early May.

After muster the next morning, all of us new arrivals in Roger Three were marched to the infirmary to be given additional shots, for there had been outbreaks of scrub typhus and dengue fever (for which there was no vaccine) among those serving in the CBI. We were told that malaria was endemic, so we were given atabrine tablets to take daily and warned never to drink water unless it was chlorinated. We could get chlorinated water from the big udder-like canvas sacks called "Lister bags" that were set up all over the camp. The pharmacist's mate who gave us this advice had a distinctly yellow tint to his complexion, and he said that it was from taking atabrine, which produces a slight jaundice.

Some of the men in our barracks were from Roger One and Roger Two, the contingents of our outfit that had preceded us at Fort Pierce. They told us they were waiting to be flown up to Kunming, the capital of Yunnan Province in China, but there were only a few seats available every day on the "gooney birds," the C-47 transport planes that flew over the "Hump," the enormously high mountains of northern Burma, the southeastern extension of the Himalayas. The only other way of getting to China was by the Ledo-Stilwell Road, which had been built by U.S. Army engineers from the northeastern tip of India down through northern Burma as the Japanese retreated, finally linking up with the old Burma Road early in 1945, so convoys could go all the way to Kunming. Scuttlebutt had it that our outfit was organizing a truck convoy that would get us up to Kunming, and I hoped that the rumor was true, because otherwise the war might end before I got to China.

There were a number of people in Camp Knox who had served with SACO in China, and from talking with them I began to get some idea of what our outfit had been doing. I learned that SACO had eighteen camps in China, along with twelve mobile columns, three raiding groups, three mine units, and nine coastal lookouts. The principal camp, called Happy Valley, was at Chengdu in Sichuan Province, about 150 miles northwest of Chongqing, Chiang Kai-shek's capital. Some of the people I talked to had served there with Admiral Milton Miles, our commanding officer, and had also met General Tai Li, the commander of the Loyal and Patriotic Army, the Chinese guerrilla force that SACO had helped to train. Scuttlebutt had it that our Roger amphibious unit would be with the LPA in the final offensive of the war, attacking the Japanese in China, while American and British forces launched an amphibious assault against the home islands of Japan. This made me all the more anxious to get into China before it was too late, and I listened for word of the truck convoy that was supposedly being organized to take us to Kunming over the Ledo-Stilwell Road.

Meanwhile, we were given a day's liberty in Calcutta, to which trucks left regularly from Camp Knox. Bill Glennon and I took a rickshaw along Chowringee, the main boulevard, and afterward we walked to the Jain Temple, which I had seen in a lithograph illustrating a travelogue I had read in Ireland, one of the exotic images that had inspired me to become a world traveler. We then went to the burning ghats to see bodies being cremated on funerary pyres, watched a staged fight between a cobra and a mongoose, avoided contact with the sacred cows, beggars, and belled lepers we encountered in the markets, and had a drink at the Great Eastern Hotel, where the British officers at the bar studiously ignored us. A gramophone was playing the "Kashmiri Love Song," and as I listened to the lyrics I thought of Peg, remembering how much the sentimental words had appealed to her romantic soul.

Pale hands I loved beside the Shalimar,
Where are you now? Who lies beneath your spell?
Whom do you lead on Rapture's roadway, far,
Before you agonize them in farewell?
Pale hands I loved beside the Shalimar,
Where are you now? Where are you now?

We then stopped in at a tattoo parlor, where a British sergeant major was spread-eagled on the floor having the crossed flags of the Allied nations tattooed on his chest and stomach. I was going to have a bluebird tattooed on my shoulder, but the tattoo artist said it would be at least another hour before he finished with the sergeant major, who wanted, in addition, to have a hunting scene tattooed on his back, with dogs pursuing a fox heading for his hole, which was guess where. So we left, and I never had the bluebird tattooed on my shoulder, which I have always regretted.

Later we went to a photographer's shop and had ourselves photographed shooting a stuffed tiger, the two of us wearing pith helmets as we aimed old rifles at the charging beast, trying our best not to laugh, because this was a picture for our family albums.

When we returned to Camp Knox I stopped at the gate to talk to the chief guard on duty, a Gurkha master sergeant who showed me the Victoria Cross he had won for bravery in World War I. He also showed me his kukri, the curved sword that the Gurkhas carry, and before he put it back in its scabbard he deliberately cut his finger, for the weapon is traditionally unsheathed only to draw blood. I resolved that on my next liberty in Calcutta I would buy a kukri as a souvenir, for I had seen them on sale in the market, though they were probably more than I could afford on the small fraction of my monthly salary that was not sent home to Peg. Even though I was getting an extra 20 percent for being in a combat zone, I had less than twenty dollars a month for spending money, about the same amount as what I had had when I was working at the Eagle Druggist Supply Company.

Later that day I had an interesting conversation with a young officer in the Indian army, who told me that Britain's days in India were numbered, for as soon as the war ended the Indian people would rise under the leadership of Mahatma Gandhi and his Congress Party to seek independence. He said that there was already a "Free India Movement" led by Subhas Chandra Bose, a dissident Congress Party member who had organized what he called the Indian National Army to fight alongside the Japanese army in Burma.

The following day a notice was posted on the bulletin board announcing that a convoy was being formed to carry supplies to China over the Ledo-Stilwell Road, with a call for volunteers who were qualified to drive a truck. I signed up immediately, though I had never driven anything other than a rented bicycle. Bill Glennon told me that I was crazy to volunteer, and he said that if I didn't die in an accident the Japanese would kill me, for they still held a large part of Burma.

But my only worry at the moment was that I didn't know how to drive, and I had to find some way to learn before the convoy left. All of those who volunteered were ordered to meet in the drill hall with Commander John Boots, the officer who would be in command of the convoy. He said that everyone who had volunteered—17 officers and 160 enlisted men—would go with the convoy, which would leave in a couple of days. There would be two men in each truck, he said, one to drive and the other to "ride shotgun," and we would be expected to spell each other. He told us to "buddy up" and passed around a list so we could sign up, two to a truck.

I signed up with my friend Ed Hill, who at least had driven his father's car a few times. We were told that the U.S. Army Quartermaster Corps would send one of their men to the motor pool at Camp Knox that evening to give driving instructions to any who needed it. Ed and I were the only volunteers who signed up for the instruction, and after evening mess we went to the motor pool for our lesson. A black sergeant was there with one of the six-by-six trucks that would make up the convoy, and he spent an hour showing us how to double-clutch and to use the low-low gear that we would need for the worst stretches of the Ledo-Stilwell Road, which he himself had driven a few months before. Ed was a quick learner, but I was hopeless, as the sergeant told me, shaking his head. After the lesson Ed and I decided that he would do all the driving, at least in the beginning, while I would ride shotgun. Later, perhaps after some practice along the way, maybe I could do some of the driving, though I secretly doubted that I would ever improve to the point where I could take over the wheel.

We were told that we would be informed about the convoy's departure and should be prepared to leave at any moment. Meanwhile, each of us was issued a carbine, or light rifle, and a Colt .45 semiautomatic pistol, along with ammunition for both weapons, as well as a combat knife, a helmet and a helmet liner, a foul-weather jacket and a waterproof poncho, a pup tent, a mess kit and canteen, and a supply of K rations. We were told that we would need the K rations principally for the first part of our journey, when our trucks would be carried on flatcars of the Bengal and Assam Railway and would not be stopping at either Indian or U.S. Army bases.

I went to the headquarters building to look at a large map of the China-Burma-India theater that was displayed across one wall, with the routes of the Bengal and Assam Railway and the Ledo-Stilwell Road marked in red. The railway would take us up along the Hooghly River to where it diverged from the main stream of the Ganges; there its track turned northeastward to follow the Brahmaputra River to what the British called the Northeast Frontier, where India borders Tibet, China, and Burma. The end of the line was near Ledo, the town that gave its name to the Ledo-Stilwell Road, which led south from there through the mountains of northern Burma to the point where it joined the old Burma Road, northeast of Mandalay, where we would cross into China and drive to Kunming.

I figured that the total distance by rail and road would be about two thousand miles, and in talking to the sergeant who had given us our driving lesson we learned that the journey would take nearly a month—that is, if we made it, for the monsoon season had already begun and we would be passing through a region that had the highest rainfall in the world, which might make the road impassable.

The following day we were informed that our convoy would be leaving the next morning, when those of us who had volunteered would be taken to the U.S. ordnance depot at Kanchrapara, thirty miles north of Calcutta. We would board our trucks there and drive them to the Sealdah rail depot in Calcutta, where they would be put on flatcars.

The next morning Ed Hill and I mustered with the other volunteers and then boarded trucks that took us to Kanchrapara, which a wit at Camp Knox referred to as Camp Shapiro. When we arrived there we mustered again and were given our assignments in the convoy. The trucks were all numbered, and Ed and I found the one to which we were assigned about halfway along the line. We stowed our gear and weapons in the back of the cab and then Ed got behind the wheel, while I stood out on the road to see what was going on. Commander Boots drove by in his jeep to check the convoy, and soon afterward I could see the first truck in line beginning to move. I jumped in beside Ed as he started up the engine.

Our drive into Calcutta was painfully slow, for our convoy was continually interrupted by civilian traffic as well as sacred cows, and we didn't reach the Sealdah station until well past noon. Then it took several hours to load our trucks on the flatcars, and another hour passed before Commander Boots made sure that all was secure before the train started, by which time it was late afternoon.

Ed and I sat in the cab of our truck and ate our first K rations as the train slowly made its way through the northern suburbs of Calcutta. Each ration consisted of a slab of American cheese—so hard that I had to pare it with my combat knife—a couple of dry biscuits that crumbled in my hand, a chunk of rancid Spam that turned my stomach, a square of chocolate that I was afraid would break my teeth when I bit into it, and a packet of powdered lemonade that proved to be insoluble in water.

If that was all we would have to eat until we reached an Army camp in Burma it would be a grim journey, so I decided that I would break into the back of our truck to see if there was anything edible in its cargo. I made my way along the flatcar to the truck, where I untied the lines on the canvas covering the wooden crates we were carrying. I then used my combat knife to open one of the crates, which was filled with quart cans of grapefruit juice, of which I took two. Then I opened a second case, which contained quart cans of fruit salad, and I took two of those as well. The other cases I broke into contained explosives and ammunition, so I just took the four cans of food and drink back to the cab of our truck, where Ed and I had a feast, pleased that at least we would have all the fruit cocktail and grapefruit juice we could consume for the rest of our journey.

Rice paddies stretching off in all directions, as seen from the railroad traveling between the Ganges and the Brahmaputra rivers, India, 1945

During the remainder of that day and throughout the whole of the day that followed our route took us northeastward across the great delta between the Ganges and Brahmaputra rivers.

Ed and I sat on top of our truck during the day to take in the view, with rice paddies stretching off to the horizon, worked by peasant farmers using water buffaloes as draft animals. Every time we stopped—usually for no apparent reason—crowds of children swarmed around us, the youngest of them naked, smiling up at us in the hope that we would give them something. I was sorry I had nothing to give them other than the chocolate in our K rations.

At night we bedded down in our sleeping bags on top of our cargo, lashing ourselves in so we wouldn't roll off in our sleep. We also had to be careful of low bridges, which we could hear whizzing by as we passed under them during the night. Whenever we needed to refill our canteens I had to climb along the side of the train to the last car, where the pharmacist's mates had set up a Lister bag in the ambulance, being careful not to be hit by the telephone and telegraph poles that flanked the railway line, for the flatcars were very wide and left little room to walk.

On the third day we came to the Brahmaputra, where we drove off the flatcars onto barges that took us across the river.

Children swarming around us, looking for treats

On the other side we drove for a short way and were then loaded onto the flatcars of another train, but in the transfer one of our trucks skidded on the road and ended up in a rice paddy. The two drivers were shaken up but not hurt, and after one of our emergency vehicles winched the truck back onto the road they were able to start it up again and drive it onto the last flatcar of the train.

Over the next several days rice paddies gave way to tea plantations, as we left Bengal behind and entered the highlands of Assam, losing sight of the Brahmaputra.

At Dimapur I saw a road sign pointing the way to Kohim, the deepest point of the Japanese penetration in their invasion of India in 1944, when they tried to cut the railway on which we were now traveling.

The following day we came within sight of the Brahmaputra again at Dergaon, where the train stopped for about fifteen minutes and we all got off and stretched our legs. A shop at the station had a variety of bottled drinks for sale, but I couldn't tell what they were because the labels were in Indian script and the owner didn't speak English. I bought a pint bottle of a ruby-red liquid whose label illustration seemed to show a cherry tree. After I got back on the train I took a swig and found that it was a cherry liqueur, but much stronger and harsher than any of the liqueurs my uncle Tom had occasionally swiped from the rectory of Fourteen Holy Martyrs and served to his guests on the holidays,

Barges carrying our trucks across the Brahmaputra, India, 1945

even us kids. That evening Ed and I sat on top of our truck drinking the alcohol, looking at the full moon silvering the Brahmaputra and listening to the howls of what we were told were jackals echoing from the hills around us.

By early afternoon the next day we reached the river port of Dibru-garh, the highest point of navigation on the Brahmaputra, where we all

Rice paddies giving way to tea plantations, Assam, India, 1945

got off to eat at a Chinese restaurant with a big sign advertising HAM AND EGGS, AMERICAN STYLE.

This was the first American food we had eaten since we left home, and it was much appreciated, though I actually preferred the Indian food we had been served in the mess hall at Camp Knox. The owner of the restaurant, who spoke a little English, told us that he had worked in the mess hall at a U.S. air base in Assam, where he had learned how to cook ham and eggs as well as French fries and other American favorites. When the first U.S. truck convoys began driving over the Ledo-Stilwell Road in mid-January 1945, he opened this restaurant, knowing that the GIs would want a good American meal after the long train ride from Calcutta and before starting the even longer truck ride to Kunming.

The following day our long railway journey ended at Margherita, a town just to the north of India's border with Burma, where we drove our trucks off the flatcars. We spent the night at a British army base outside town, where the mess hall served even better Indian food than we had eaten at Camp Knox.

After supper we were invited to a play that the British garrison put on, a comedy of manners that I thoroughly enjoyed, not just for the play itself, but for the experience, sitting in an improvised outdoor theater in the highlands of northeastern India, the mountains of Burma just to our south and the even higher peaks of the Himalayas in easternmost Tibet less than a hundred miles to the north.

I knew that we were in Nagaland, the now-autonomous tribal region between Assam and the northern tip of Burma. I remembered having read an article about the Nagas in *National Geographic,* to which my aunt Nell gave me a yearly subscription every Christmas. It said that they were headhunters before their general conversion to Christianity in the late nineteenth century. Scores of Nagas had come in from the surrounding villages to watch the play, and they seemed to be enjoying it as much as I was, for although they had not the faintest idea of what the actors were saying the comedy was so broad that they laughed at the same things we did.

After the play was over I lingered in the outdoor theater until it was time to return to the barracks where we were spending the night. By then the moon had risen, still almost full, and in its ashen light, brilliant in the clear air of the Naga highlands, I could see the snow-shrouded

Riverboats at port on the Brahmaputra

peaks of the Himalayas in the eastern tip of Tibet. I had always dreamed of traveling to Tibet, and I was thrilled that I was now at least gazing at its easternmost ramparts, which reminded me of the film *Lost Horizon* with Ronald Colman, which I had seen with Peg at the Colonial Theatre. I would tell her all of this when I got home, whenever that would be, for I was now halfway around the world from Brooklyn, though within sight of a romantic place I had seen in a movie house there.

The transient barracks at the British Army base in Ledo were luxurious, all the more so given the conditions we'd endured over the past two months of constant and grueling travel, which had taken us halfway around the world. All in all, I reckoned that in the past two months I'd traveled about fourteen thousand miles almost without a break.

At the British camp at Ledo we had a delicious curry for evening chow, and afterward we watched the *Road to Morocco,* with Bing Crosby, Bob Hope, and Dorothy Lamour ("We're three happy chappies / with snappy serapes. / Like Webster's dictionary / we're Morocco bound"). It was a ridiculous film, corny beyond belief, but I enjoyed it anyway, as did the tribal people who had made their way in from the surrounding jungle.

I hit the sack, pleasantly exhausted. But I was so wired with excitement that I couldn't get to sleep until the soft mattress and pillow wound me down. I slowly drifted into the twilight zone until I was back home in Brooklyn, talking with Peg in one of our nocturnal dialogues, until her melodious Irish brogue lulled me into the country of dreams.

The next morning, before our convoy started out, I looked at the large-scale map in the British Army administrative building and saw that we were less than a hundred miles from Tibet. The peaks that I'd seen the previous night, and that I now saw again in the pellucid light of day, were those of Mount Yulong, Jade Dragon Snow Mountain, 18,360 feet high, about halfway between Ledo and the eastern tip of Tibet. A British lieutenant told me that the highest of its thirteen peaks—Shanzidou—was just nine miles north of Lijiang, an old town in southwestern China.

The lieutenant went on to say that the indigenous people in Yunnan and Sichuan provinces were not Han Chinese, but were from one or another of a score of minorities, most of them Tibetan in origin because this borderland region was historically part of Tibet. The most interesting of these were the Naxi and the Mosuo. The Naxi predominated in Lijiang and the Mosuo in Lake Lugu on the Yunnan-Sichuan border.

The Mosuo refer to this lost Eden as the "Kingdom of Women," because women dominate their society in both peace and war. A new world opened for me in this remote Shangri-la, where in the days that followed, after we crossed the border into China, I would come upon some of these tribes living in the shadow of Jade Dragon Snow Mountain.

Soon we left Ledo for Margherita. Ledo was the Indian town for which the Ledo-Stilwell Road was named. "Stilwell" had recently been added to the name to honor General Joseph Stilwell, better known as "Vinegar Joe," who had been commander of the China-Burma-India theater until he was removed at the insistence of Chiang Kai-shek, whom he referred to contemptuously as "Peanut Brain."

Ledo was only ten miles or so from Margherita, so we arrived there before noon and parked our trucks at the U.S. Army Transportation Corps base that served as the headquarters for the maintenance and repair of the Ledo-Stilwell Road. We were told that each day's drive would end at a U.S. Army bivouac station. Gasoline and oil for the vehicles were available at a POL (petroleum, oils, and lubricants) station near each bivouac location. If any of our trucks broke down along the way we were to stand by and wait for one of our emergency vehicles, which would tow us to the next POL station.

Most of the American soldiers at the base were with the various engineering and supply units that repaired the Ledo-Stilwell Road and handled the supplies on the truck convoys, and I could see that about half of them were black. I spoke to a black sergeant—"Sarge"—who happened to be from Brooklyn, as I could tell from his accent. He told me that he and most of the other GIs at the base, black and white, had been in Burma since 1942, with no home leave: "Ain't gone nowhere, ain't done nothin', nothin' but sit on my ass here in this motherfuckin' jungle."

When we went to the mess hall, Sarge pointed out a large group of white soldiers eating by themselves. They were the survivors of Merrill's Marauders, the U.S. infantry unit that had borne the brunt of the fighting in Burma since February 1944 and had opened up the Ledo-Stilwell Road by pushing back the Japanese. They looked as if they had been to hell and back, and they ate in silence and left without speaking to anyone else in the mess hall.

After we left the mess I joined Sarge in his tent, where other black soldiers in his outfit were drinking and gambling. Among them were a number of much smaller dark-skinned soldiers who at first I thought were Puerto Ricans, but they were speaking a language that I'd never heard before, along with some pidgin English. Sarge explained that they were Kachins, indigenous tribal people of northern Burma, who had been serving as scouts for the U.S. Army. They were highly effective soldiers, he said, though it had proved impossible to break them of their habit of cutting off the ears of their Japanese victims, which they kept in bamboo tubes attached to their waists. At that he spoke to one of the Kachins, who took the bamboo tube at his waist and pulled out the stopper, after which he turned it upside down and dumped a pile of blackened objects on the ground. Sarge laughed, saying, "Divide those by two and you'll know how many Japs he's killed."

I accompanied Sarge to the stockade, where he went to visit a buddy of his who had just come back to the camp after having been AWOL for several weeks. His friend had "gone native," attracted by the bare-breasted Naga women he had seen in a tribal settlement in Assam. He had apparently lived like a king in the settlement, for when he returned to the camp he was wearing a chieftain's headdress, accompanied by several Naga warriors armed with large knives, with two bare-breasted women following behind him. Sarge shook his head. "Poor motherfucker, he'll do serious time in the slammer. Ain't no ass nowhere worth that, no way."

Later in the afternoon I took a walk around the camp and met someone from my old neighborhood in Brooklyn. It was John Crowley, the older brother of Steve Crowley, a classmate of mine at Fourteen Holy Martyrs. I recognized him at once even though I'd not seen him since the war began, for all the Crowleys, boys and girls, were very good-looking in the black Irish way, with raven hair, aquiline noses, and aquamarine eyes. He seemed much tougher and more serious than I remembered him, but he lit up in a big smile when he spotted me.

"Freely, what in God's name are you doing here? I thought you were in the Navy."

"I am in the Navy, but I'm serving in a commando unit called SACO."

"Yeah, I've heard of your outfit. Tons of ammo and supplies have come through here in trucks marked 'SACO,' including some of the stuff I've got stashed away in my tent."

He invited me into his tent, which was lined with cases of canned beer he'd diverted to his own use from the supplies shipped over the

Ledo-Stilwell Road. We sat around for an hour drinking beer and talking about our old neighborhood. He hadn't been home in three years, and I gave him what news I had of our local characters, particularly my uncle Tom, who was one of his father's drinking pals. I reminded him that they both moonlighted as roofers and housepainters, and he laughed at the memory.

"I remember the pair of them sitting up on a roof one night, with two pots of paint and a big pot of beer between them. It's a wonder they weren't killed."

We laughed as we downed our beer, the first I'd ever had, since the legal drinking age in the United States was twenty-one, as were the rights to drive and to vote, though it was legal to volunteer for the Navy at seventeen and go off to war, as I had done, and now here I was in the CBI, ready to fight Japanese I'd never met.

John told me he'd been here with an Army supply unit since the beginning of work on the Ledo-Stilwell Road. He agreed with Sarge that life in Ledo was a form of Limbo, with nothing to do except think about home. He and Sarge were good friends here in Burma, but back in Brooklyn they couldn't live in the same neighborhood, eat in the same restaurant, or drink in the same bar.

I had noticed recently that whenever I met someone from Brooklyn, and the longer I had been away and the farther I got from the United States, memories of home arose in me unbidden. Meeting John and drinking with him and Sarge caused me to remember Boyle Brothers, on Halsey Street, across the street from the Broadway Arena, where I had gone with my father and my uncle Tom to see Irish Pat McCoy fight the black boxer Kid Chocolate, and how no one cheered for the Kid when he knocked out McCoy because there were no blacks in the audience.

And I recalled that the first black people I ever saw were on Halsey Street, all of them waiting for the trolley that would take them to their own neighborhood farther away in the Bedford-Stuyvesant district. The only black kid I knew was Patrick Irish, the tall skinny guy who was my teammate on the JV basketball team at Brooklyn Tech who passed because he had red hair, blue eyes, and freckles. I knew the black ghetto in Bed-Stuy only too well, since I delivered the Brooklyn Eagle *there through a bitterly cold winter, although I hardly ever saw any of my customers, for they didn't answer the bell when I came to collect on Saturday, sticking me with the bill and leaving me nothing to show for three months of hard work.*

John had the usual pinups on the canvas walls of his tent, starring Hedy Lamarr, Betty Grable, and Lana Turner, but directly above his cot there was a photograph of my classmate Albert Kreyl's beautiful older sister. He saw me looking at it, and in answer to my unspoken question he said, "She sent me a Dear John letter after I went off in the Army." And that was it for John's love life these past three years, as he said with a rueful smile.

"I'd go off with one of those bare-breasted Naga dames, but I don't want to end up in the stockade with the Sarge's friend. He'll probably get twenty years in Leavenworth for desertion."

Then he smiled.

"You were sweet on Mary McCabe, weren't you?"

"Kind of. She was very pretty, and also the smartest girl in the class."

"Did you ever go out with her?"

"Just the once, when we graduated from Fourteen Holy Martyrs. A bunch of us went out on a quadruple date. We ate chop suey at a Chinese restaurant and then went to hear Frank Sinatra at the RKO Paramount. Nothing happened. We were both so shy we never even held hands."

He laughed.

"Has she sent you a Dear John?"

"No need to. I never saw her again after that evening. Anyway, we've been on the move since early June and our mail hasn't caught up with us yet."

"I get mail every few months, and only from my mother. She's very worried about Steve. He's on a destroyer in the Pacific and she hasn't heard from him for a long while."

We sat in silence, wrapped in thoughts of Brooklyn, until he spoke again.

"Be careful, John, the road is very dangerous."

"So I've heard."

"One of the worst spots is just a couple of hours' drive from here, at Pangsau Pass. Be very careful when you drive over the pass; a lot of GIs have been killed there."

I hesitated for a moment before I spoke.

"I don't know how to drive. My buddy Ed Hill will be driving, and I'm riding shotgun."

He laughed.

"Jesus, Mary, and Joseph! Then in that case say a couple of Hail Marys."

We laughed and then bade each other goodbye, saying we'd meet again after the war, God willing. But the war might go on forever, the way it had been going, since 1941 in the United States, 1939 in Europe, and 1937 in China, where we might still be fighting the Japanese on Judgment Day, both good guys and bad guys entering the next world together, them to hell and us to heaven, with a brief stop in purgatory to lick our wounds.

Later I took a look inside the headquarters building. There was a small lending library, though it was of no use to me since I would be moving on the following day. But there was a free twenty-page booklet entitled *Stilwell Road: Story of the Ledo Lifeline,* a veritable gift from heaven, as I learned when I began to read it.

This booklet has been provided to give you some worthwhile information about the places to be seen along the great military supply line, about the customs and religions of the people who inhabit this remote corner of the world. You will see a strange mixture of people as your convoy winds its way toward Kunming, passing through regions which few Americans have ever been privileged to enter.

Outstanding among the tribes to be seen in the Ledo area are the Nagas, thick-legged muscular aborigines who abound in the jungle hills. These scantily-clad, primitive people bob along in a dog trot, carrying a dau, a square-blade knife slung across their middle. Headhunters only a generation or two ago, even today they engage in tribal wars and hang skulls of their victims in their native dwellings. They are extremely friendly to Americans, however, and have proved invaluable in helping rescue pilots and soldiers lost in the dense thickets.

Farther on you will see the Kachins, fierce tribal residents of northern Burma. The Kachins resemble the Nagas, but have finer features, and like them, live in bustees, bamboo huts built on stilts.

They carry the long-bladed daub and both men and women wear the bustee, a skirt-like attire which falls to the ankles. Kachins have served with our forces as scouts. Enjoying a reputation as ferocious fighters, they resisted all Japanese attempts to bring them into the fold.

The Nagas and Kachins are native worshippers known as animists. Their primitive state is reflected in their religious worship, hence you will see no temples in the Patkai Hills or Upper Burma. The Kachins believe they are plagued with a variety of devils, and villages have weird looking gadgets on top of thatched shrines as a tribute to things of nature.

On the back wall there was a large map of the China-Burma-India theater, similar to the one I'd seen at Camp Knox, with the course of the Ledo-Stilwell Road marked in red. But this map was on a larger scale, focused on Assam, northern Burma, southwestern China, and the eastern tip of Tibet.

I could follow the route we'd taken over the past several days before we reached Ledo. I traced the course of the Brahmaputra River above where we had left it at Dibrugarh, and I could see the point where it emerged from the Tibetan Plateau just 100 miles to the north of where we had been just two days before. And just 200 to 250 miles east of that I noted where three other great rivers poured down from the eastern tip of Tibet—first the Salween, next the Mekong, and then the Yangtze. We would cross the Salween and the Mekong once we made our way from the Ledo-Stilwell Road in Burma to the old Burma Road in China, and if we continued on from Kunming to SACO headquarters in Chengdu, as scuttlebutt said we might do, then we would cross the Yangtze as well.

This brought to mind an article I'd read in *National Geographic*. As I recalled, the article said that the Brahmaputra, the Salween, the Mekong, and the Yangtze had, since antiquity, been revered by the people of the lands below the Tibetan Plateau as the Rivers of Paradise, because they nurtured life in the lands through which they flowed.

I noticed a cross marked on the map some twenty miles south of Ledo. There was a black staff sergeant sitting at a desk, and I asked him about this. He said there was a big military cemetery for all the Allied soldiers

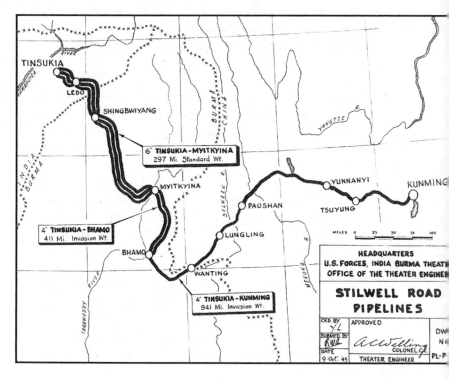

Ledo-Stilwell Road map

who had been killed on the Ledo-Stilwell Road: Americans, Brits, Indians, Kachins, and Chinese.

"There's about a thousand marked graves, mostly GIs and Limeys."

"And the others?"

"They're all buried in a mass grave. Nobody even knows or cares who the poor fuckers were. They're just dead soldiers. Dead's dead."

Our convoy passed the cemetery an hour or so later. It was just to the left of the road, the white grave markers arrayed in five lines of a couple of hundred each. There was a huge earthen mound in the dead center of the burial ground, and, so far as I could see, there was no marker on it. Even as a gravedigger's son I was saddened. Dead's dead, and there is no redemption.

We'd been told that each day's drive along the Ledo-Stilwell Road would end at a bivouac station—unless it didn't, which was almost always. There were shower and latrine facilities at the bivouac stations, but in most places each convoy had to feed itself on K rations. Each of us had an aluminum mess kit, comprising a plate, knife, and spoon, along with a kidney-shaped canteen. We each carried a canvas shelter half, which two men could put together to form a pup tent in case we were benighted between bivouac stations, which happened more often than not. The shelter half doubled as a poncho we could use to keep off the rain, since the truck cabs were not waterproofed. Our helmet was fitted with a plastic liner with canvas suspension and chin-straps. The helmet could also serve as a seat, washbasin, pillow, or all-purpose pot, which we filled with water to dissolve or cook the various components of our K rations: compressed beef and pork loaf, processed American cheese, powdered lemonade, bouillon tablets, instant coffee, sugar cubes, dried milk, and a compressed chocolate bar. The pack also contained a small package of toilet paper, a pack of matches, halazone tablets to further purify our chlorinated drinking water, and two packages of eight cracker biscuits each. I gave the four-pack of cigarettes included in each K ration to Ron Fuller, and the five sticks of chewing gum to the naked children who thronged around our trucks. They were so hungry that they ate the gum after they chewed it dry, so I gave them the extra K rations we were carrying as cargo, along with the compressed chocolate bars and our pilfered quart cans of grapefruit juice and fruit cocktail

K rations came in a waterproof waxed-cardboard carton, which I opened with my combat knife. Ed and I used the cardboard to start a little campfire on the rare evenings when the monsoon rain was not bucketing down. Otherwise we ate our rations in the truck, wrapped in our ponchos and wearing our helmets and helmet liners to keep off the rain.

When the rain stopped, clouds of mosquitoes swooped in, making their final attack like kamikazes, their engines whining as they dove in for a bite before I splattered them in a small pool of blood. I was forced to put on my mosquito netting, which fastened to the rim of my helmet liner and tied tightly around my throat. But the mosquitoes got in anyway and were dive-bombing my face as well as my neck, wrists, and ankles, some even biting my bollocks, as I slapped and scratched everything from my face to my no-longer-so-private parts. Ed was in an even worse fix than I was, since he was wedged tightly behind the steering wheel and gear shift. The two of us thrashed around in the cramped cab of the truck, soaked to the marrow and sweating like bulls.

Suddenly, the squadrons of mosquitoes abated and a veritable Niagara engulfed us, turning the cab into a shower stall. Ed was by nature phlegmatic, but when the monsoon let up and a second wave of dive-bombers whined in, he groaned and shouted into the night, "What the fuck are we doing here, anyway?" There was no answer.

When the monsoon finally slowed we tried to sleep in the truck, encumbered by our helmets, field packs, seabags, duffle bags, and mess gear. We also had our weapons and ammunition, which we cradled under our ponchos lest the rain render them inoperable. I prayed for the long night to end, although it would just mean another grueling and bone-jarring day on the road.

Before we started out, our pharmacist's mates drove along the length of the convoy to give each of us our daily tablet of atabrine, the antimalarial drug that gave us a jaundiced yellow appearance—which, as my pal Ron Fuller said, "made me look like a Chinese laundryman." Japanese propaganda had it that atabrine made you impotent, but my friend Pete Echeverry said, "Ain't nothin' wrong with mah pecker!" But, to tell the truth, the misery of our daily and nightly life lowered our libido, except for Pete, who advised everyone to "keep yer fuckin' pecker up!"

We were vaccinated against every tropical disease known to medicine; nevertheless, GIs serving in Burma were stricken by bush typhus, dengue ("breakbone fever"), amoebic dysentery, and other diseases and disorders, including pellagra, beriberi, and fungal infections, particularly the two we called "rotten crotch" and "jungle rot." I'd had a deep tan from our commando training in Florida and exposure to the equatorial sun in the Pacific and Indian oceans, but weeks in the overarching jungle of Burma and the coolness of the mile-high Yunnan Plateau had left my skin a dead white, along with a yellow pallor from the atabrine. All of this had ended any romantic notions I'd had of being on an odyssey, but even the misery didn't dispel the feeling that I was off on a great adventure—although that too would vanish when I smelled the sickening stench of death on the road to Mongyu.

Our first day's journey would take us across the border into Burma as far as Shingbwiyang, a drive of 103 miles that would probably be the most difficult of the whole route, because this stretch had been washed away by the monsoon and had only been hastily repaired over the past few days.

We formed our convoy and started off, just as the rain started to pour down. The road was soon flooded and churned up into mud by the first trucks in the convoy, so those of us farther back had heavy going. Ed was having great difficulty shifting gears and double-clutching as we continually stopped and started and several times almost slid off the road over the steep precipice beside it. I took over the steering for a while so that Ed could concentrate on the gears, and just as we did this the road descended in a steep grade and we hurtled down to a narrow bridge at a river crossing. Two Indian army soldiers were standing guard at the bridge, but when they saw us speeding down the road with me steering from the wrong side of the cab they fled for their lives.

I continued steering for a while after we crossed the bridge, but when Ed got the hang of the gears he took over the wheel again and we proceeded in a more normal fashion. But we kept getting stuck in the mud, as did every other truck and jeep in the convoy. We were told to put chains on our tires for better traction, and that helped for a while, but as the rain increased in intensity the mud deepened and we proceeded in fit and starts, with the emergency vehicles shuttling back and forth to pull out trucks that were stuck in the mire, some of them in danger of toppling into the deep canyon below. At times we seemed to be hovering on the brink of the abyss, and I held my breath in sheer terror until

Ed managed to get us fully back on the road, his face white and drawn with fear.

I was able to follow our slow progress by the mileposts the Army engineers had erected along the way. At mile 29 we crossed from India into Burma, where a sign informed us that we were passing Hellgate, the convoy control station at the beginning of the Ledo-Stilwell Road. The gate was well named, and the black GI who waved us through laughed and said, with a Georgia drawl, "Good luck, guys, you sure gonna need it!"

The rain stopped and the sun emerged, so that we could view the scenery along the first stretch of the road. I knew from the map in Ledo that the heights ahead were part of the Patkai Mountain Range, which here formed the border between India and Burma, with peaks up to nine thousand feet high, covered with deep jungle all the way up.

At mile 33 the road started steeply upward in a succession of hairpin turns, and for the next five miles we made our way around one bend after another, sometimes stalling in the mud and waiting until we were pulled out by an emergency vehicle, at other times coming close to tumbling off the sheer side of the mountain where the road had been washed away by the rain.

We finally went over the Pangsau Pass, 4,500 feet above sea level, as indicated by a roadside sign put up by the U.S. Army engineers. This was the border between India and Burma, and we meandered down eight miles of steep, undulating road, the turquoise waters of the Forbidden Lake glittering to the south.

During the war this came to be called the Lake of No Return, because of the large number of Allied airmen who had disappeared into its mirroring turquoise waters. I presumed that the pilots had tried to make a soft landing there after being damaged by Japanese fighter planes or antiaircraft fire. None of them has ever been found, and they rest peacefully at the bottom of the lake, dreaming deep in the well of memory.

Ahead of us I could see what I recognized from the map in Ledo to be the Huang Valley, shrouded by a curtain of heavy clouds that brought more rain down upon us. It was almost dark by the time we reached the village of Namyang, where we started the steep descent into the valley, crossing streams on Bailey bridges and passing the burned-out and bullet-riddled wrecks of Allied trucks and jeeps and small Japanese tanks, relics of the battle that had raged along this route during the past eighteen months, taking the lives of more than sixty thousand Chinese and Japanese soldiers.

At mile 79 we reached the summit of Tagap Hill, the farthest point of the Japanese advance into northern Burma. In March 1943, a large Japanese patrol reached the Kachin village at Tagap, but they were forced to turn back when their native porters and elephant handlers deserted, leaving them utterly alone in the impenetrable highland jungle.

It was past midnight when we reached Shinbwiyang, a large Kachin village that in times past was connected with the outside world by trails that were passable only during the dry season; it was drenched with continuous rain during the monsoon, when it endured seasonal rainfalls exceeding two hundred inches, five times greater than New York's precipitation. And here we were at the height of the monsoon, with the road virtually invisible in the rain.

At the bivouac station outside Schinbwiyang, we found two other convoys backed up because the road ahead was washed out. We had to camp in the field behind the barracks, using our entrenching tools to dig a temporary toilet—known as a slit trench—which we filled in after we used it. I tried to defecate, but failed, for I was completely blocked up by the hard American cheese of our K rations and the other rocklike jawbreakers I'd been eating on the road. A blood-sucking leech attached itself to my right leg while I was squatting over the trench, and I had to scrape it off with my combat knife, which gave me the shudders and left a welt that oozed blood for hours afterward.

The liquid mud came pouring through our two-man pup tent, so Ed and I abandoned the tent and went back to our truck, where we broke out our K rations, wearing our helmets and wrapped in our ponchos to keep off the rain that leaked through the roof of the cab. I'd never spent a more miserable night in my life, and I wondered what in God's name I was doing here, when I could be sunning myself on the beach at Rockaway. And this was just the beginning of what promised to be a journey through hell.

The next day we set off after the two convoys ahead of us had left, heading southeast across the Huang Valley in a driving rain. About noon we crossed the Chindwin River on a Bailey bridge, passing the wrecked Allied and Japanese vehicles that had been bulldozed out of the way to clear the road.

As the afternoon wore on we crossed a series of tributaries of the Chindwin on Bailey bridges, all of which were flanked by the shot-up wrecks of trucks, jeeps, armored vehicles, and tanks. Then the convoy stopped when we came upon a detachment of U.S. Army engineers who were repairing a stretch of road that they had reopened only that morning, but that had been chewed up again by the two convoys ahead of us. After conferring with the engineers, Commander Boots passed the word that we would once again spend the night in our trucks.

The rain had let up, so I went foraging for food in a small settlement of beehive-shaped huts that I could see on the hillside above the road, hoping to buy some eggs to supplement our K rations. The settlement appeared to be empty, and when I peered into one of the huts I saw that its only furnishings were half a dozen straw mats with bedding rolls raised up on low bamboo bed frames. I was so exhausted that I was tempted to lie down on one of the beds, but at that moment I heard the tinkle of bells. I looked out and saw a group of people I recognized as Kachins emerging from the jungle and heading for the settlement. They were naked except for loincloths, and the men were carrying spears and bows as well as primitive tools, the younger women bearing infants slung on their backs. As they came closer I could see that some of them, particularly the older ones, had withered limbs and patches of piebald skin. They were wearing bells, just like the lepers I'd seen in Calcutta, the tinkling meant to warn others to keep away from those suffering from this most dreaded of all diseases. I realized that I'd come upon a leper colony, and I left as quickly as I could, warning others from my outfit who were heading toward the settlement to stay away, feeling ashamed as I did so.

At mile 178 we drove over the Jambu Pass, where in March 1944 American and Chinese infantry had defeated the Japanese in a fierce weeklong battle that turned the tide in the northern Burma campaign. The battlefield was still littered with artillery shell casings, and I gathered that thousands of dead Chinese and Japanese soldiers were buried in shallow graves in the jungle, haunting it.

The next bivouac station, at mile 189, was Warazup, a little Kachin village on the Mogaung River that in March 1944 had been the scene of the biggest tank battle of the war in Burma. As we drove by part of the battlefield, I could see the wreckage of several one-man Japanese tanks,

Trucks held up by the mud along the Ledo-Stilwell Road

along with other bullet-riddled vehicles. Whoever might have been buried here would now have been washed away, since the narrow streams had been turned into violent torrents by the monsoon rains. The entire valley had become one vast swamp, and we were able to drive through it only because the roadway had been built as high as fifteen feet above the floor of the valley.

The next day we reached Myitkyina, where again we had to camp out. At Ledo I'd heard stories about the battle for Myitkyina, which the Allies, including Merrill's Marauders, had captured the previous summer after a particularly bloody seven-week siege. An open field near where we parked our trucks was still littered with shell casings from the battle, along with the burned-out remains of military vehicles, including a small Japanese tank. I climbed up on the tank and looked inside, only to be driven back by the awful stench; although the remains of whoever had been inside had been removed, the unmistakable smell of death remained.

Soon after starting off the next day we crossed the Irrawaddy, the longest and widest river in Burma, on a pontoon bridge. I noticed immediately that the people south of the Irrawaddy were very different in appearance from those we had encountered thus far in northern Burma. The women in particular were quite beautiful, with almond eyes shining from mocha-colored oval faces, all the more attractive with the colorful costumes they wore even when working in their fields. I immediately consulted *Ledo Lifeline* so I could learn about these distinctive people, the Shan.

> Soon after you leave Myitkyina and cross the Irrawaddy, you will enter the Northern Shan States. These people resemble Chinese, simply because they are of Lao-Tai stock, blood brothers of the Siamese and Tai of southern China.

The road then took us south along the Irrawaddy Valley, the landscape to our east dominated by peaks rising to more than eight thousand feet along the mountainous border between Burma and China.

It was dark by the time we reached Bhamo, a once-beautiful old market town and river port on a bend of the Irrawaddy that I'd read about in *National Geographic*. I was curious to learn more about Bhamo, so again I took out my copy of *Ledo Lifeline*. The short description captured the town exactly as I was seeing it, utterly ruined by a war that had been exported from the outside world: "Bhamo was once the third largest city in Burma. Today it is a shambles of demolished pagodas and burned-out buildings sprawled dead and grotesque among groves of teak trees on the Irrawaddy River."

A Buddhist temple in northern Burma

We parked at the bivouac station, where I sought aid at the base clinic for an acute case of hemorrhoids that I'd developed from long days of rough riding in a truck and eating rock-hard K rations. But the only person on duty at the clinic was a medic from the Chinese army who introduced me to his pet monkey, with whom he was sharing a bottle of rice wine. He laughed and offered to carve out my hemorrhoids with a rusty bayonet. I accepted a swig of wine but declined his treatment, which both he and the monkey thought was very funny, so I bade them good evening and left.

The next day I found it too painful to sit in the cab, so I climbed on top of the truck, where I laid on my stomach, lashing myself to the tarpaulin that covered the cargo so I wouldn't fall off. I spent a thoroughly miserable day, feeling every jolt as we drove up into the mountains along the border between Burma and China.

Late in the afternoon, after crossing on a suspension bridge over the Shweli River, a tributary of the Irrawaddy, we reached the ancient town of Namkham, just inside Burma's border with China. Commander Boots decided we would camp there for the night, since there wasn't enough daylight to reach the next bivouac station at Mongyu, and the road ahead was too dangerous to navigate in the dark.

It turned out to be my lucky day, for Namkham had a U.S. Army field hospital that had been set up by Dr. Gordon Seagrave, the famous "Burma Surgeon," an American medical missionary who for years had been treating the Burmese tribal people. Dr. Seagrave had been commissioned as a colonel in the Army when the war began, and had set up field hospitals along the Ledo-Stilwell Road, staffed with the Burmese nurses he had personally trained. He himself wasn't there at the time of our visit, but his nurses took good care of me, giving me salve to relieve the pain of my hemorrhoids and herbal tea to unblock my constipation. The medication worked, and by morning I was able to take my seat in the truck once again.

On our way through Namkham, now shattered by years of war, I saw the famous Buddha of the Golden Eye. The colossal Buddha, his golden eyes shining, was smiling down upon me benevolently. He had a shell hole right through the middle of his chest, indicating that some barbarian gunner—more likely a GI than a Japanese soldier—had taken a potshot at him just for the hell of it.

The next stage of our journey took us from Namkham to Mongyu along the south bank of the Shweli, which here formed the border between Burma and China. Around noon we encountered a Chinese army convoy going the other way. I learned that it was headed for Ledo, carrying casualties from the fighting still going on farther south in Burma. At one point we were stuck next to a truck that gave off an awful stench, and when I got out to check its cargo I found that it was full of dead Chinese soldiers, stacked like sides of beef, with clouds of flies buzzing about them. I backed off with a bad case of the dry heaves, and I staggered down the road until Ed could drive clear and pick me up. I was so shaken by the sight that I began trembling, knowing that a truckload of Chinese boys was going to be dumped in a mass grave in the cemetery outside Ledo. War was indeed hell, and I feared what was to come.

About an hour before sunset we reached Mongyu, a small Shan village at the point where the Ledo-Stilwell Road keyed into the old Burma Road, which led up from Mandalay. This was the focal point of the last great battle of the Burma campaign. After two months of continuous fighting, the battle had finally ended on January 27, 1945, when U.S., British, and Chinese forces forced the Japanese out of Mongyu and the surrounding region between the Shweli and Salween rivers.

This made possible the way from Burma into China, and the following day the first U.S. truck convoy rolled through Mongyu, having come down the Ledo-Stilwell Road from Ledo. It then continued along to the old Burma Road, heading for Kunming, thus opening up an overland route connecting unoccupied China with the sea. I'd seen a photograph of this historic event in the administrative building at Ledo, showing the first truck passing under an archway with two arrows pointing in opposite directions, one with the words BURMA: LEDO ROAD—LEDO 478 MILES, the other reading CHINA: BURMA ROAD—KUNMING 566 MILES. We were almost halfway there, and we'd soon be crossing the border into China. I'd had a bellyful of Burma, but I feared that China might be even worse.

At the U.S. Army camp at Mongyu, we were told that thousands of Japanese soldiers were still holed up in the mountains to the south, where they were probably starving to death, since all of their supply lines were now controlled by the Allies. They were still dangerous, though, for just a couple of days before they had ambushed a Chinese patrol sent south from Mongyu, and some of these casualties were undoubtedly those I'd seen earlier in the day.

We were all assigned watches on the defense perimeter around the camp that night, because Japanese stragglers had been caught as they attempted to sneak into the base under cover of darkness, trying to find food. They were desperate and dangerous, we were warned, and soldiers on sentry duty were ordered to fire without warning at any intruders. Kachin scouts would be interspersed with those of our unit who would be on duty, one of them positioned out of sight between each pair of us.

My watch was from midnight to four in the morning, and I was awakened by the captain of the watch, in this case one of our ensigns. He then woke up my pal Tunney King, and we met the Kachin scout who would be on sentry duty with us. Without speaking, the Kachin led us out into the moonless night to relieve those who were going off their watch.

It was pitch-dark when I got up to go to my sentry post. I was armed with my carbine and .45 pistol, as was Tunney, but the Kachin bore only his lethal-looking dau, which I noticed when he positioned me and Tunney in shallow foxholes. He then crawled out into the jungle somewhere between us. I could see neither him nor Tunney, though I sensed they were not far off to my left.

The only sounds were the startling birdcalls, the rustling of the trees and underbrush when a sudden breeze blew up, and the echoing howl of a lonely jackal from deep in the menacing jungle. I'd never felt so alone and vulnerable, and I worried that any moment someone would spring on me from the surrounding darkness.

Then, about halfway through my watch, I suddenly heard someone screaming in the darkness to my left. The scream continued for a few seconds, ending in a gurgling sound before it stopped abruptly. I was stiff with terror, and I held my rifle on the ready as I stared into the darkness, waiting for someone to emerge. But I saw nothing, and when my relief took over at four o'clock I returned to our tent, where Ed was still sound asleep.

At morning chow I saw Tunney and asked him if he knew what had happened in the middle of our watch, but he said it had been too dark to see anything. He had been too terrified to go and look, just as I'd been. There was no sign of the Kachin scout who had been on sentry duty with us, and so, on reflection, I figured that he had caught a Japanese soldier sneaking into our camp and had cut his throat, in which case he would have now added another pair of severed ears to his collection. I was horrified, though I knew that if the intruder had come at me I'd have had it, and at the mere thought of it I suffered a sudden spasm in my sphincter. Fortunately, I didn't mark my laundry, as GI slang would have it, at a moment of sudden terror, though my sphincter ached for minutes afterward. I realized then that I was a coward.

At morning chow I mentioned the incident to several of my friends, but none of them had heard anything, since they were too exhausted to even dream. Ron Foster had been told by one of our ensigns, who'd seen the corpse, that the Japanese soldier was just an unarmed, emaciated kid. Pete Echeverry laughed. "Who gives a shit? The only fuckin' good Jap's a dead Jap."

I was profoundly shocked, although I'd heard that remark many times. The Japanese were the enemy and we were conditioned to hate them, and as far as we were concerned it was either kill or be killed. I'd always had a reverence for Japanese culture, beginning with the first image of Japan I ever saw, a picture of Mount Fujiyama over the hearth of our cottage in Ireland, next to a holy picture of the Blessed Virgin Mary. The first of the many travel books I'd read was Lafcadio Hearn's Glimpses of Unfamiliar Japan. *And the first opera I'd ever heard was* Madame Butterfly, *which Jean Caputo played for me one afternoon in Brooklyn, translating the Italian into English. I particularly recalled the beginning of act 1, scene 5—"Ancora un passo" ("One step more")—where Cio-Cio San can be heard guiding her friends to the top of the hill, jubilantly telling them, "Over land and sea, there floats the joyful breath of spring. I am the happiest girl in Japan, or rather in the world." And then I heard the awful scream of the boy whose throat was cut in the jungle the previous night, the last sound he made on earth before descending into Yomi-no-kuni, the Land of Darkness, the Japanese Country of Dreams, where he joined the army of the dead who would live forever, eternally young.*

I said nothing about the incident to Ed, because he was struggling to keep our truck from sliding over the precipice immediately to our right.

A couple of hours' drive from Mongyu, we crossed from Burma into China at Wanting, where there was a Chinese army border post. We had to get out of our trucks to have our ID cards and our cargo checked, which seemed to be a ridiculous formality. I handed my ID to an arrogant Chinese army captain, who shouted at me in primitive English to hand over my .45, which he obviously intended to keep for himself. I told him in English to go to hell. I knew he understood me, because he drew his pistol and pointed it at my head. One of our ensigns came along in a jeep at that moment with a Chinese major, who shouted at the captain and made him put his gun away. The ensign told me and Ed to go back to our truck and get going. We did, and as we drove past the captain I had to force myself not to give him the arm gesture that I'd learned from my Italian friends in Brooklyn.

There seemed to be nothing to see, so I took out my copy of *Ledo Lifeline* to find out if I'd missed anything. I learned that this had been the site of the bloodiest battle of the Salween Valley campaign, which in six weeks during the previous year had squandered the lives of seventeen thousand Chinese and fifteen thousand Japanese soldiers, all of them buried in unmarked graves at the border post between Burma and China, soaking the earth in the blood of young men.

A precipitous turn on the old Burma Road

We were now on the old Burma Road, which, even to me, seemed very different from the Ledo-Stilwell Road. Once again I consulted *Ledo Lifeline* to learn about this ancient thoroughfare, which for millennia had been southwest China's only link with the outer world. Its last phase had, beginning in 1920, been constructed by some 100,000 Chinese coolies, whose unmarked graves in their hundreds line the course of the roadway, unremembered.

The Burma Road section of the Stilwell Road has a history all its own. Cutting over the Himalaya Hump, it is the newest of many communications routes developed by the Chinese during the past 4,000 years. The Burma Road started from Kunming in 1920 along the general route of an old, little-used spice, tea, and caravan trail toward Burma. By late 1939 it was opened to Wanting, a Yunnan Province border village, to which place the government of Burma had built arteries to connect with their Irrawaddy River ports of Bhamo and Rangoon and the railhead of Lashio. The course of the road is not new, for Genghis Khan and Marco Polo in the twelfth and thirteenth centuries, respectively, visited places along today's route.

Our route for the rest of that day took us along the south bank of the Shweli River and then beside one of its tributaries, as the road brought us higher and higher and higher into the mountains of Yunnan, the southwesternmost province of China, which in earlier times had been part of Tibet, along with Sichuan Province to its north.

The road was pockmarked with shell holes and flanked by the burned-out and bullet-riddled wrecks of Japanese and Allied vehicles and artillery left over from the battle that had raged down this valley the previous winter. On either side, carved out of the treeless terrain, were myriads of foxholes, trenches, machine-gun emplacements, and bunkers. And above them on the terraced hillsides were the carefully tended graves of what the Chinese call "the summoned dead," marked by funerary urns and incense pots. There was nothing to mark the graves of the young men who were killed in the fighting along this road of death, nothing except mounds of raw earth, covering Chinese and Japanese boys alike, all of them summoned by death before their time.

The villages through which we passed were all in ruins, but life seemed to be going on in them all the same, and in one of them I saw a class of

Chinese students in a partially destroyed school watching as our trucks went by

young children being taught in a schoolroom whose walls and roof had been completely blown away. The children waved to us as we passed, while their teacher, an old man in traditional Mandarin dress with a long and wispy white beard, bowed gravely as he tried to get his students back to their lesson.

We spent the night at the bivouac station just outside Lungling, where I again consulted *Ledo Lifeline,* for it looked like a very interesting old Chinese town.

> Lungling is a walled city on the edge of the Burma Road. The largest populated center on the road west of the Salween River, it served as the principal Jap supply outlet in the Salween country, and was captured by the Chinese in November, 1944, after a six-month battle. (Translation of Lungling: Lung = dragon, Ling = royal tomb.)

I spent an hour or so before evening mess wandering around the town, something I'd been unable to do elsewhere on our journey. I noticed that the people looked very different from the Chinese I'd seen in New York, much taller and with features somewhat resembling those of the Native American chiefs whose pictures I'd collected as a boy in chewing gum packages. I'd been told at Margherita that the people in Yunnan and Sichuan provinces were not Han Chinese, but from one or another of a score of minorities, most of them Tibetan in origin. As I recalled, the most interesting of these were the Bai, Mosuo, and Naxi, all of them matrilineal, where descent is traced through the female line rather than the male. Marriage was unknown in their communities, and women held all the power. I couldn't wait until I told all of this to Peg, for she always said that the world would be a better place if women ruled.

I strolled through the market, where scores of itinerant peddlers—all of them women with big wicker baskets on their backs—were selling fruits and vegetables, which seemed to be in very short supply, for their baskets were virtually empty. I'd heard that famine was rampant in the surrounding countryside, and I presumed that these women were selling produce from their own little farms, though no one seemed to have any money to spend. Several of the women approached me, showing me the few pathetic things they had to sell. I was bewildered, not knowing what to do, for I would gladly have given them all the cash I had on me, which in any event was just the "funny money" we'd been given in Ledo at four hundred yen to the dollar.

Then I was confronted by a young woman with a basket of gnarled yams on her back. She said nothing, but held out two of the earth-encrusted yams for my inspection. I gave her all the money I had in the pockets of my fatigues, and she handed me the yams. We stood there for a moment, the two of us looking at each other across a cultural gulf as wide as the world itself. She was a bit taller than I was, crowned with an enormous nimbus of coarse black hair, her half-closed agate eyes gazing at me, a faint smile on her astonishingly beautiful face, mesmerizing me as if she were the goddess of the moon. Then, without a word, she turned and walked away, leaving me there with the yams, struck through the bones by her beauty. She was my wounded Amazon, sister of the one I'd seen at the Metropolitan Museum, and now she too was gone, except for the lingering memory of her serene beauty.

Nine miles farther along we passed Sungshan (Pine Mountain), the scene of yet another battle in the seeming endless war between China and Japan in this blood-drenched valley of death. Sungshan is a seven-thousand-foot promontory that had been known as the Japanese Gibraltar of the Salween. A Japanese garrison of two thousand had been exterminated here after three months of fighting on the steep slopes of the mountain. The stronghold finally fell on September 7, 1944, when

Chinese engineers set off explosives that blew the top off the mountain and killed a large portion of the Japanese garrison. This was one of the most decisive battles of World War II for China, since it opened up the Burma Road for the Allies. But it was a Pyrrhic victory, taking the lives of some 7,600 Chinese soldiers and 3,000 Japanese, most of the defenders pulverized when their stronghold was blown up, reducing the garrison to the dust from which they emerged, their brief lives now a forgotten dream.

Looking down on the great gorge of the Salween,
one of the Rivers of Paradise

At around noon the next day we came to the great gorge of the Salween, known in Chinese as Nu Jiang, the second of the Rivers of Paradise that we would cross.

We would drive across the river on the Huitong Bridge, the lowest point on the Burma Road, at 2,960 feet above sea level. The original bridge was just a wooden catwalk on which one file of Chinese soldiers could cross at a time. This had been blown up in 1943 by American commandos to stop the Japanese from penetrating farther into Burma, effectively trapping them in the southern portion of the country. The young soldier I'd heard die a few nights ago would have been one of these unfortunate wretches.

It took us about an hour to wind our way down to the river through a succession of hairpin turns. Then, after we reached the approach to the bridge, we and the two convoys ahead of us had to wait while final repairs were made to the suspension bridge, which had been blown up by an American commando during the battle for Mongyu. (Thirty years later, at a party in Athens, I met the commando, a Greek American named Ernie Tzikagos, who told me that he almost lost his sight when the explosives he had placed on the bridge went off prematurely.)

While we waited to cross, the local children crowded around our convoy, trying to trade worthless copper coins for food. I gave one little boy a couple of my K rations and a can of fruit cocktail, and he handed me a large coin in return. I tried to give the coin back to him, but he wouldn't take it, indicating with a wave of his hand that it was worth nothing to him. I scraped the coin clean and found that it was a Sun Yat-sen gold dollar and probably very valuable indeed. I thought to go in search of the boy to return his coin, but at that moment the convoy started up and I had to get back in our truck.

After crossing the bridge it took another hour to wind our way up around the succession of hairpin turns on the other side. When we reached the top I had an eagle's view of the Salween, which, from my memory of the map in Ledo, I knew flowed all the way from Tibet through southwestern China and then Burma before it emptied into the Andaman Sea.

We spent that night and all the next day at the bivouac station at Paoshan, for most of the trucks were in need of repair. While Ed worked on our engine I took the opportunity to explore Paoshan, an old walled town on the southern branch of the Silk Road, which Marco Polo had

The entrance to the bridge across the Salween River, August 1945

passed through on his way to Kublai Khan's summer capital at Xanadu.

Much of the town was in ruins from the fighting that had taken place in opening up the Burma Road this past winter, and I was told by a GI at the base that there was a serious shortage of food because the Japanese had stripped the country bare and the war had disrupted the caravan trade on which this region had depended since the days of Marco Polo and before.

That evening I saw a long line of Chinese waiting outside the mess hall, and when I finished supper I learned that they were to be given what we had left on our trays. Instead of emptying our leftover food into garbage cans in the scullery, we scraped it into bowls and other containers held out by the emaciated Chinese waiting in the line, most of them old people and women with children, the young men having been taken off in Chiang Kai-shek's army. I felt ashamed at having so little on my tray when I scraped it off into a tin can held out by a little girl, so I went through the chow line a second time and gave it all to an old woman, who took it without a word and limped away.

The mess sergeant noticed what I'd done and told me that he tried to feed everyone in the line with the food that was left over, but it was an impossible task, and he was afraid that when the U.S. Army left everyone in this region would starve to death.

I learned from *Ledo Lifeline* that the population of Paoshan in 1942 had been 400,000, but now it was less than half that. On May 4, 1942, the

*Looking down on the Salween River and its bridge
after the crossing*

Japanese army had shelled the city heavily, killing 10,000 townspeople. Some of the shells contained germs causing cholera and bubonic plague. More than 60,000 people in the Paoshan area died of cholera in the weeks after the bombing, and thousands more succumbed to bubonic plague, which was still endemic in the region.

The next morning we started off for Yungpin, a distance of a hundred miles, which we were told would be the most difficult stage of our journey in China, because parts of the road had been washed away by the monsoon and had not yet been fully repaired. About two-thirds of the way there we crossed a pontoon bridge over the Mekong River, which flows down from Tibet through Yunnan Province in China and then through or between Burma, Laos, Thailand, Cambodia, and Vietnam, before emptying into the South China Sea, passing Mandalay on the way.

After we crossed the Mekong, the third of the four Rivers of Paradise, the monsoon set in again and we were struck by a torrential rainstorm, which turned the road into a river of mud and washed even more of it away. By sunset there was no sign of Yungpin, though Commander Boots sent a messenger back from the head of the convoy to inform us that we didn't have far to go. The convoy was now strung out so far that we couldn't see the trucks at either end. With the failing light and torrent of rain our visibility was very limited. Finally word came from the commander that Yungpin was in sight. But by the time we reached the side road that led into the camp we had great difficulty finding our way through the canopy of jungle that surrounded and arched over us.

One of our ensigns was there in a jeep, waving a flashlight to draw our attention. He handed me the light and told me to stand there by the side road to direct the trucks behind us into the camp. I did as I was ordered and Ed drove off behind the ensign into the camp, though after they left I could barely see where the side road led off from the Burma Road.

The trucks behind us came along every minute or so at first, and as they approached I waved my flashlight to direct them into the camp. Then the interval between trucks became longer and longer, as I waited in mud up to my ankles, and although I was wearing my poncho I was as drenched as if I'd been swimming in my clothes. One of the trucks got stuck in the mud as it turned into the side road, though the driver did manage to maneuver it so it wasn't blocking the way. The driver and his buddy decided to abandon the truck for the time being and walk on into the camp, locking the cab because they had stowed their weapons there.

I was already so drenched that it hardly mattered, but I thought that I'd take cover under the truck, where I would at least be out of the rain. I crawled under the tailgate and wrapped myself up in my poncho, emerging whenever I heard the roar of an approaching truck so I could wave my flashlight to direct the driver onto the camp road.

The ensign who had given me the flashlight eventually returned in his jeep and told me that there were still trucks stuck out on the road. An emergency vehicle would try to get them started, but he thought that some of them might be stuck out there for the night, though they would try to bring the men into the camp. He told me to stay at my post until told otherwise, and he would try to find someone to relieve me so I could get some chow before the mess hall closed.

About an hour later a truck appeared, and I directed it into the camp road. The driver and his buddy told me they didn't think any more trucks would make it that night, for even our emergency vehicles were now stuck in the mud, and they offered to give me a lift into the camp. But I told them that I'd been ordered to stay at my post until relieved, so I crawled back under the truck, where I wrapped myself in my poncho and resumed my vigil.

I'm sure no other trucks arrived during the night, for although I dozed off I would have been awakened by the roar of their engines. When I did wake up I could see from under the truck that the sun was shining, though the road was still a morass of liquid mud. Then I became aware that someone standing behind the truck was nudging me with his boot, and I crawled out to find a tall black American soldier standing over me, his stripes and insignia identifying him as a top sergeant in the Army engineers. He had a big smile on his face as he looked down and helped me to my feet.

"Wake up, soldier," he said, "the fucking war's over!"

He told me that the U.S. Army news broadcast on the previous night had announced that the Japanese government had surrendered unconditionally earlier that day, August 15, 1945. We'd been out of touch with the rest of the world since we left Ledo, and once again I'd lost track of the days—this time on dry land rather than at sea—so I knew nothing of the events that had led up to this astounding news. The war had become a way of life, always in the background of my thoughts since my early teens. And now it was over! I felt as if the curtain had been brought down before the drama ended.

On the way into the camp, the sergeant told me that on August 6 the United States had dropped a powerful new weapon called an atom bomb on the Japanese city of Hiroshima, obliterating its center and killing a large part of its populace. Three days later, he said, an even more powerful atom bomb had destroyed Nagasaki and incinerated everyone in the city center. President Truman had demanded that the Japanese surrender unconditionally, and they had announced their submission on August 15, with the details of the formal end of hostilities to be worked out in the coming days.

I was stunned, for nothing in my past experience had prepared me for this incredible news, which seemed to mean that the war had suddenly come to an end, just as my great adventure was beginning. But by now the death and destruction and near starvation I'd seen during the past weeks, along with the unrelieved misery of our way of life, day and night, had eroded the notion that my journey was an adventure. I was deeply confused.

I remembered all of us sitting in the living room on Sunday, December 7, 1941, when we heard the news that Pearl Harbor had been bombed, on what Present Roosevelt called "a date which will live in infamy." I had followed the progress of the U.S. forces in Europe, North Africa, the Pacific, and the Far East, hoping that I could enlist in the Navy as soon as possible, never dreaming that I would end up in China, hundreds of miles from the sea, thinking the war would never end. And now it had ended, abruptly. I didn't know what to think.

I thought again of Cio-Cio San jubilantly telling her friend, "I am the happiest girl in Japan, or rather in the world." And then I heard the death cry of the boy whose throat was cut at Mongyu. It was all over, except for the awful memories.

The sergeant said that the whole base was whooping it up, and he invited me to join him and his pals in their barracks. They'd collected enough booze to get them through the war, and they sure weren't going to leave any behind. I thanked him for the invite, but I said that I had to check in with my outfit and have some chow, since I hadn't eaten anything since the morning of the previous day.

He pointed out the mess hall, and as I started in that direction I passed a barracks where some white GIs were having a party. One of them saw me and said, "Hey, take a look at that fucking sad sack!," drawing a big laugh at my expense, for I must have looked like a drowned rat that had been dragged through the mud.

I made my way to the mess hall, where I joined Ed and the rest of our outfit for breakfast, the first real food we'd eaten since leaving Ledo. We mustered after we left the mess, and Commander Boots told us that we would be staying in Yungpin for the rest of the day and our convoy would resume its journey the next morning. Although the government of Japan had agreed to surrender, the war was still going on, he said. The Japanese troops in the field were still a threat, and although their army had been defeated in the battle for Mongyu, there were thousands of them in the highland jungles around us who had not given up. We'd have to be on our guard at night because they were desperate for food, as I knew from my experience at Mongyu.

Ed led me to our barracks, where I showered off the mud that had caked all over my body. I was also covered with leeches from sleeping on the ground, and I had to peel them off one by one, each of them leaving a bloody welt on my skin. My "rotten crotch" was quite painful in the hot shower, the first one I'd had since we left Calcutta. I washed my only set of skivvies in the shower, for I'd ditched the rest of my underwear and my only pair of socks because they were in such foul condition. I sat outside, naked, waiting for my skivvies to dry, but there was no sun and I had to wear them still wet, putting on my mud-encrusted combat boots with exquisite care so as not to further aggravate the painful jungle rot on my ankles. Then the sun emerged from within the clouds long enough to buoy up my spirits. I was happy to be alive.

We joined a big party that was going on in the base headquarters, where everyone I spoke to, most of them black, told me that they had been in the CBI for three years or more without leave, and all they could talk about was going home. Everyone got very drunk, including the pet monkey that had become the base mascot—the second drunk monkey I'd seen in recent days. I wondered how these poor creatures would adjust to life in the jungle when the GIs left. I also wondered how the GIs themselves would adjust to normal life after years of war, death, and destruction. Most of them had left behind wives and children, as well as grandparents who had died since they left, and infant sons and daughters they knew only from the photographs they showed me.

The guys in my own outfit were much younger, virtually all of them in their late teens or early twenties. A few of them were married, and most of the rest were engaged or going steady. Pete Echeverry had been run out of his hometown by the sheriff, "just cause ah was shackin' up with his wife. Gotta find another place to live when ah go home!"

Ed Hill was a very private person, and although we'd endured a month together in our truck I knew virtually nothing about him, other than that he was a very nice guy. Now, after he'd downed a few swigs of rye whiskey, he loosened up a bit and showed me a photo of a quite beautiful girl with long auburn hair. He said nothing, and then put the picture back in his wallet.

I didn't have a wallet, nor did I have a photograph of anyone, not even Peg. But all of this had stirred the well of memory, as the Irish say, bringing to its surface a succession of almost forgotten images, some of them of them happy, others painful.

I was back in Brooklyn, in the playground at PS 96, around the corner from Fourteen Holy Martyrs. I'd been playing basketball with my friends, and I was taking a break, sitting with my back up against the chain-link fence. I'd just gotten a crew cut at Louie's barbershop. He charged me only a dime, which was all the money I had, and my head felt cold in the spring breeze. Marie Nolan was standing behind me, watching the game. She'd watched me play touch football and stickball and roller skate hockey. She never said anything, but she smiled whenever I gave her a glance. She was only fifteen, two years younger than I was. She was small even for her age, but very pretty, with a big mop of curly blond hair, and she always wore a black corduroy jacket that had been handed down from her older brother. She put her hand through a gap in the fence and ran her fingers through my blond stubble. Ed Kettle saw this and laughed. "How could anyone love a head like that?" I blushed, and Marie did too. Then I said to her, "Would you go to the movies with me on Friday night?" She smiled and nodded her head, and I said, "See you at seven." She smiled again.

During the week I earned a couple of dollars scavenging with Jimmy Anderson, and I borrowed John Mione's sport coat. Marie's father worked with my father in the Evergreens Cemetery, so he'd given permission for her to go out with me. It was her first date, and mine too, not counting Mary McCabe.

It was a beautiful spring evening and the few trees in Brooklyn were beginning to green, perfuming the night air. I took Marie by the hand as we crossed Bushwick Avenue even though there wasn't a car in sight. We walked to the RKO Gates, on Broadway and Gates Avenue. The film was The White Cliffs of Dover, *starring Irene Dunne and Alan Marshal, with Elizabeth Taylor in a supporting role. There was a long line for tickets, but one of my pals worked there and let us jump the queue. The minimum age for evening admission was eighteen, and minors were allowed in only with an adult. But I was tall for my age and passed, even with my crew cut, and I pretended that Marie was my kid sister, though we didn't look at all alike. The woman selling the tickets looked me over very suspiciously, but she finally let us through. Marie and I tried to make ourselves invisible while everyone milled around in the lobby, and then we did the same when we went in to see the film, finding two seats in the middle of the theater where we wouldn't be noticed. The newsreel had already started, and we saw British Lancaster bombers blowing Nuremburg to bits. Then, after a* Tom and Jerry *cartoon,* The White Cliffs of Dover *began.*

It was a romantic tearjerker, and many of the women in the audience were dabbing at their eyes. I heard Marie sniffling too, so I put my arm around her and drew her close. She rested her head on my shoulder and I held her tightly by the hand. I was suffused with happiness, and I paid no attention to what was happening on the screen, for Marie and I were engaged in our own romance, and I wondered if she felt the same way that I did. She looked up at me and smiled.

I didn't see Marie again until late September, at the end of my first home leave in the Navy. My leave was coming to an end, and I was walking back along Wilson Avenue toward the subway station. As I passed Decatur Street I saw Marie standing there wearing her brother's black corduroy jacket, an early-autumn breeze ruffling her mop of blond hair, her eyes what the Irish call "a most unholy blue." She'd heard I was home, she said, and I told her that I'd spent the whole week with my family, which was true, and neither of our families had a telephone—nor did anyone else we knew—so I had never gotten in touch with her. But there was no need to, knowing each other as we did. So I just took her by the hand and we walked together to the Wilson Avenue subway and said goodbye.

And that was the last I ever saw of Marie, for when I came home again in late spring, just before going overseas, I was told that the Nolans had moved to Long Island, and no one knew their address. Marie slowly sank into the well of memory, the deepest of wells, only coming to the surface here in the black night of southwest China.

I was back in the barracks at Yungpin. The party was over, for everyone was dead drunk or sound asleep or both. I left the barracks for a few minutes to catch some fresh air, but it was damp and humid and smelled of rotting vegetation. The only sounds were the occasional howls of jackals and the rustling of the trees and brush in the surrounding jungle when a slight breeze blew up. Then I heard the Japanese boy screaming and I fled inside, stuffing the pillow over my head to shut out the awful sound. The screaming stopped and I just lay on my cot trembling before I fell asleep and escaped my memories for a few hours.

We started off at the crack of dawn the next day, for we'd been told that there was a very long and dangerous stretch ahead of us. We would drive 121 miles to Yunnanyi, which would take us over the Quingshuillang Mountains, whose highest peaks rose to nearly nine thousand feet. By noon we were high in the mountains, snaking from one vertiginous ridge to another, with the edges of the road partially washed away by the monsoon in many places. We were making our way cautiously along the side of a steep canyon when the truck in front of us stopped so suddenly that we almost ran into it. I jumped out to see what had happened, and I saw that the second truck in front of us had skidded off the road and rolled down several hundred feet into the canyon, where it had tumbled onto its side, wheels still spinning.

I climbed down to the wreck with about a dozen others and we found the driver unconscious behind the wheel, while the other man in the truck, who'd been thrown clear, was conscious, bleeding profusely from a gash in his forehead. I recognized the driver as Coxswain John Jacob Esau, and the other man as Ensign Dawson.

We were soon joined by others from the convoy, including the two pharmacist's mates, one of whom looked after Esau and the other Dawson. They strapped Esau in a stretcher tied to the cable of our emergency vehicle, which then winched it up to the road as we lifted it along the way. Dawson was brought up the same way, and then when they were both laid out in an ambulance it set off toward Yunnanyi, where there was a small field hospital.

When we arrived in Yunnanyi, we were told that Esau and Dawson had been sent off to Kunming in a regular ambulance with a doctor and a nurse in attendance. Dawson was stable but Esau had a fractured pelvis along with internal injuries and was in critical condition, and was being taken to the U.S. Army base hospital in Kunming.

The next day we started out for Tsuyung, the penultimate stage of our journey, a drive of eighty-three miles that brought us up onto the mile-high Yunnan Plateau, the easternmost extension of the great Tibetan Plateau. Tsuyung, at the southern tip of Lake Erhai, is the "New City" of the beautiful medieval town of Dali, which I'd read about in *National Geographic,* and which I could now see on the western shore of the lake directly under the majestic Cangshan Mountains, their peaks rising to nearly thirteen thousand feet. I figured we were only some two hundred miles from the snow-plumed peaks at the eastern tip of Tibet, which I'd seen from Assam and could now see again from China since our route had taken us halfway around the eastern approaches of the Roof of the World.

Here again, as in the other towns we'd passed along the Burma Road, the locals looked very different from the Chinese I knew in New York, and I was sure that most of them were from the Bai, Mosuo, and Naxi tribes. I could see a range of enormous snow-shrouded peaks to the north, which I recognized as Jade Dragon Snow Mountain, to the north of Lijiang, the regional capital, inhabited almost entirely by Naxi. Farther north, around Lake Lugu on the great bend of the Yangtze, was the home of the Mosuo, who called their domain the Kingdom of Women.

I wandered around the marketplace, which seemed to be run entirely by big strapping women with moonlike faces, regal in their bearing, though lacking the surpassing beauty of my Lost Amazon. I spoke to them in my smattering of Chinese, but they didn't seem to understand a word I was saying. I managed to buy a couple of eggs from one of them, and that evening I boiled them in my helmet over a fire that Ed had lit outside our pup tent.

At Tsuyung the Burma Road was joined by two other roads, one from the north and the other from the south. The road from the north was the old caravan trail from Tibet, while the other was the continuation of this route down to southern Yunnan and Burma. We were told that the Chinese divisions that had been fighting in southern Burma were now being evacuated along this route before turning onto the Burma Road and heading for Kunming, marching day and night without stopping, for they had no food. Once they reached Kunming, they would be expected to march in a parade to celebrate Chiang Kai-shek's "glorious" victory over Japan.

We set out the next morning on the last stage of our journey to Kunming, a distance of 120 miles. We found ourselves driving between two seemingly endless columns of Chinese soldiers, their rifles slung over their shoulders, who hardly glanced at us as we passed. They wore only sandals, and their tattered uniforms hung like shrouds from their emaciated bodies as they staggered along, some of them barely able to walk. Once we had to swerve to avoid a dead Chinese peasant lying faceup in the road, his body swollen and covered with flies, not even noticed by the soldiers as they marched by impassively.

It was dark by the time we reached Kunming, and as we approached the city we were met by a U.S. Army jeep that led our convoy to where we would camp for the night. Our campsite was on the edge of the airfield on the southern side of Kunming, where we set up our tents just beyond the end of the runway.

I was so exhausted that I got into my sleeping bag soon after I finished my K rations, but it took me a long time to fall asleep because of the succession of airplanes coming in to land just over our heads. The planes were still landing when I awoke at dawn, most of them C-47 transport planes that had been carrying troops and supplies over the Hump from India to China for the past three years.

Every now and then a fighter plane landed as well and taxied to our end of the runway. I went over to look at one of them and saw that the nose of its fuselage was painted to resemble a shark's head. I recognized this as the symbol of the Flying Tigers, the 1st American Volunteer Group, which was founded in 1941 by General Claire Chennault, who commanded the Chinese air force and then later became head of the U.S. air forces in China.

I talked to the pilot after he emerged from the plane. He told me that he had just made his last flight, because now that the Japanese had surrendered he figured he and his comrades would soon be going home, although no official orders had yet been received. Like the other Flying Tigers, he had been flying combat missions for more than four years. He was sick of war and just wanted to go home and live a normal life, though he could hardly remember what normal life was like.

Commander Boots spoke to us when we mustered after morning chow at the mess hall. He'd just received word that the Japanese were going to sign a formal document of surrender aboard the battleship USS *Missouri* in Tokyo Bay on September 2, 1945, two days from then, and we cheered, though we'd seen only the tail end of the war. It had been enough, I thought, thinking of the road to Mongyu and the boy screaming in the jungle.

The commander said that we'd drive to a parking area in Kunming, and from there we would be taken to the main SACO base in Kunming—Camp Hank Gibbins—where we would receive orders for our individual assignments. Some of us would go on with the convoy to Chengdu in Sichuan Province, where SACO had its main headquarters, but each truck would now have only one driver, for since hostilities had ended it meant that plans would change for half of us. We would not be flown over the Hump to Calcutta to be shipped back to the United States, but otherwise, he said, the details were still uncertain.

Kunming is more than six thousand feet above sea level, rimmed by mountains on three sides, giving way to terraced hills with rice paddies whose pools were glistening in the sunlight when I looked at them early in the morning after our arrival. The high altitude made it deliciously cool, and we had to break out our foul-weather jackets before the convoy started up. We were told that we were headed for a *godown,* or depot, on the western outskirts of Kunming, where we would park our trucks and await further orders.

We mustered again after we parked our trucks in the *godown,* which looked like a caravansery I'd seen in a travelogue on Central Asia. It consisted of wooden structures with pagoda roofs surrounding a huge square crowded with oxcarts and coolies carrying enormous loads suspended from bamboo poles. Commander Boots said that most of our outfit would be put up at Camp Hank Gibbins, but due to lack of space a few of us would be temporarily housed in the main camp of the Chinese 1st Army Group, where General Tai Li's Loyal and Patriotic Army was based. One of the ensigns read out the list, and I found that I was one of five assigned to the Chinese army base. My group reported to a lieutenant in the Chinese army, who in broken English told us to get into the back of a truck, and in a few minutes we drove off from the *godown,* waving goodbye to the rest of our outfit.

The Chinese army base was in the hills above Kunming, and on the approach road we passed between the same columns of ragged and emaciated soldiers I'd seen on the previous day. When we reached the base we were taken to a separate enclosure for the LPA, where the Chinese soldiers seemed healthier and better clothed than those of the regular Kuomintang army—all of them, so far as I could see, wearing American uniforms and combat boots just like our own. They were housed in tents with screens on the sides to keep out the mosquitoes that had plagued us along the Burma Road, while the soldiers in the regular army slept in overcrowded barracks.

The lieutenant assigned each of us to a tent together with a Chinese soldier who would be our interpreter while we were in the camp. My interpreter was a private in the LPA who introduced himself in very basic English as Ching Ging Too, which he wrote out for me in both English and Chinese, after which he led me to our tent, whose only furnishings were two U.S. Army–issue folding cots. He was a slender young man, about my age, taller and darker than the regular Chinese soldiers, and from his moonlike visage I figured that he was from the Naxi or one of the other tribes in the Tibetan borderlands.

Ching offered to take me to the mess hall, "but the food was pretty bad," he said. Giving me a quick lesson in Chinese, he said that *ding how* meant "good" and *boo how* was "bad." Then when I said "*Ding how,*" he laughed and replied, "Don't *ding how* me, you *boo how* bastard," a phrase that his American comrades in SACO had taught him.

I suggested to Ching that we use what was left of my "funny money" to buy some food and rice wine—we could have our own party to celebrate the end of the war on September 2, two days hence. He thought that was a great idea, so he got permission for us to leave the base. We bought our food and half a dozen bottles of wine in the local village. He purchased enough food to last us for at least three days, including rice cakes, Azabi beans, and "crossing the bridge" noodles, a Kunming specialty, along with a dozen slabs of *baba* bread.

I learned that Ching was twenty years old, a year older than I was, and that he was from a small village southwest of Kunming, under Jade Dragon Snow Mountain, where his family had a tiny farm. He had served in the LPA for two years and had fought against the Japanese in several hit-and-run guerrilla raids led by Americans in SACO.

After we ate, Ching took me for a walk around the camp and pointed out a large complex of Quonset huts in the valley below, which he identified as the Associated Universities of Southwest China. The students and faculty were from all over China, he said, and they had been moved here during the war to keep them out of the hands of the Japanese. (Twelve years later, at Princeton University, I met two Chinese physicists, Tsung-Dao Lee and Chen Ning Yang, who had just won the Nobel Prize, and I learned that both of them had graduated from the Associated Universities of Southwest China, and that they were there during my brief stay in Kunming.)

Ching said that he had hopes of going to this university when he was discharged from the army, because he dreamed of being a science teacher. But it might be a long time before he got out of the army, he said with a sigh. He explained that Tai Li would undoubtedly keep the LPA under arms even though the Japanese had now surrendered, for another war was about to begin between Chiang Kai-shek's Kuomintang army and the Communist People's Liberation Army (PLA) of Mao Tse-tung. He told me that Mao had spies and organizers right here in this camp, and he himself had been approached by them. (Forty years later, at Harvard, I met a prominent Chinese editor who was in the United States on a Newman Fellowship, and he told me that he had been at the Chinese army base in Kunming while I was there, spying and recruiting for Mao's PLA.)

Ching said there was going to be a military review at the base on September 2 to mark the official Japanese surrender, and he expected that all of Kunming would join in the celebration. He suspected that things might get out of hand in town, for there would be thousands of armed soldiers on the loose and many of them would be drunk and disorderly. They had been at war since 1937, when Ching was twelve years old, so he hardly remembered what China was like in times of peace, before the killing began.

The review was held early in the afternoon of September 2 on the huge drill field of the base. Ching identified the various contingents of the LPA and of the regular Chinese nationalist army as they passed in review, led by their generals and other officers. I was hoping to catch a glimpse of General Tai Li, the commander in chief of the LPA, but Ching said that he was probably still in Chongqing along with SACO's American commander, Admiral Milton Miles.

Toward the end of the review, Ching pointed out the women's battalion of the LPA, and he said that many of them were from the Bai, Miao, Mosuo, and Naxi minorities in Yunnan and Sichuan provinces, some of whom I'd seen in Dali. The sight of them reminded me again of the Amazon I'd seen at the Metropolitan Museum, but whereas she had been forlorn and defeated these Chinese Amazons were triumphantly celebrating China's victory over Japan.

After the review, which lasted all afternoon, Ching and I went back to our tent and had supper, which we washed down with the first of the half-dozen bottles of rice wine we'd bought in the village. After the first bottle of wine, Ching began to sing what he said was an old Naxi folk song, which I found quite beautiful, though I didn't understand a word of it. When he finished he said that it was called "Waves Washing the Sand." He translated a few lines for me, which were to the effect that time passes like the waves of the sea lapping upon the shore, and memory is the faint pattern left by the ripples on the sand, soon to be washed away.

Our party was suddenly interrupted by a burst of fireworks, and we rushed out of the tent to look at it. We could see that there were two separate fireworks displays, one on the drill field of our camp and the other in the city below, in what Ching said was the main square of Kunming. The displays lasted for about fifteen minutes, and when they ended we went back into our tent to continue our party.

Soon afterward the party was interrupted again by what we thought at first was a resumption of the fireworks, which surprised us. When we went out to see what was going on we quickly realized that it was not fireworks we were hearing, but gunfire, including bursts of machine-gun fire, sounding as if there was a battle being fought between the two sides of the camp. We went back inside the tent and took cover, for we could hear bullets whizzing over our heads. I crawled into my sleeping bag and lay down under my cot for whatever extra protection that might furnish, having brought a bottle of rice wine with me. Ching did the same, and as we sipped our wine we chatted during intervals in the gunfire until we dozed off.

When I awoke the next morning Ching was already up, and he showed me about a dozen bullet holes in the sides of our tent, some of them very close to where we had been sitting. He said that what we had heard was a fixed battle between two armies in the camp, one commanded by General Lung Han, the Yunnan warlord, who had apparently defected to Mao Tse-tung, and another led by General Tu Yu-ming, one of Chiang

Kai-shek's right-hand men. It seems, from what Ching had heard, that Chiang Kai-shek had ordered Tu Yu-ming to take control of Kunming before the Americans pulled out, and though the battle was a standoff Ching was sure that the two armies would resume fighting before long. He was right, and I later learned that the battle I'd heard was part of the prelude to the Chinese civil war.

(Julia Child, in her autobiography, wrote that she was giving a big dinner party that evening in Kunming, where she was with the staff of Lord Mountbatten, the commanding general of the Allied forces in the China-Burma-India theater. All hell seemed to have broken loose in the Chinese army base, and when shrapnel began falling in the city she was forced to call off the dinner.)

Later that morning a U.S. Army truck came with orders to take the five of us from SACO down to Camp Hank Gibbins, for it was obviously too dangerous for us to remain on the Chinese base. So Ching and I said goodbye, promising to try to get in touch with each other after we returned to our homes—but we knew that there was little likelihood that we'd ever see each other again.

Camp Hank Gibbins was in the village of Hai-ling, ten miles south of Kunming. When we arrived in the camp there were still no bunks available for the five of us, so we laid out our sleeping bags in one of the storage sheds. We mustered with the rest of our unit after chow the next morning. Commander Boots said that we could all spend the rest of the day on liberty in Kunming, and that trucks would be available to take us into town and back to the camp in the evening.

Ed and I spent the day wandering around Kunming, surrounded by curious crowds staring at us wherever we went. At one point we were walking along the main avenue when a motorcade of American jeeps and staff cars appeared, slowly making its way through the mass of humanity that blocked the way. The lead jeep stopped next to us for a moment, and I asked the GI who was driving it what was up. He said that the civilians in the staff cars were members of an American congressional delegation, who had stopped off in Kunming before going on to see Chiang Kai-shek in Chongqing.

As the motorcade drove by, the congressmen all turned to look at me and Ed, for we had on our Navy uniforms, surrounded by a sea of Chinese wearing the padded jackets that everyone in China wore in those days. I thought that the congressmen must have wondered what two American sailors were doing in this remote part of the world, hundreds of miles from the nearest ocean.

Three days later we learned that John Jacob Esau had died of his injuries in the U.S. Army hospital in Kunming. The following day we buried him on a hillside above Kunming, where a small military cemetery had been laid out for the American servicemen who had perished in Yunnan during the war. An Army chaplain conducted a brief service, then a bugler sounded Taps while a guard of honor fired a volley as his coffin was lowered into the grave. Commander Boots took the American flag that had covered the grave, and he said that he would make sure that it was delivered to Esau's parents. I wondered how his parents would feel when they learned that their son had passed away four days after the official end of hostilities, one of the last American fatalities of World War II, buried half a world away from his home. I hardly knew him, but he seemed like a very nice guy. In his brief tribute to John Jacob Esau, Commander Boots said that he had just turned twenty-one. He, like so many others, would never grow old, deprived of life just as he had come of age.

The next day I moved into the barracks, as there were now vacancies made by those who had been flown back to Calcutta. Meanwhile, new arrivals were coming in from China and even beyond, including some SACO commandos who had been training Mongol cavalry for the LPA in the Gobi Desert and others who had made contact with Mao and his forces. Those who had been out in the field told me that a civil war in China was imminent, which I'd seen for myself just a few days before, and they were all sure that Mao would prevail over Chiang Kai-shek, for he had far greater support among the Chinese people. I guessed, however, that the congressional delegation I'd seen a couple of days before would be assuring the generalissimo that the United States was solidly behind him.

Two days later a notice was posted on the bulletin board informing us of our next assignments. I learned that I was one of a group of thirty who would be flown back to Calcutta on September 15, while all the others in the convoy, including Ed Hill, would drive the trucks on to Chengdu, starting the following day. There would be only one driver in each truck, which was why I'd been left off the list of those going on with the convoy, for Commander Boots knew I couldn't drive. Nevertheless, I was very disappointed, for scuttlebutt had it that at Chengdu the trucks would be put on barges that would take them and their drivers down the Yangtze to Shanghai, where they would be shipped back to the States. The rumor turned out to be true, as I learned several months later when I received a postcard that my pal Ron Fuller sent to me from Shanghai.

I spent the intervening days wandering around Kunming with Ed, surrounded by crowds everywhere we went. We saw the two Tang Dynasty pagodas, the Yuantong Temple, and the Nancheng Mosque. The mosque surprised me, for I hadn't known that there were Muslims in that part of China.

That evening I spoke to an ensign at Camp Hank Gibbins who had studied Chinese history, and he told me that the Muslims in Yunnan were Mongols, descendants of the warriors that Kublai Khan had led in his march of conquest. Marco Polo mentioned these Muslims when he passed through the city later in the thirteenth century, when it was known as Yachi, later changed to Yunnanfu, and later still to Kunming.

Around noon on September 15, I said goodbye to Ed and my other friends who were continuing with the convoy to Chengdu. We'd been through a lot together and I would miss them, particularly Ed. Although we still weren't that close as friends, we'd been side by side constantly for two months, day and night. When I shook his hand, I knew somehow I'd never see him again.

The thirty of us who were leaving were taken in trucks to the airfield. We boarded a C-47 cargo plane, one of the famous gooney birds that had carried troops and supplies over the eastern extension of the Himalayas between China, Burma, and India. Hundreds of these planes had crashed or been shot down during the previous three years, but at least now we wouldn't have to worry about encountering Japanese fighter planes. Still, I was very nervous when I boarded the C-47, for I'd never flown before, though I'd been fascinated by airplanes ever since I first heard of Charles Lindbergh's solo flight across the Atlantic in the *Spirit of St. Louis*.

We sat on canvas bucket seats facing one another across the central aisle. The flight engineer, a young lieutenant, told us that the ride might be very rough, which was why they called flying the Hump "Operation Vomit." He said we should put on our foul-weather jackets, because we'd be flying at a high altitude and it would be very cold; because the cabin wasn't pressurized, we also might have trouble breathing.

The lieutenant said that we would be taking off as soon as the last passengers arrived, which puzzled me, since there were no seats left. A few minutes later a black GI from the Transportation Corps came up the ramp leading a line of five mules, which he tethered to a rope along the center aisle of the aircraft. He laughed when he saw the expressions on our faces, and said the U.S. Army was abandoning its trucks and jeeps as it pulled out of China, but not its mules, which had carried supplies and weapons all through the war and now were being taken back to the States to spend their remaining days in honorable retirement.

As soon as the mules were tethered we took off, and after a few minutes of sheer terror I relaxed and tried to enjoy the scenery, craning my neck to look out the window behind me, since the view through the window across the aisle was blocked by the hindquarters of a mule. The lieutenant pointed out some of the landmarks along the way, starting with the peak of Jade Dragon Snow Mountain, at 18,500 feet, towering off to the north within the great bend of the Yangtze, the only one of the Rivers of Paradise that I'd not crossed, but which I'd now, at least, seen. The flight engineer then pointed out the Mekong, the Salween, and the Brahmaputra, the other three Rivers of Paradise, and far to the north I could see where all four of them poured down out of the Tibetan Plateau, flowing from the Roof of the World to bring their life-giving waters to farms, tea plantations, and rice paddies all the way from China to India, as if they were indeed coming down from paradise. But I reminded myself that the countryside through which we'd passed during these past few weeks had been turned into what had literally been a hell on earth. And even now, when peace had returned to the rest of the world, war was about to resume here in this lost Eden.

The flight from Kunming to Calcutta took about five hours, whereas our journey overland had taken about a month. This gave me the same feeling of wonder I felt when I first heard of Lindbergh's flight across the Atlantic, after my own early transatlantic voyage.

After we landed at the Dum Dum airfield we had to wait for the mules to be led off before we could disembark. I was immediately struck by a wave of moist heat, which was all the more uncomfortable since I was wearing my foul-weather jacket and laden down with my seabag, carbine, .45 pistol, combat knife, helmet, entrenching shovel, and mess gear. We were suddenly surrounded by the seething mass of humanity that is Calcutta, so profoundly different from the cool and sparsely inhabited highlands of Yunnan that we had left only a few hours before. We had come down from the Roof of the World to an inferno.

We boarded trucks that took us back to Camp Knox, where we were all assigned bunks in one of the SACO barracks; they were luxury accommodations after the primitive conditions in which we had lived for the previous month. As I drifted off to sleep that night I thought of Ching Ging Too singing "Waves Washing the Sand," as he and the world of war passed into what Homer, in the last book of the *Odyssey*, called the Country of Dreams.

On the morning after our return to Calcutta we mustered with the other SACO personnel at Camp Knox. We were told that all of us would soon be shipped back to the United States, and that in a day or two lists would be posted with our assignments.

Those of us who had just returned from China were marched off to the infirmary for a physical exam, which was even more thorough than usual, we were told, since we had been exposed to scrub typhus, dengue fever, and malaria, which were endemic in the CBI. We were all given a clean bill of health, though we had all lost a lot of weight and were suffering from sores caused by leeches and insect bites, as well as jungle rot, whose scars I still bear on my right ankle. (Happily, my hemorrhoids seemed to have been cured by Dr. Seagrave's nurses in Burma.) We were also infested with lice, so all our body hair was shaved off and our heads, armpits, and crotches were painted with purple ointment, which made us the laughingstock of the base, all the more so since our skin had turned yellow from the atabrine we had been taking to ward off malaria.

The day after my return Bill Glennon and I went into Calcutta on liberty, where I bought a Gurkha kukri sword as a souvenir. We then had lunch at a little restaurant in the market quarter off Chowringee Road. While we were sitting there two American sailors came into the restaurant, one of them, who was missing a leg, walking on crutches. We invited them to sit down and they joined us. They said they had been on the USS *Houston,* a heavy cruiser that had been sunk in the Java Sea on March 1, 1942, as a result of which half of their crew of 1,061 had been killed. The survivors had been picked up by the Japanese and taken to a concentration camp in Burma, where they had spent the next three and a half years. By the time they were liberated, just two weeks before, there were only 368 survivors, most of whom were now in the main U.S. military hospital in Calcutta. The sailor on crutches said that his leg had been amputated by a Japanese medic in the prison camp, without an anesthetic, and that he was lucky to be alive. They were waiting to shipped back to the United States, and we said that we were too and hoped we would end up on the same ship.

Five days later a notice was pinned on the bulletin board saying that all the personnel of the Roger amphibious unit at Camp Knox would be shipped out on September 28. We would travel on the troopship *General W. F. Hase,* AP-146, which would take us to New York via the Suez Canal. I spent the intervening week exploring Calcutta, for I had no idea what the future held in store for me, and it might be a long time before I got back to the Orient.

Since we were U.S. Navy personnel, we were the first to board the *Hase* on the morning of the twenty-eighth. The *Hase* was a sister ship of the *Collins,* the troopship that had brought us to Calcutta. But the *Hase* would be carrying three thousand troops, a thousand more than had been aboard the *Collins,* which had been made possible by converting much of the cargo space into dormitories. The minute I learned that, I stowed my gear and took my sleeping bag up to the searchlight platform on the mast amidships, the same spot that had been my refuge on the *Collins*. I was relieved to find that I was not assigned to work in the engine room, as I had been aboard the *Collins,* and since the war was over there was no need to man the antiaircraft guns. I went up to look at the 20mm gun on the starboard side of the flying bridge that had been my battle station on the *Collins*.

We cast off early in the afternoon and spent the rest of the day making our way down the Hooghly River, and I took my last look at India from my perch on the crow's nest. When I awoke the next morning there was no land in sight, as we steamed southwestward through the Bay of Bengal, heading into the Indian Ocean. The mood was much more relaxed than it had been aboard the *Collins,* since we no longer had to be on the alert for Japanese submarines or air attack, and we were going home instead of off to war. All the GIs spent the day lying around on deck or on the cargo hatches, sunning themselves and listening to the songs playing on the PA system, everyone's favorite being "Sentimental Journey," which was repeated over and over again; whenever I heard it afterward, it reminded me of that long voyage home.

Gonna take a sentimental journey,
Gonna set my heart at ease.
Gonna take a sentimental journey,
To renew old memories.

The GIs whom I spoke to had been overseas for as long as three and a half years, and all of them talked about nothing except their longing to see their girlfriend or wife or children. They also talked about getting back to their jobs or school, and I heard some of them mention the GI Bill, a law passed by Congress that would give returning veterans benefits that included a free university education, which I thought wouldn't apply to me since I hadn't finished high school. They expected to be discharged as soon as they returned to the States, but I was younger than they were and hadn't been in the service as long. I figured I would probably be the last World War II serviceman to return to civilian life. But that didn't bother me in the least, for I had nothing to go back to, neither girlfriend nor wife nor school nor job, unless I could manage to find work as a merchant seaman and continue my travels around the world.

Then I learned that the GI Bill also included unemployment benefits for up to a year, which I thought I would be eligible for, since my only skill was the demolition work for which I had been trained at Fort Pierce. If I qualified for this unemployment relief, then I could spend a year reading, and that led me to search in my seabag for the catalog that the chaplain on the *Collins* had given me, the Great Books program at St. John's College in Annapolis. I found it at the bottom of my seabag, and when I looked through it I saw again that the list of Great Books was headed by the *Iliad* and the *Odyssey,* and I was excited by the thought that on my homeward journey I would be crossing the track of Odysseus on his long voyage back to Ithaca.

A few of the GIs didn't talk at all, but sat on the deck or on the hatches staring off toward the horizon with expressionless faces, referred to by other soldiers as "zombies." When I mentioned this to others around them they attributed the condition of the zombies to shell shock and combat fatigue, which was compounded by the tranquilizers they were given by the pharmacist's mates in sick bay, where I often saw many of them lined up. When I visited a friend in sick bay one day I saw that there were a number of zombies there, some of them restrained by straps, along with some men who were recovering from their battle wounds, including amputations, as well as from malaria, scrub typhus, and dengue fever. A pharmacist's mate told me that all of the patients would be transferred to military hospitals in the United States, including many of the zombies whom I had seen on deck. He said that most of the zombies were suffering from profound depression that may have had little to do with their combat or other military experience, and that they would probably spend the rest of their lives under psychiatric care.

Because there were a thousand troops more than had been aboard the *Collins,* the chow lines for the two meals a day were much longer. The chow was the same inedible "shit on a shingle" and "horse cock" that we had been given aboard the *Collins,* so I decided I would try to pass myself off as one of the crew and eat with them. I managed to persuade one of the Marine guards that I was a new member of the ship's company who had come aboard in Calcutta. Whenever he was on watch I was allowed into the crew's mess hall, where the chow was much better and there were three meals a day, and I began gaining back some of the weight I had lost in Burma and China.

Because I was a sailor rather than a soldier and had made friends among the ship's company, I soon had the run of the *Hase,* whose layout I knew intimately from my voyage aboard its sister the *Collins.* Some of the friends I made among the crew stood watches on the bridge, and that gave me an opportunity to look at the charts and follow the progress of our voyage to New York, which I learned would take about a month.

Our first landfall was after we passed through the Palk Strait between Ceylon and India's Coromandel Coast, a name that conjured up exotic images of the East. We then made our way down the western coast of Ceylon to Colombo, where a pilot came aboard to steer us into the harbor. We dropped anchor in the middle of the harbor, and I was told that we were stopping to pick up a single U.S. Navy petty officer, who was brought out to the *Hase* in a launch. While we waited for him I looked around the harbor and was surprised to find that most of the port installations were in ruins, and I could see the bombed-out wrecks of several half-submerged vessels. I learned from a petty officer on the bridge that a Japanese carrier force had attacked Ceylon early in the spring of 1942, and in two air raids on Colombo they sank five ships, some of whose half-submerged wrecks were still lying in the harbor.

After leaving Colombo we headed westward, passing Cape Comorin, the southern tip of India, and steamed on into the Indian Ocean toward the Gulf of Aden, which I figured we would enter in about six days. I kept track of our overall progress through the ship's daily four-page newspaper, *Westward Ho,* which on its masthead each day gave the distances to New York and Calcutta. I still have a yellowed and crumbling copy of *Westward Ho* dated October 5, 1945, with the distances given as "Miles to New York 7,959" and "Miles to Calcutta 2,056," along with an apology from the staff for having given the mileages incorrectly for the two previous days.

The headline in *Westward Ho* that day was MACARTHUR OUSTS JAP POLICE, with the subheading "Cabinet Member Also Removed in New Move to Free Political Thought." The second paragraph was entitled "Communists Among Those Freed," which I read with great interest, for I found it hard to believe that Reds would be let out of jail in occupied Japan when they faced prison in the United States, as I remembered from my last reading of the *Daily Worker,* which had led Peg to call me "Class-Struggle Freely."

The other article on the front page was entitled STRIKES CONTINUE, with the subheading "New York Dock Walkout Spreads; Truman Acts to Solve Oil Tie Up." According to the article, the strike of dockworkers in New York, "which has already tied up more than 100 ships spread to additional waterfront workers and threatened to paralyze the whole port," which made me wonder if the *Hase* might be directed to another harbor. My sympathies were with the strikers, for I remembered John's struggle to earn a living shaping up on the New York docks, where longshoremen like him had no more rights than the coolies I had seen unloading our ship in Calcutta.

The third page of *Westward Ho* had an article about SACO entitled NAVY IN CHINA: REVEALED HOW NAVY MEN WORKED WITH CHINESE AGENTS IN UNDERCOVER WAR. This was followed by a parenthetical note from which I learned that I had missed the first article in the series: "This is the second in a series of articles describing the highly secret activities of a group of U.S. Navy men in China during the war. The group of 188 men now aboard this ship as passengers participated in the operation." The article described some of the activities of SACO, including the weather observers and coast watchers in Japanese-occupied China, the laying of mines in coastal and river waters used by enemy shipping, and the rescue of downed American airmen. I missed the subsequent articles in the series, but I learned that they covered SACO's training of Tai Li's Loyal and Patriotic Army, as well as its commando raids behind Japanese lines and the training of Mongol cavalry in the Gobi Desert.

Most of the rest of *Westward Ho* was devoted to sports reports, the main story being the victory of the Detroit Tigers over the Chicago Cubs in Game Two of the World Series, tying the teams at one game each. Despite my great interest in baseball, I read the story as if it were news from another planet, and it was hard to believe that able-bodied men had been playing ball all through the war while millions of their countrymen were fighting; I wondered if the professional baseball players had punctured eardrums like Frank Sinatra.

There was also a column in *Westward Ho* called "Now Hear This," which included information on when and where ice cream and Coke would be available in vending machines—which did me no good, since it said that only half-dollars, quarters, or dimes would be available at the change booth, and the only currency I had was the Chinese "funny money" I had been paid with at Baoshan, as well as the Sun Yat-sen gold dollar I had obtained before we crossed the Salween River.

The "Now Hear This" column ended with a notice that the evening film would be *Dancing in Manhattan,* with Ann Savage and Jeff Donnell. As I watched it on a sheet hung up on the quarterdeck—once more left-right inverted—I couldn't help wondering what the Naga and Kachin and Naxi tribespeople whom I had been among this past month would think of this make-believe Hollywood world I was watching in the middle of the Indian Ocean.

Our first landfall after crossing the Indian Ocean was the island of Soqotra at the entrance to the Gulf of Aden. Once past Soqotra, it took another two days to make our way through the Gulf of Aden to Bab-el-Mandeb, between Yemen to the east and Djibouti to the west, the latter providing my first view of Africa and bringing the list of continents I had seen up to five. (South America and Antarctica still awaited me, and still do to this day.)

It took us four days to make our way up the Red Sea, with first Yemen in view to the east, followed by Saudi Arabia, while to the west we passed Eritrea and Sudan before coming to Egypt, as I followed our course on the charts on the bridge, but both coastlines looked exactly the same, with nothing to distinguish one artificial national boundary from another. When we passed Sharm el-Sheikh to enter the Gulf of Suez I could see Gebel Katherina, its peak towering more than eight thousand feet above the southernmost promontory of the Sinai Peninsula. I borrowed a pair of binoculars from a sailor on the bridge to try to catch a glimpse of the famous monastery of St. Catherine on Gebel Katherina, which I had read about in *National Geographic,* but I could see no sign of it on the barren mountain.

At the northern end of the gulf we anchored for the night off Suez, the southernmost town on the Suez Canal. The following morning we took aboard a pilot to steer us through the canal, which I was told would take at least fifteen hours, and I went up on the flying bridge so I would have a good view of our passage. It seemed that we would be the first American troopship to pass through the canal since the war had ended, for the waterway had been blocked at many points by sunken ships, whose bombed-out and bullet-riddled wrecks I could see pulled up onto the shore on either side.

When we reached the halfway point of the canal at Lake Timsah I saw a motor launch come out from Ismailia, the town on the western bank. The launch pulled up next to the port side of the *Hase* and all the GIs rushed over to take a look. At first I couldn't see the launch, but when I looked down from the port side of the flying bridge I saw a somewhat portly young man in a naval uniform wearing a red fez. I recognized him as King Farouk from newspaper photographs I had seen, and I cheered along with the GIs when he gave us the royal wave.

We spent the rest of the day making our way through the straight northern half of the canal, passing the ruins of an ancient fortress at Qantara. As we passed the fortress a band of Bedouins on camels waved their rifles at us and fired into the air in greeting, reminding me of a scene from an illustrated version of Lawrence of Arabia's *Revolt in the Desert*.

We spent the night at Port Said to take on supplies and replenish our tanks of diesel oil and drinking water. I stayed up half the night looking down to see what I could of the town, watching camel caravans making their way to and from the docks, where half-naked porters loaded and unloaded vessels ranging from warships and freighters to dhows with lateen sails, reminding me of lithographs in old travelogues of Ottoman Egypt.

The next morning we left Port Said and headed westward across the Mediterranean. This was the part of the voyage I had looked forward to most, for the next few days would take us across the route that Odysseus had followed on his homeward journey. Just before dawn the next day, looking out to starboard from the flying bridge, I caught sight of what I could identify from the charts on the bridge as the Greek island of Gavros, south of Crete, marking the southernmost point of Europe. Soon afterward I could see Cape Elafonissi, the southwesternmost promontory of Crete, and here I remembered that the disguised Odysseus, in a lying tale to Penelope, told her that he had passed this way on his homeward journey from the war in Troy, just as I was passing it now on my long voyage home from the war in China.

Shortly after sunrise, looking out on the port side, I could see that we were passing the northernmost cape of Libya, after which we started across the immense gulf known as Khalij Surt, stretching from Benghazi to Tripoli, which we passed during the night. At dawn the next day we began turning northwestward to go through the Strait of Sicily, with the coast of Tunisia visible on the port side, as we passed the deeply indented Gulf of Gabes. By sunset we emerged from the strait as we passed Cape Bon to port, turning westward as we came within sight of Tunis, the site of ancient Carthage. I didn't know it at the time, but that day I had crossed the path of Odysseus twice, the routes he took to and from the coast of North Africa, where he went ashore in the Land of the Lotus-eaters, which Homeric scholars have identified as Djerba in Tunisia.

We then skirted the coast of Algeria for more than two days, passing Algiers on the second day and Oran early in the morning of the third. After we passed Oran I could see the mountains of Morocco to the south and those of Spain to the north, the opposing shores of the Mediterranean converging as we approached the Strait of Gibraltar. As we passed through the strait I strained my eyes to see the famous Rock of Gibraltar, and although I finally identified it I was somewhat disappointed, for it wasn't as impressive as it appeared on the emblem of the Prudential Insurance Company, which I remembered from the hundred-dollar life insurance policy that Peg had cashed in when we were flat broke during the height of the Depression.

The mood changed when we steamed out into the Atlantic, which we took twelve days to cross, bucking high winds and heavy seas that drove most of the GIs belowdecks, where many of them lay seasick in their bunks puking their guts out. I went below only to eat in the crew's mess hall, spending the rest of the day up on my old perch on the searchlight platform, watching the ship nose into one tremendous wave after another, sometimes engulfed in a shower of wind-blown spray that left only the masts visible above the water. As I stood there I remembered our last voyage across the Atlantic twelve and a half years before, when Peg kept us out on deck in all kinds of weather. In my mind's eye I could still see her peering intently westward, and I knew she had been hoping that fortune would be kinder in America this time than it had been in the past.

The last issue of *Westward Ho* came out on October 26, 1945. The headline informed us that we would be arriving in New York the following day. Nine other troopships would be arriving with us, four of them having been diverted from the Pacific via the Panama Canal. There would be a gala reception for us in New York Harbor, and the welcoming committee would be headed by President Harry Truman.

The next day I was up on the flying bridge at dawn to see our first landfall in the United States and our approach to New York Harbor, where we were the last of the ten troopships to enter the port. I was thrilled to see the Statue of Liberty again, the fifth time I had passed it on ships entering or leaving the harbor.

It was about noon when we finally entered the harbor, where a fireboat was making an aquatic display and a launch carried a brass band of WACs, the Women's Army Corps, playing patriotic songs, while all the ships in the harbor repeatedly sounded their horns. A launch came alongside the *Hase* and put aboard a number of civilians, including some women, and from their notebooks and cameras I figured they were journalists. I hoped to check the papers the next day to read what the reporters wrote about us, and to see if any of the guys in my outfit appeared in the photos.

We followed the other troopships in turn as they passed the reviewing stand at Battery Park, where another Army band was playing. I borrowed a pair of binoculars from one of the crew on the bridge and as we passed Battery Park I scanned the reviewing stand, where I could see President Truman waving to us along with a crowd of dignitaries that included generals and admirals and what I presumed were high-ranking officials and politicians with their wives.

I realized that our welcome home had been stage-managed for the publicity it gave the president, for the moment we were past the reviewing stand we were no longer the center of attention, just ten troopships crammed with thousands of war-weary GIs anxious to get home and resume their lives. But it didn't bother me in the least, because for a short while I had been part of a truly historic occasion, which in my imagination I compared to the return of the victorious British fleet after the Battle of Trafalgar. And as our ship pulled up to the dock at Pier 88 I could take pride in the fact that I had just completed a journey around the world.

As soon as we docked I went below to get my gear, struggling to make my way through the crowds of GIs who were trying to do the same thing. Once again our outfit was the first to debark, and I went down the gangway behind my friend Tunney King. When we reached the dock we said goodbye, for we would probably not see each other again, or at least not for a while. He said that if I ever found myself in Greenville, Maine, I should look him up. I did, forty years later almost to the day, and one of the first things he said to me was, "Who do you think was screaming in the jungle that night in Mongyu?"

As soon as we were all on the dock, we mustered, and Commander Boots told us that we would be taken to the Navy Armed Guard Center near the Brooklyn Navy Yard, where we would be processed for discharge or further assignment. He explained the point system that would be used to determine the order in which we would be discharged, with a point for each year of our age, another point for every year that we had been in the Navy, and extra points for time spent in combat as well as for any decorations we had received. All of this seemed to put me at the bottom of the list, so I figured it would be a while before I got out.

We then boarded trucks that had neither windows nor seats in the back, more suitable for cattle than humans, which led me to moo like a cow. Soon I had everyone mooing and laughing at the same time, while we tried to keep our footing as the truck lurched through the streets of Manhattan on its way to Brooklyn. When I stopped mooing and laughing I felt a deep sense of resentment, wondering if President Truman knew that some of the servicemen he had just welcomed home from the war were now being transported like cattle on their way to a barn.

We were, in fact, going to a barn of sorts, for the Armed Guard Center turned out to be an old trolley barn, converted into a barracks for Navy personnel who manned the guns on American freighters in the Atlantic. We were given bunks and told to check the bulletin board to learn our next assignment, but in the meantime we were confined to base. We had to turn in our carbines and our .45s, along with our combat knives, helmets, mess kits, ponchos, shelter halves, and foul-weather gear.

There weren't any facilities for making telephone calls, because the center was just a temporary facility for transferring naval personnel from one ship or shore station to another, with no conveniences or frills of any kind. In any event, no one in my extended family had a telephone, nor did anyone else I knew, and I was also probably going to be shipped out again right away, so there was nothing I could do.

After evening mess I met Bill Glennon, who was in the same fix that I was. Even though his family lived in the Bronx there was no way he could get in touch with them, since neither they nor anyone they knew had a phone, which I said was evidence of how far up the economic ladder Irish immigrant families like ours had progressed in America.

Bill and I decided that we would try to get out of the center that evening, because we had been cooped up on a troopship for a month and were desperate for a little freedom. We talked it over with a few friends who felt the same way, and we planned to see if there was any way we could get out. I found that there were only two guards at one of the side gates, and both of them were very busy checking the IDs of the base personnel who were entering and leaving. So we decided that we would all try to bluff our way through the gate at the same time, and if any of us were stopped the others would just keep going. Our plan worked up to a point, for all of us got through except for Bill, who was stopped by one of the guards, whereupon he raised such a fuss that the rest of us were able to get away.

None of us had a penny, so there seemed nowhere we could go, but at least we were able to take a stroll, though the area around the Armed Guard Center and the Brooklyn Navy Yard was a wasteland, as I knew from my months of working at the Willis Paint Company. I was the only one in the group from New York, so the others let me decide where we might go. At that moment we passed the entrance to a subway station, and I suggested that we go to Coney Island. So we went down and waited till we heard a train coming, and then we jumped the turnstile, for I knew that even if the ticket agent called the cops we would be long gone before they arrived, a trick I had learned from my youthful adventures with Jimmy Anderson.

When we arrived at Coney Island we found that the Steeplechase and all of the other entertainment facilities were closed for the winter. But it didn't matter, for we were able to go down to the beach and stretch our legs for the first time in months, joking and singing as we walked along the sand in our bare feet, running away from the sea every now and again to avoid the incoming waves. As we strolled along I wondered if President Truman could even imagine that some of us were spending an evening such as we were, absent without leave on the deserted beach at Coney Island without a penny in their pockets.

We jumped the turnstile successfully at Coney Island, but as we approached our stop near the Navy Yard I began to worry that we would be caught trying to get back in to the center. But when we got there we found the two guards were again busy checking IDs, and we managed to slip through with a crowd of returning base personnel without getting caught.

The following morning I learned that Bill had been arrested by the SPs and was now in the brig. I went to see him during visiting hours.

The brig turned out to be a Navy frigate from the War of 1812 that had been refitted as a floating jail, with its old leg irons still in place, though unused. Bill said that he was facing a captain's mast and would probably get a month of hard labor, which had been my sentence at Camp Sampson, but he didn't really care, for he expected to be discharged sometime that winter anyway. Bill was a year older than I was and had been overseas longer, since he had previously served a year in the Caribbean. From my reckoning of the point system I would have to serve at least seven months more than he would, probably on sea duty, for that was where the Navy was shorthanded, according to scuttlebutt.

That afternoon I checked the bulletin board and found my name on the roster assigned a troopship, the USS *General Harry Taylor* (AP-145), a sister ship of the *Hase* and the *Collins* that had entered New York Harbor yesterday in our flotilla. The notice said that those assigned to the *Taylor* should report to the duty officer at ten the following day with all their gear, ready to ship out.

The next morning I reported to the duty officer in charge of the roster for the *Taylor,* along with about a dozen other men, all of them about my age, and none of them looking very happy. After he checked off our names we were herded aboard the same kind of truck that had brought me to the center, but this time I didn't moo like a cow, for I no longer saw anything funny in my situation.

The truck brought us to Pier 90, where we boarded the *Taylor,* which was berthed next to the *Hase,* both of them taking on supplies in preparation for sailing. I expected that I would go to the quarters of the electrician's mates and other engine room ratings, but to my surprise I was taken to the compartment of the cooks, bakers, and stewards, all of whom were black. They were equally surprised, but they made me welcome and invited me to join them in a card game called pitty-pat, which seemed like a primitive form of rummy. I was beginning to enjoy myself when a chief cook came in and told me that there had been a big mistake. I followed him as he took me to meet the chief electrician's mate, a Puerto Rican man named Gonzalez, who led me to my quarters with the other engineering ratings, all of them white.

After I stowed my gear Chief Gonzalez brought me to the workroom and meeting place of the electrician's mates, a couple of small compartments at the stern of the ship, below the fantail deck and just forward of the twin screws, the two propellers. There he introduced me to the other electrician's mates, two petty officers, and two firemen first class. The chief was regular Navy, and from his three hash marks I could tell that he had been in for at least twelve years, and he would probably serve until his retirement, usually after twenty years. The other electrician's mates were, like me and virtually everyone else in the wartime Navy, USNR—U.S. Navy Reserves—and we would serve until we had enough points. They were all somewhat older than I was and had been in the Navy longer, and they expected to be discharged in the next couple of months.

Chief Gonzalez told me that on our coming voyage, which would begin the following day, we would go first to Le Havre in France, from where we would take German prisoners of war to Bremerhaven in Germany. Then we would bring GIs from Bremerhaven back to New York. He told me that my duties would include standing regular watches in the engine room, along with checking all of the electric motors on the ship as well as the tilt indicator, the degaussing apparatus for protection against magnetic mines, the remotely controlled auxiliary steering gear, and the searchlight on the foremast, which had been my perch on both the *Collins* and the *Hase*. I told him frankly that I was totally incompetent in matters electrical, because I had failed my course in electrician's mate school, and all I knew was how to operate an antiaircraft gun and blow things up.

The chief was very patient and said he would teach me everything I needed to know. He gave me circuit diagrams for all the electric motors on the ship, as well as instruction manuals for the tilt indicator, degaussing apparatus, remotely controlled steering gear, and searchlight. Then he took me down to the engine room and introduced me to the chief motor mechanic, who told me that my principal duty when I stood my watches there would be to monitor the twin generators to make sure that neither of them drew so much current that they overloaded and tripped the main circuit breaker. I nodded in agreement, remembering that a little more than four months earlier my lapse in monitoring the twin generators aboard the *Collins* had left it drifting helplessly in a war zone in the Pacific.

When the *Taylor* departed the next morning I was on duty at the auxiliary steering gear, which was in the stern of the ship next to the twin screws. Chief Gonzalez was there to explain to me that the auxiliary steering gear would be used only if the main steering mechanism on the bridge malfunctioned, and he told me what to do if that happened. He said that the auxiliary steering gear was normally used only when the ship was entering or leaving port, and that I should remain there until the helmsman on the bridge called on the intercom to inform me that I was free to leave.

When the helmsman told me I could go I went topside and stood on the fantail deck looking back along our wake toward New York, watching the towers of Manhattan until they disappeared in the maritime mist on the western horizon, thinking that just three days before President Truman had welcomed us back from the war and here I was now heading back across the Atlantic without even having seen my family.

While we were crossing the Atlantic I was busy standing watches and checking my circuits, which took me into every nook and cranny of the ship. I also checked the tilt indicator and the searchlight, both of which were on the same platform high on the foremast, my favorite spot. The tilt indicator was just a pointer that swung back and forth as the ship rolled, with red markers on either side of the scale to indicate the limits of stability, which if exceeded would set off an alarm on the bridge. I just had to make sure that the servomechanism was working. The searchlight was to be used when visibility was limited by fog or when we entered or left a port at night, and I had to turn it on for a few minutes every day to make sure that the carbon-arc light source was functioning properly.

I tried to arrange my work schedule so I could spend as much time as possible on the searchlight platform, particularly when the sea was rough and the pointer on the tilt marker approached the red lines. On those days the seascapes were magnificent, and when the ship turned its prow into a huge wave it was often so engulfed that only its masts appeared above the surface until we emerged in the trough, the twin screws shuddering and the superstructure and decks shedding streams of seawater.

It took us two weeks to cross the Atlantic and enter the English Channel, our first landfall being Cap de la Hague, the headland east of Cherbourg. The next morning, as we approached Le Havre, I went below to man the auxiliary steering gear, and I didn't emerge until we were tied up at the pier. I was shocked at the destruction I saw: the harbor was full of wrecked ships, and the city was in utter ruins as far as I could see, the shells of a few burned-out buildings still standing like skeletons amid the mounds of rubble.

I received permission to go ashore while we took aboard the German prisoners—three thousand of them—who were confined in a huge stockade ringed with barbed wire and guarded by armed American soldiers. We had only recently learned of the Jewish Holocaust, and this was in my mind as I passed the stockade on the way into town. The prisoners stared at me as I passed, most of them a few years older than I was, their faces showing their exhaustion and what I could sense was a feeling of utter defeat, but they were in far better physical shape than the ragged and barefoot Chinese soldiers I had seen staggering toward Chiang Kai-shek's victory parade in Kunming.

I had thought I could buy some wine in town, but the quarter around the port had been so thoroughly bombed that there was not a single building standing, and the only people I saw were waiting in long lines to obtain bread, which I was told was provided for them by Allied relief agencies. So I went back to the ship and watched the German prisoners being herded aboard by their guards, who were to accompany them on their voyage to Bremerhaven.

We left Le Havre early the following morning, and later that day I had my first sighting of England as we passed within view of the white cliffs of Dover, which I had heard of so often during the war, particularly in the song that had been played over and over again on the *Hase* on our return voyage from Calcutta, along with "Sentimental Journey."

There'll be bluebirds over
The white cliffs of Dover,
Tomorrow,
Just you wait and see.

There'll be joy and laughter,
And peace ever after,
Tomorrow,
When the world is free.

Two days later we passed the East Frisian Islands, and as we approached Bremerhaven I went below to take up my post at the aft steering gear. Soon afterward the bridge contacted me on the intercom to say that the main steering gear had stopped functioning and that I should activate the remote-control mechanism. I almost panicked, for I didn't really know how to operate it, but at that moment Chief Gonzalez appeared and took over. A few minutes later the bridge called again to say that the main steering gear was now functioning and I could switch off the auxiliary unit, which Chief Gonzalez did for me. Then the chief left, saying that he hoped I could operate the mechanism myself next time. I resolved to start studying the instruction booklet he had given me.

Bremerhaven was in an even more ruinous state than Le Havre, and the whole area around the harbor and as far as I could see was a scene of utter destruction. I watched as the German prisoners were herded off the ship into a stockade at the end of the pier, and I wondered what was going through their minds as they returned to the wreckage of the Third Reich, which their Führer had told them would last for a thousand years.

That evening I went with a group of my shipmates to a makeshift café that had been set up in the substructure of a bombed-out warehouse. Electrical power had not yet been restored in Bremerhaven, and the café was illuminated only by candles. The only customers were American and British soldiers and sailors, some of whom had picked up German women who seemed to be well known to the older men who ran the café. All they had to drink was beer, which tasted as if it was homemade, and one of my friends, a Texan, compared it to the home brew his grandpa cooked up in a still.

The entertainment was provided by a ravaged-looking blonde who played an accordion while she sang in German in a throaty voice, after which she repeated the lyrics in English. The climax of her performance was, of course, "Lili Marlene," and whenever I heard the song in later years it brought back memories of her voice echoing through the candlelit café beneath the ruins of Bremerhaven.

> *Underneath the lantern, by the barrack gate,*
> *Darling, I remember the way you used to wait.*
> *'Twas there that you whispered tenderly*
> *That you loved me, you'd always be . . .*
> *My Lili of the lamplight, my own Lili Marlene.*

The next day some three thousand GIs filed aboard the ship, and I could tell from their shoulder badges that most of them were infantrymen, along with others from the various support branches of the Army. I was surprised to see that some of the infantrymen were black, for I thought that the Army was just as thoroughly segregated as the Navy. One of the black GIs told me that during the European campaign a number of African American infantry, cavalry, and field artillery units were created, and he himself was in the 92nd Infantry Division, one of the most highly decorated in the Army. He then spoke with some bitterness, saying that it was going to be tough going back to segregation in civilian life, in his case in rural Mississippi, and then I remembered my own experience delivering newspapers in the black ghetto in Bed-Stuy.

That evening I went ashore with a few of my shipmates, who had heard of a cache of captured German weapons that we might be able to pick up as souvenirs. We found the weapons in a ruined warehouse not far from the café we had gone to the night before. I was surprised to find the warehouse unguarded, but I was told that the Allies no longer had the manpower to guard such weapons, most of which were so damaged that they weren't usable. I managed to find two rifles that were in reasonably good condition and brought them back to the ship, where I gave one of them to a machinist's mate in the engine room who had covered for me while I was supposed to be on watch. I now had a souvenir from the European theater to match the kukri I had bought in Calcutta.

We left Bremerhaven the next morning, when I once again took up my station at the aft steering gear, this time without incident. The next day, as we headed through the North Sea toward the English Channel, we ran into the worst storm I had ever experienced at sea, and all of the GIs were ordered to stay below. The crew who had to go out on deck had to be attached to safety lines and wear life jackets, for the decks often flooded when the ship hit a big wave. I was sent up the foremast to check the tilt indicator, for its alarm was going off. At times I had to hang on for my life as colossal waves broke over the ship and submerged its superstructure.

When I got up to the searchlight platform I found that the tilt indicator was, in fact, working properly; when the ship rolled severely, the pointer went beyond the red markers on the gauge, setting off the alarm on the bridge. I also had to clean the lens of the searchlight, which had become coated with salt from the sea spray.

The storm grew even worse that night, and when I finished my eight-to-midnight watch in the engine room I was almost washed overboard making my way back to my bunk. I was so exhausted that I fell asleep almost immediately, despite the violent pitching and rolling of the ship, which set everything movable sliding across the decks and crashing into the bulkheads. But then I was awakened by a tremendous crash and almost thrown out of my bunk, and my first thought was that we had struck a mine, for we had been warned that many of them had broken loose from the mine fields in the North Sea and the English Channel.

A General Quarters sounded over the PA, and I had to go out again to make my way to the electrician's mate station under the fantail deck. When I went out on deck I could see that the bow of our ship had been damaged, though I couldn't tell if it had been caused by an explosion or the sea. When we assembled, Chief Gonzalez said we would be part of a damage control unit to examine the bow and make whatever emergency repairs we could. We found that the damage had, in fact, been caused by the sea, which had ripped open a large hole on the starboard side of the hull near the bow. The officer in charge of the damage control unit said that we were in no immediate danger of sinking, since the internal bulkheads were watertight and confined any intake of seawater to the small forward compartment, which was being pumped out. He went on to say that we would be changing course to head up along the east coast of England, where we would be shielded from the full force of the storm.

The machinist's mates rigged up a metal plate over the hole in the bow and sealed the leak, after which Chief Gonzalez put our unit to work checking the electrical apparatus and repairing any damage. While the repair work went on I was relieved to see that the storm was abating, with the wind diminishing in intensity and the waves no longer so high and powerful.

By the time the repairs were finished it was beginning to grow light, and since the storm was now virtually over I decided to remain out on deck by the prow to see where we were. Soon after sunrise I spotted land to the northwest, and as it took form I could see that we were heading into the calm waters of a large bay, where a number of what looked to be fishing boats were heading toward us. One of the boats came alongside us just as we dropped anchor, and an older man in oilskins waved and called up to me. I waved back to him and asked, "Where the hell are we?" He smiled and said, "You're in the Humber, lad!"

When the repairs were finished, the captain and the chief engineering officer came to inspect the hull. They decided that the ship was seaworthy, and because the weather forecast was favorable we set out again in a couple of hours, resuming our voyage across the Atlantic to New York. It took us ten days.

After we docked in New York and the GIs disembarked we were informed that we would remain in port until our bow was fully repaired. All of us with engineering ratings would be needed for these repairs and would not be granted liberty, particularly since many of the crew were now eligible for discharge and their departure would leave the *Taylor* shorthanded. Once again I was back in New York and unable to go home and see my family.

I so resented this that on our second evening in port I tried to sneak past the SPs who were guarding the gateway of the dock area. They brought me back and handed me over to the officer of the day on the *Taylor,* who put me on report. The following day I was brought before the captain, who gave me a severe dressing down and told me that as long as I was aboard the *Taylor* I would be denied shore leave, and if I ever tried to go AWOL again I would be given a general court-martial and sent to Portsmouth Naval Prison. He told me that if I wanted to know what life in Portsmouth was like I should talk to some of the new crew members who were about to come aboard, for they had been released from the prison to replace some of our ship's company who were eligible for discharge.

When I went back on deck I saw that about a dozen new crew members were about to come aboard, herded up the gangway by a detachment of Marine guards. They were all black, so I knew they were cooks, bakers, or stewards assigned to the mess hall, where I spoke to some of them as I passed through the chow line that evening, welcoming them aboard. I later learned that each of them had been given a general court-martial for having gone AWOL and missing the ships they had been assigned to, and they told me they were happy to be serving out their sentence on the *Taylor* rather than in Portsmouth, which they said was indeed a hellhole.

I managed to get a letter off to Peg telling her that I was okay and that I hoped to be home in a few months. But I didn't mention that I was in New York, for she would think it strange that I wasn't able to get on the subway and come back to Brooklyn. I spent Christmas aboard the *Taylor,* and I saw in the year 1946 with my black friends in the quarters of the cooks and bakers and stewards, who had smuggled aboard enough alcohol to last them through a round-trip voyage across the Atlantic.

We left New York in mid-January, once again scheduled to pick up German prisoners in Le Havre and bring them to Bremerhaven, from where we would take GIs back to New York. That voyage passed uneventfully, as did the two that followed, though on all of them we ran into storms in the Atlantic. When we began what would be my fourth round-trip across the Atlantic we were told that this would be our last trip, because by then, mid-April 1946, most of the GIs in Germany who were eligible for discharge had been brought home, and we would be bringing the last lot of German prisoners back from France.

When we docked in Le Havre, I realized that I might not see France again, and I felt bad that I hadn't been able to visit Paris. Then the PA announced that all the ship's company except a skeleton crew would be given three days' liberty in Paris, which made me feel even worse, since my attempt to go AWOL in New York had cost me my liberty. I was astonished when I found my name on the list of those who were eligible to go to Paris; the captain had either forgotten my infraction or had forgiven me because of my subsequent good behavior.

In any event, I got to spend a weekend in Paris, traveling there and back by troop train from Le Havre. Waiters in the sidewalk cafés on the Champs Elysées, Montparnasse, and Saint-Germain told us that we had brought with us the first spring days since the end of the war, whose effects I could see in the bullet marks on the facades of buildings, in the scarcity of food, wine, and other things to buy, in the threadbare and out-of-fashion clothes the women wore, and in the almost total absence of men of military age. But the city was coming to life again and regaining its old gaiety, or so it seemed to me on Saturday night in Pigalle, where some us made the rounds in the company of Senegalese troops in the French army who were also seeing Paris for the first time.

On Sunday morning I went to mass at Notre Dame, and as I took in its splendor I thought of the basement church at Fourteen Holy Martyrs in Brooklyn, and of the first time I had attended services there with Jimmy Anderson, and I wondered if he had survived the war.

We sailed from Le Havre after the German prisoners were brought aboard, the last to leave France by sea. At Bremerhaven we took aboard both GIs and German war brides, and some war babies as well, probably the first time that an American troopship had ever carried children. I was allowed a day's liberty in Bremerhaven, which was as somber as Paris was gay, the city still in ruins and its inhabitants showing the bitterness of humiliating defeat.

A few of the GIs aboard the *Taylor* made disparaging remarks about the youthfulness of our crew, for many of the new ship's company who had replaced those who were discharged were straight out of boot camp and looked it. One of the GIs said to me, "Hey, kid, who let you out of school?" I shot back at him that I had been in the Navy for two years and had served in the Pacific and China-Burma-India theaters of war, as well as seven months on troopships in the North Atlantic carrying dogfaces like himself. Later, when we hit a bad storm, I had the satisfaction of seeing this wise guy puking out his guts on the deck, and I stopped to ask him if he was having a pleasant voyage home.

I went up to my perch on the searchlight platform, where I sat peering westward into the eye of the storm, which would probably be the last one I would see for a while, for we were nearing New York. Then I remembered how Peg and I had done the same on my boyhood crossings of the Atlantic, and I recalled a line from a poem by Yeats describing how the Irish hero Cúchulainn "fought the ungovernable sea." The wild sea was in our blood, she said, and so it was.

As we approached New York Harbor I arranged my work schedule so I would be on duty up on the searchlight platform. It was a beautiful morning in late May, and I watched as the skyline of Lower Manhattan came into focus along with the Statue of Liberty. The sighting of Lady Liberty marked the completion of my thirteenth crossing of the Atlantic, which in addition to my circumnavigation of the globe gave me the satisfaction of having achieved my boyhood dream of being a world traveler—and I wasn't yet twenty, with no idea of what I would do next.

After all the GIs were disembarked the PA called for the crew to muster on the foredeck, where the captain announced that the *Taylor* had made its last voyage and would be decommissioned. He wished us good luck on our next posting, which for some of us would be civilian life. As he bid us farewell, I silently thanked the captain for allowing me the weekend of liberty in Paris, even if unknowingly, even though he had kept me from seeing my family for seven months.

The chief boatswain's mate then took over, reading off the lists of assignments, which for the newer additions to the crew were usually the Navy Armed Guard Center in Brooklyn. Those who were slated for discharge would be taken to the Naval Separation Center at Lido Beach, Long Island, and my heart leaped when I heard my name being called out among those on this list.

I went below and packed my kukri in my seabag, though I had to carry my German rifle separately. When I was packed I said goodbye to my friends, particularly the black mess cooks in the galley, who were going to the Armed Guard Center for further assignment. Then I saluted the officer of the day at the head of the gangplank and disembarked from the *Taylor*, the third and last of the three ships on which I had served in the Navy, not counting the LSM(R) to which I had been assigned in Little Creek before I had volunteered to join SACO.

I spent less than forty-eight hours at Lido Beach, where my records were examined in preparation for my honorable discharge from the Navy. I still have the single-page document that was given to me by the yeoman's mate who processed my records, where he recorded that I had served for exactly two years, and that I was awarded the Victory Medal, the American Campaign Medal, the European–African–Middle Eastern Campaign Medal, the Asiatic-Pacific Campaign Medal with one battle star, and the Presidential Unit Citation ribbon for service with the U.S. Naval Group China. (I did not receive the Good Conduct Medal, because of my captain's mast.) I later learned that as a member of SACO I also received two service ribbons from the Chinese Nationalist Government.

The yeoman was surprised that my rank was only fireman second class, and so, being a nice guy, he arbitrarily changed it to fireman first class—a rank I held for approximately one hour, my last in the Navy. The document also records that I received a mustering-out allowance of $100 plus a final salary payment of $39.15, which included a transportation allowance of $1.15, the latter paying for a $1.10 dollar ticket on the Long Island Rail Road and a nickel for the subway. At the bottom line of the document is my signature, the imprint of my right index finger, and the date, May 26, 1946, exactly one month before my twentieth birthday.

I had an hour before my train was due to depart, which I spent in a lounge at the base headquarters. Soon afterward I spotted Pete Hansen, one of my friends from boot camp at the Sampson Naval Training Center. We embraced each other and swapped stories about what we'd been doing since we left boot camp. Pete told me that he had been on a destroyer in the Pacific and had been in action in the landings on Okinawa and also at Saipan and the Philippines. I told him that I had originally been assigned to an LSM(R), one of a dozen that were slated to go to Okinawa, and I asked him if he had seen any. He said that he had seen the wreckage of six of the twelve LSM(R)s on the beach at Okinawa, all of them destroyed by Japanese artillery.

Then I asked Pete if he had any news of Charles Shelmerdine and our other friends in boot camp who had shipped out on the USS *Dickerson*. He was silent for a moment before he handed me a copy of *Our Navy* magazine, telling me that I could read all about it there. Then he said goodbye, for his train was about to leave, and that's the last I ever saw of him.

The lead article in the magazine was about the *Dickerson* and its role in the U.S. amphibious landings on Okinawa, which began on April 1, 1945. According to the article, on the second day of the landing, a Japanese kamikaze made a long, low glide and sheared off the tops of two of the *Dickerson*'s four smokestacks before crashing into the base of her bridge, toppling her mast and starting intense gasoline fires. Almost simultaneously, another Japanese plane dropped a five-hundred-pound bomb on the five-inch gun on the forecastle, killing all of the gun crew and tearing a hole in the deck almost the whole length of the ship. The article gave the names of the gun crew, and among them I saw that of Seaman Second Class Charles Shelmerdine, aged eighteen.

I was so shocked that it took a while before I could continue reading the article, which went on to say that 54 of the *Dickerson*'s crew of 113 were killed, including her commanding officer, and that the ship was scuttled two days later with the captain and most of her dead crew still aboard.

I was still somewhat shaken when I boarded the train. I had always wondered why I had never heard from Charles, who had promised to write as soon as he had an FPO address. I looked at the article again and saw that those who had been killed with him, manning the five-inch gun on the forecastle, included two other boys who had been in our recruit company at Sampson, Ed Grant and a Greek American named Spiro, both of them also aged eighteen.

I got off the train and changed to the Eighth Avenue subway line, attracting some attention because of the German rifle I was carrying. I got off at Wilson Avenue, looking down the tunnel toward the freight yard where Jimmy Anderson and I used to sneak into the station without paying our fare. Then I began wondering if Jimmy and Phil Gould had survived the war.

I left the station and started down Wilson, passing Paul Hesse's bar. Paul saw me and waved, so I walked in to say hello, and he showed me my name on the World War II honor roll above the bar, along with that of my uncle Mike, who had a silver star next to his name because he had been wounded. The names of Jimmy Anderson and Phil Gould were there too, but there were no silver or gold stars next to their names, so I supposed that they were okay.

Paul told me that my father stopped off for a beer every day when he finished work at the Evergreens Cemetery, hoping that he would see me emerging from the Wilson Avenue subway station, returning home from the war. Then Paul laughed and pointed at the old *Daily News* article framed on the wall at the end of the bar by the door—S T O R K   S N A R L S   T R A F F I C. I was truly home, for this was the historic event that had led to the first of my thirteen voyages across the Atlantic, and the last of which had just brought me back to Brooklyn after I had traveled all the way around the world.

After I left the bar I walked along Wilson and turned left on the far side of Cornelia Street, where Mr. Hellman waved to me from his grocery store. He came out to welcome me home, saying that my family had been anxiously awaiting my return. They would all be there waiting for me, he said, because my father had already come home from the cemetery and my mother had the day off, for it was Saturday.

When I rang the bell my brother, Jimmy, answered the door, and when he saw me he let out such a yell that it brought the rest of the family into the hallway, first Dorothy and Nancy and then John and Peg. They hugged and kissed me and welcomed me home, and then we all sat around the kitchen table and talked while Peg prepared supper.

I told them where I had been and what I had done since I last saw them, showing them my kukri, my German rifle, and the Chinese "funny money" that I still had in my dungaree pockets. Then Peg gave me all the family news, telling me that my uncle Mike was now in a VA hospital, and that he was all right except for his drinking. I asked about Jimmy and Phil and she said that they had come home and were fine. Jimmy had dropped by and was waiting to hear from me.

After supper, Mr. and Mrs. Simmons came down to join us. Mrs. Simmons brought along her nephew Jan and his wife and their baby daughter, who had just arrived as refugees from Poland and were living in the back bedroom off the hallway behind mine. Jan could speak a little English and told me that he had been in the Polish army and had been captured by the Germans. He had been freed by the Allies and made his way back to his hometown in Poland, where he married his childhood sweetheart. After their daughter was born, he managed to get in touch with Mrs. Simmons, who brought them to the States. I showed Jan my German rifle and made a show of going through a drill with it— something I had learned to do in the Catholic Boys' Brigade but never in the U.S. Navy.

On Sunday morning, everyone went to nine o'clock mass at Fourteen Holy Martyrs except me and Peg, for we had stayed up half the night talking and slept through till almost noon. John said he had spread the news of my return at church, and his brother Tom and my aunt Chris would be giving a welcome-home party for me at their flat on Central Avenue.

The party at Tom's was the first family get-together I had been to in almost two years, and everyone in our extended clan was there, including my uncle Mike, who had gone AWOL from the VA hospital, and my aunt Mary Freely's French Canadian husband, Phil Pelletier, who had served two years in the Army despite the fact that he had only one eye. Mauris Guiheen had brought along his accordion, which he played while he and others sang alternately in Irish and English. One of the songs was my uncle Tom's favorite, "Down by the Tanyard Side," which he sang whenever he was drunk, never missing a word.

I am a rambling hero, and by love I am betrayed.
Near to the town of Baltinglass, there dwells a lovely maid.
She's fairer than Hypatia bright, and she's free from earthly pride.
She's a darlin' maid, and her dwellin' place is down by the tanyard side.

Before he passed out, Tom told me that he had run into Jimmy Anderson, who had said he would be waiting for me at two o'clock on Monday afternoon at John's Bar and Grill on Central Avenue and Hancock Street. When I arrived there on the dot of two I found Jimmy at the front end of the bar, the only one there except the bartender. We embraced and stood back to look at each other, for we hadn't met in more than four years. I hardly recognized Jimmy at first, because he looked tough and hard, but after we exchanged a few old jokes and stories, particularly about our days scavenging together, I saw again the shy smile I noticed when we first met in Fourteen Holy Martyrs the day I started school there.

The bartender asked what we wanted, and Jimmy and I decided that we would drink our way through the cocktail list posted on the wall, which started with a Tom Collins and ended with a pousse-café, whatever that was. We each put a hundred-dollar bill on the bar, most of our mustering-out allowance, for 90 percent of our service pay had been sent home to our mothers. The money on the bar was far more than what we had earned between us in our years of scavenging and other odd jobs, and as we drank our cocktails we reminisced about walking to the Museum of Natural History and back, having squandered our return subway fare on a dime's worth of bananas.

Jimmy told me that he had fought all through the Guadalcanal campaign, and in the landings at Saipan and Okinawa, but although his outfit had suffered heavy casualties he had come through it without a scratch. He said that Phil Gould had also fought at Guadalcanal and Okinawa, and that he too had made it through unharmed, though both of them had come down with malaria. He said that Phil wasn't around at the moment, for he was shacking up with a model he'd met at a bar in Manhattan.

Jimmy told me that he himself was engaged to a girl who was serving in the women's branch of the Marine Corps, and that they would be married as soon as she received her discharge in the coming weeks. He asked me to be his best man, and I said I would be happy to do so, but that I hoped the wedding would be informal because I didn't have a suit to wear. He said not to worry, because neither did he.

We didn't make it through the whole cocktail list before we called it quits for the day, hardly making a dent in our hundred-dollar allowances. Jimmy was going off the next day to see his fiancée at the Marine Corps base in Quantico, Virginia, and he said he would look me up when he got back.

Later that afternoon I went to see Jean Caputo, who was working as a secretary at *The New York Times*. She had seen the photograph of the returning troopships that had appeared on the front page of the *Times* on October 28, 1945, and she had saved it, thinking that I might have been aboard one of the ships. She gave me a copy of the front page, which had a close-up photo of a young female reporter going aboard the *Hase,* the same scene I had viewed from the flying bridge of the troopship.

Jean told me that she was engaged to marry Bob Batchelder, a very nice guy, and I wished her well. She asked me what I was going to do with my life, and I said I had no idea, but for the time being I was going to collect unemployment relief for a year and read through all the Great Books. Jean suggested that I might go to college on the GI Bill, but I said I hadn't finished high school before I joined the Navy. She said I should go back and finish high school, or, if I didn't want to do that, I could take an equivalency exam that would allow me to start college without a secondary school diploma. I said I would think about it in the fall, but first I wanted to enjoy the summer, because for the last six years I had been either working or in the Navy, and for the next two months I just planned to swim and lie on the beach and read. Jean smiled and asked simply, "Alone?," to which I could only reply, "Time will tell." Then she put on a recording of *Rigoletto* and we listened together in silence, just as we used to before I went off to war.

Then I took a stroll around the neighborhood, looking at the houses I'd lived in on Cooper Street, Chauncey Street, MacDonough Street, Aberdeen Street, De Sales Place, and Central Avenue; the schools I had attended at Our Lady of Lourdes and Fourteen Holy Martyrs; the trolley line on which John had been a conductor and the cemetery where he still dug graves; the streets where we'd played stickball and hockey; the school yard where we'd played basketball and softball; the vacant lot where we'd played baseball; the field where we had roasted stolen potatoes; the playground where I had won medals in the sack race and the three-legged race; the apartments to which I had delivered the *Long Island Press* and the *Brooklyn Daily Eagle;* the abandoned ice house where Jimmy and I had had our clubhouse and stored some of the junk we had scavenged; the house where Joe Bauch had lived before he passed away; Mr. Thompson's shop, with its photos of famous people before and after he applied makeup to their black eye; the Boyle Brothers bar, with its window full of stuffed birds and animals; Otto's ice cream parlor, where I could still see one of the bulletholes made by Billy De Witt's pistol; the movie house where I had seen *King Kong* and *Frankenstein;* the boxing arena where I had seen Kid Chocolate knock out Irish Pat McCoy; the abandoned vaudeville theater where I had watched the amateur hour on Saturday afternoons; the candy store where I had bought chewing gum and swapped baseball cards for Japanese-atrocity cards; the public library; the church hall where Richard Holtzman and I were trained in the Catholic Boys' Brigade; and Friel's, where Peg had pawned her wedding ring and then redeemed it.

After supper that evening we all sat out on the front steps, together with Mr. and Mrs. Simmons and their nephew Jan and his wife and baby. When the Good Humor truck came by I bought ice cream for everyone, and when we finished my sister Dorothy went off on a date while Nancy and Jimmy went to play Ringelevio and Hide and Go Seek with their friends on the street. I took a pitcher from the kitchen and had it filled with beer at the Decatur Street Bar and Grill, which I poured into mugs for John and Jan. I didn't have any myself because I didn't want to drink in front of Peg.

Later they all went inside to listen to Jack Benny on the radio, while I made my round of the local bars looking for old friends I hadn't seen since I went into the Navy. At the Gay Café (that was its name) on Bushwick Avenue and Decatur Street I ran into John Crowley, whom I had last seen at Ledo in northern India, at the beginning of the Burma Road. He said that most of the other returned veterans in the neighborhood were at Pike's Bar on Broadway and Cooper Street.

They were indeed, so I spent the rest of the evening drinking in Pike's with pals who had fought in Europe with the Army or in the Pacific with the Navy or the Marines. I learned that veterans would rather talk about their experience with other veterans, and that when they do their stories are usually about the comic or bizarre side of war, life turned upside down, such as my own tale of how I had learned that "the fucking war was over" in China. But even as we laughed at our war stories I thought of Charles Shelmerdine entombed in the hulk of the *Dickerson* off Okinawa; John Jacob Esau buried on a hillside above Kunming; the nameless Chinese soldiers whose corpses I had seen along the Ledo-Stilwell Road; and the Japanese boy I had heard screaming in the jungle that night at Mongyu. I wondered what would happen to Ching Ging Too in the civil war that was now about to tear China apart while the rest of the world was beginning to enjoy peace.

All of this whirlpool of memories troubled my sleep that night, until I realized that I was in my own bed for the first time in two years, and no longer in a bunk on a crowded troopship or in a pup tent in the muddy and mosquito-ridden jungle. I was home, and I now had a future to look forward to. As I finally drifted off to sleep, I wondered what I would do with myself. I resolved that I'd return to Crete one day, and then I would check the color of the sea there in all kinds of light, to observe if it was really sable or wine dark or midnight blue as it had been in the last hour before dawn when I passed Cape Elafonissi on the *Hase,* so different from the pale green of the North Atlantic that I had first seen on my voyages to and from Ireland with Peg. Surely I'd be able to get to Crete again and to Ireland and even to China and the Rivers of Paradise, for I had three weeks to go before I was even twenty, which Peg always said was just the first quarter of a man's life, quoting the old Irish proverb I had first heard from Tom of the Winds. I can still hear her soft brogue as she tells me this, speaking to me from the Country of Dreams. "Twenty years a-growing, twenty years in blossom, twenty years a-stooping, and twenty years declining. Such is the life of a man."

Part Three

Memory

a year after the war I met and fell in love with a very beautiful girl named Dolores, known to her family as Tootsie, which I shortened to Toots, because the jukebox in the tavern where I met her along with her family was playing "Toot, Toot, Tootsie, Goodbye."

Toots had just graduated from high school, and, like me, dreamed of being a world traveler. A month after we met we signed a pact in blood on a parchment scroll swearing that we would spend our lives traveling together around the world. She had just started work as a secretary at the Matson Steamship Lines in Rockefeller Center, where she ran the Hawaii Visitors Center, thinking that this would lead to a life of travel.

When I met Toots she was headed for a career as a singer and dancer, for she had a superb voice, particularly when she sang the blues, and she had been trained in dance ranging from ballet to tap. She was also a talented painter and had attended art school in the evening, but she gave up thoughts of a career when she signed her blood pact with me.

Toots and I were married on July 21, 1951, and in the next nine years we had three children: Maureen (1952), Eileen (1955), and Brendan (1959). Meanwhile, I had gone to school on the GI Bill and had received a BS in physics from Iona College in New Rochelle, New York. I then enrolled in the evening graduate program at New York University, from which I obtained a PhD in physics in 1960, while during the day I worked as a research physicist, first at the U.S. Army Signal Corps Laboratory (1951–55), and then in the controlled thermonuclear fusion center at Princeton (1955–60). Later I did postdoctoral studies in the history of science at All Souls College, Oxford. During those years I published several research papers in atomic physics in the *Physical Review,* the most prestigious physics journal in the United States.

In 1957, while I was working at Princeton, Chen Ning (Frank) Yang and Tsung-Dao Lee won the Nobel Prize in physics. The *New York Times* article on their prize mentioned that they had completed their under-graduate studies at the Associated Universities of Southwest China at

Kunming in 1945. I saw Yang and Lee at a tea held in their honor at the physics department in Princeton when they won their prize, but I wasn't able to speak to them.

Some years later I met Professor Yang at a seminar in Istanbul, where I learned that he too had been in the camp of the Chinese 1st Army Group in Kunming when the war ended. He had also been struck by the extraordinary matrilineal tribespeople in the Tibetan borderlands of China, so different from Han Chinese like himself, particularly the fearfully independent and astonishingly beautiful women. Over the years we corresponded, and he put me on to several interesting books on the subject, most notably works by Joseph Rock and Peter Goullart, travelers who lived for two decades prior to 1945 in Lijiang, the most important town in the region inhabited by these tribes.

After I received my PhD at NYU I was offered a permanent research position at Princeton. But, after consulting with Toots, I regretfully turned down the job and accepted a teaching post as professor of physics at Robert College in Istanbul, now known as Bosphorus University. In September 1960 Toots and I flew off to Istanbul with our three children, beginning the life of travel that we had agreed to in our blood pact. I was Odysseus and she was my Penelope—except that I was taking her and the children with me rather than leaving them at home.

We lived in Istanbul from 1960 to 2015, with intervals in Boston, New York, Princeton, Oxford, London, Athens, the Greek Islands, Crete, and Venice. During that time I published more than sixty books, most of them on history, biography, the history of science, architecture, and travel, all of which have been based on our extensive travels around the Mediterranean and through western Europe, the Balkans, Asia Minor, and the Middle East. After Dolores died in 2015, I moved to Bath, England, to be near my daughter Maureen.

My most recent book, *A Traveler's Guide to Homer,* begins with my sighting of Cape Elafonissa on my journey home from the war in China, when my troopship crossed the track of Odysseus on his homeward voyage from Troy. This is where, in Book 19 of the *Odyssey,* Odysseus tells Penelope, "In the middle of the sable sea there lies an isle called Crete, a ravisher of eyes . . ." I also wrote of this incident in my book on Crete, where I stand on Cape Elafonissa and look out across the Mediterranean, where the sight of passing ships reminds me once again of my crossing the course of Odysseus on my homeward voyage from our war, a journey that in my case still continued, with my Penelope at my side.

During the fall of 1998 I was in New York doing research on my history of Robert College–Bosphorus University. One day, on an impulse, I went to the Metropolitan Museum of Art, which I hadn't been to since 1944, just before I went off to war. I went straight to the gallery of classical art. There she was, the wounded Amazon, all by herself in the long shadows of late autumn, just as I had seen her in my youth, unaware of the years that had passed, dreaming eternally in the night of time like the dead boys who had served with me during the war. They were all living in the Country of Dreams, and I would go there myself and speak to them, as Odysseus does in Book 11 of the *Odyssey,* before he finally returns to his home in Ithaca.

Late in the spring of 2000 my friend Cem Kozlu, president of Turkish National Airlines (THY), held an event to honor me for all the books I had written about Turkey. I was awarded two free round-trip first-class tickets, so Toots and I could fly to any city in the world to which THY operated flights.

I had always wanted to go back to Kunming, China, for I had never forgotten the promise that Ching Ging Too and I had made to seek each other out after the war. I knew that it was very unlikely that I could ever find him again, but at least I would be able to show Toots a part of the world that I had been telling her about since we first met.

I looked through the THY schedules and saw that they had direct daily flights from Istanbul to Beijing as well as Shanghai, and that Air China, the national airlines, had direct daily flights to Kunming. I worked out an itinerary that would take us from Istanbul to Beijing, then, in turn, to Kunming and Shanghai, from where we would fly back to Istanbul. I found that there were daily flights between Kunming and Lijiang, the beautiful medieval town and old caravan city near Dali, which our truck convoy had passed along the Burma Road in late August 1945. I remembered Ching Ging Too telling me that he was from a village near Lijiang, so I added Lijiang to our itinerary, which I figured we could complete in the fortnight we had set aside for our trip in mid-September; I would be back in Istanbul just in time for the beginning of the fall semester at the university.

The first leg of our journey took us almost the whole width of Asia. As I peered down on the bleak Tibetan Plateau and the ochre sands of the Gobi Desert, I recalled looking at the maps on the blackboard during geography classes at Fourteen Holy Martyrs School, daydreaming of the places I was now seeing.

My memories of war-torn and starving China were hard to reconcile with what we saw during our three days in Beijing, where bulldozers were demolishing the last pagodas of old Peking and cranes were erecting skyscrapers in their place. The streets were thronged with well-dressed younger people and one-child couples, filing into the same brand-name shops and fast-food restaurants that we ourselves had avoided in New York, and we had trouble finding a simple Chinese eating place.

Our hotel was within walking distance of the Forbidden City and Tiananmen Square, so we spent the first two days of our stay sightseeing in that part of the city. On the third and last day we went on a tour that took us to a stretch of the Great Wall of China known as the Simatai, at Mutlangu, some thirty miles northeast of Beijing. This was a sight that I had been longing to see ever since I first read about the Great Wall in *A Pictorial Journey Around the World,* and the long line of crenellated walls and watchtowers marching along the crest of the wooded hills looked just like the lithograph I had pored over in that long-lost book nearly seventy years before.

The next day we flew diagonally across virtually the whole of China from Beijing to Kunming. As we came in to land I recognized the ring of mountains that encircled the city on its mile-high plateau, and I could see that the airport was in exactly the same place that it had been when I was last in Kunming. But then it had been an unpaved military airstrip in an open field, whereas now it was a modern international airport. The date was September 15, 2000, fifty-five years to the day since I had left Kunming from this same field on a C-47 troop transport, with a half-dozen U.S. Army mules among my fellow passengers.

Kunming had changed profoundly since I last saw it, for then it was still a medieval town, whereas now it was to a large extent a modern city, though far less developed than Beijing, so that it had not completely lost its old Chinese character. Kunming was different from Beijing in other ways as well, for its remoteness had spared it from Mao's Cultural Revolution, and also because its native population was not primarily Han Chinese, but consisted of one or another of the twenty-six ethnic minorities that inhabit Yunnan and Sichuan provinces, each with its own distinctive language and culture—most notably the Bai, Mosuo, and Naxi, who were still matrilineal.

I inquired about the U.S. military cemetery where we had buried John Jacob Esau on September 6, 1945, and I was told that the five hundred or so Americans who had been laid to rest there had long since been brought home and reinterred. The 1st Army Group camp where Ching Ging Too and I had been stationed along with the LPA was now the headquarters of the 14th Army Group of the People's Liberation Army, and it was off-limits to the public.

I had been advised not to mention my SACO wartime service during our visit to China, because our outfit and the LPA had been demonized by the Communist government. After the Communist takeover of China in 1947, the former members of the LPA who remained in the country were hunted down and exterminated to a man or woman. So I knew there was very little chance of finding Ching Ging Too in Kunming. In any event, he had been from the more tribal areas in the Tibetan borderlands, which was why I had decided that we should spend a few days in Lijiang. So we left Kunming and my wartime memories, and started on the last stage of my quest, boarding a flight to Lijiang.

The flight took just forty-five minutes, landing us in a beautiful valley within sight of the snow-covered mountains of easternmost Tibet, which I remembered from the last days of the war. A taxi took us to a modern hotel on the edge of Lijiang's old section, a labyrinth of ancient wooden and adobe houses with pagoda roofs, built along the cobbled banks of a maze of canals spanned by stone bridges, the crystal-clear water flowing down from Jade Dragon Snow Mountain to the north.

The market square in the old town was filled with Naxi women, distinguished by their blue blouses and trousers covered with blue or black aprons, a T-shaped cape with crossed straps holding up the huge wicker baskets hanging on their backs. They were formidable women and obviously ran the town, the men apparently relegated to a secondary role.

The town was filled with tourists, most of whom were prosperous Chinese who seemed to be from elsewhere in the country. Toots and I were continually being photographed, and were sometimes asked to pose with the companions of the photographer, who usually thanked us with a thumbs-up sign.

On our second evening in Lijiang we went to a performance by the Naxi Classical Orchestra, which was given in a beautiful old theater on the main street of the Old Town. We arrived early so as to get a good seat, finding a place in the second row left of center.

I sat back to look at the members of the orchestra as they came from the wings to take their seats on stage and tune their instruments. I counted about fifty musicians, most of them old men with long white beards, dressed in traditional embroidered robes, along with a number of somewhat younger players, including a woman with a broad moonlike face who kept staring at me, just as I was transfixed by her, the two of us looking at each other across a cultural gulf as wide as the world itself, as had happened when I bought two yams from that beautiful young woman in Lungling more than half a century before.

Then the master of ceremonies came on stage, introducing himself in both Chinese and perfect English as Xuan Ke. He explained that the members of the orchestra were all Naxi, and they would be playing a type of Taoist temple music that had been lost in the rest of China. As he introduced some of the older musicians he described their instruments, many of which had also disappeared elsewhere in the country. It was left unsaid, but I knew that the Cultural Revolution had destroyed much of the precious heritage of ancient Chinese culture, and only the remoteness of Lijiang had allowed these old masters to preserve the music we were about to hear.

Xuan Ke then introduced each of the musical pieces in turn, in one of which a young woman sang the "Love Song of the Walking Marriage," referring to the temporary matrimony that a girl from one of the matrilineal tribes like the Naxi goes through with her first lover.

This was followed by a number of orchestral compositions whose haunting melodies put me into a trance, which was suddenly broken when I heard Xuan Ke say, "The next piece of music our orchestra will play for you is 'Waves Washing the Sand.' This song was written by the last Tang Dynasty emperor, Li Ya." I was astonished and deeply moved, for this was the song that Ching Ging Too had sung for me during our little party in Kunming on September 2, 1945, celebrating the end of the war. Though fifty-five years had passed I recalled his explanation of the song: time passes like the waves of the sea lapping upon the shore, and memory is the faint pattern left by the ripples on the sand, soon to be washed away.

The war was at last over for me, and I could now consign my painful wartime recollections of China to the house of memory, along with the lingering memories of my youth in Ireland and Brooklyn, all part of the lost world that Homer called the Country of Dreams.

ALSO BY

JOHN FREELY

ALADDIN'S LAMP
How Greek Science Came to Europe Through the Islamic World

Aladdin's Lamp is the fascinating story of how ancient Greek philosophy and science began in the sixth century B.C. and, during the next millennium, spread across the Greco-Roman world, producing the remarkable discoveries and theories of Thales, Pythagoras, Hippocrates, Plato, Aristotle, Euclid, Archimedes, Galen, Ptolemy, and many others. John Freely explains how, as the Dark Ages shrouded Europe, scholars in medieval Baghdad translated the works of these Greek thinkers into Arabic, spreading their ideas throughout the Islamic world from central Asia to Spain, with many Muslim scientists, most notably Avicenna, Alhazen, and Averroës, adding their own interpretations to the philosophy and science they had inherited. Freely goes on to show how, beginning in the twelfth century, these texts by Islamic scholars were then translated from Arabic into Latin, sparking the emergence of modern science at the dawn of the Renaissance, which climaxed in the Scientific Revolution of the seventeenth century.

History

VINTAGE BOOKS
Available wherever books are sold.
www.vintagebooks.com